AMERICAN NATIONAL SECURITY
A Presidential Perspective

AMERICAN NATIONAL SECURITY
A Presidential Perspective

Cecil V. Crabb, Jr.
Kevin V. Mulcahy

Louisiana State University

Brooks/Cole Publishing Company
Pacific Grove, California

Brooks/Cole Publishing Company

A Division of Wadsworth, Inc.

Printed in the United States of America

10 9 8 7 6 5 4 3 2 1

Library of Congress Cataloging in Publication Data

Crabb, Cecil Van Meter, [date]–
    American national security : a presidential perspective / by Cecil V. Crabb, Kevin V. Mulcahy.
    p.   cm.
    Includes bibliographical references.
    ISBN 0-534-14022-X
    1. United States—Foreign relations—1945–   2. United States—National Security. 3. Executive power—United States. 4. National Security Council (U.S.) I. Mulcahy, Kevin V. II. Title.
    E744.C795   1990
    327.73—dc20   90-36371
                                                                                        CIP

Sponsoring Editor: *Cynthia C. Stormer*
Editorial Assistant: *Cathleen Sue Collins*
Production and Design Coordination: *Marlene Thom*
Manuscript Editor: *Lynne Fletcher*
Permissions Editor: *Marie Dubois*
Cover Design: *Katherine Minerva*
Cover Illustration: *Cloyce J. Wall*
Typesetting: *Patricia K. Douglass*
Printing and Binding: *Malloy Lithographing, Inc.*

For
Ian Hamilton Davis
Colin Farrell Davis
and
Harriet Crabb

About the Authors

Cecil V. Crabb, Jr., is a professor of political science at Louisiana State University in Baton Rouge. He obtained his doctorate from Johns Hopkins University. He served as an intern in the Department of State and has traveled and lectured widely within the United States and abroad. He is the author of numerous books and articles dealing with American foreign policy and international relations, including: *American Foreign Policy in the Nuclear Age* (Harper & Row, 1987); *Invitation to Struggle: Congress, the President and Foreign Policy,* 2nd ed. (Congressional Quarterly Press, 1984); *The Doctrines of American Foreign Policy: Their Meaning, Role, and Future* (Louisiana State University Press, 1982); and *American Diplomacy and the Pragmatic Tradition* (Louisiana State University Press, 1989).

Kevin V. Mulcahy is an associate professor of political science at Louisiana State University in Baton Rouge. He received his Ph.D. degree from Brown University. Dr. Mulcahy is the founder and past director of LSU's Government Internship program and serves as a member of the Public Administration Institute in the College of Business. Specializing in the study of public administration with emphasis in cultural policy making and the conduct of American foreign policy, Dr. Mulcahy has lectured on the national security policy making process at the National War College in Washington, D.C. He is also the author of *Public Policy and the Arts* (Westview, 1982), co-author of *America Votes* (Prentice-Hall, 1976), and has written numerous articles and essays in journals such as the *American Political Science Review*.

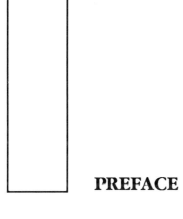

PREFACE

Whether there are two presidencies—one for domestic affairs and another for foreign affairs—may be debatable as a constitutional matter. Unquestionable, however, is that political practice, public expectations, and judicial approval have placed the modern presidency in a paramount position in the conduct of American external relations. As the nation's chief diplomat and commander in chief, the president presides over the diplomatic and military undertakings that constitute national security policy. A president may assign responsibility for the administration of these two spheres to his secretaries of state and defense; however, the formulation of overall national security policy and the coordination of what are inevitably interdepartmental initiatives are necessarily exclusively presidential responsibilities. The presidential perspective is what gives coherence to national security policy; its absence virtually guarantees a fragmented and diffuse external policy.

The principal presidential agency for the management of American national security has been the National Security Council (NSC). Established in 1947 as the United States began its assumption of global leadership in the aftermath of World War II, the NSC has emerged as the central forum for the articulation and integration of "decisions of the highest order."* The development of this decision-making process and its consequences for national security policy making are central concerns of this book and will be discussed in great detail.

We can, however, note four key facts about this process at the outset. First, the concept of national security is extremely broad and transcends traditional categories such as diplomacy, the military, intelligence, and international

---

*See *Decisions of the Highest Order: Perspectives on the National Security Council*, ed. Karl F. Inderfurth and Loch K. Johnson (Pacific Grove, Calif.: Brooks/Cole, 1988), for a comprehensive set of readings on this subject.

economics. Second, responsibility for the administration of national security affairs is consequently outside the province of any one department of government; the NSC functions as a transdepartmental forum for the formulation and coordination of such policies. Third, the NSC is explicitly set up as an advisory body composed of the president (as chairman), the vice-president, and the secretaries of state and defense, with the director of central intelligence and the chairman of the Joint Chiefs of Staff consulted as necessary. Fourth, the president is always free to accept or reject whatever advice is forthcoming from the NSC, the cabinet, or any other source. The NSC (much like the cabinet) serves to assist, rather than to circumscribe, presidential decision making.

With the increasing centrality of the National Security Counsel as a forum for decision making came a rise in importance of the NSC staff and, in particular, its director. Indeed, one of the most significant developments in postwar foreign policy making has been the emergence of the NSC's director as an equal of, and in some cases superior to, the secretary of state. The national security adviser, or assistant to the president for national security affairs (ANSA), is now a permanent actor in the formulation and direction of American international relations. How this process came about is a major topic of this book. It can be noted here, however, that the emergence of the national security adviser is related to the more general rise of presidential government. Many presidents have often felt that they could not trust the foreign policy bureaucracies (especially the State Department); even presidential appointees have been suspected of "going native"—that is, of representing a narrow, departmental view rather than a presidential perspective. As an internal White House expert with no external constituency, the national security adviser has been ideally situated to serve as a presidential functionary (although not all ANSAs have been models of objectivity devoid of personal policy agendas).

As will be discussed, national security advisers have played various roles under different presidents. For all the admitted variability, we have identified four basic types of roles played by national security advisers. A few have served as simple *administrators,* maintaining the policy-making machinery; others have become active *coordinators,* seeking to facilitate interdepartmental cooperation; some well-known examples have acted as *counselors,* enjoying a close personal relationship with the president; and at least one conspicuous figure became a presidential *agent* who effectively displaced the secretary of state in the policy-making process. Though we will evaluate the relative strengths and weaknesses of each role, we emphasize that presidential preference is the sole determiner of which ANSA role is appropriate and likely to be played. No amount of theorizing or statutory provisions can really inhibit the president's decision-making freedom in the realm of national security. As an old adage has it, in making foreign policy decisions the president is free to consult with whomever he wishes—including even his barber and chauffeur.

These observations are not meant to suggest, of course, that a president enjoys carte blanche in the conduct of international relations. Congress, in particular, exercises explicit constitutional and statutory prerogatives, and no president, as a matter of practicality, will fail to consult with the department heads who serve as members and advisers of the National Security Council. However, experience has shown that any constraints on a president's freedom of action as chief of state, particularly as chief diplomat and commander in chief, are very limited. Not all observers may agree with our point of view, which admittedly takes a presidential perspective. Yet we do not believe that the historical record since World War II, political realities, or the exigencies of national security decision making in the postwar period support a contrary viewpoint. Presidential judgment in internal and external policy alike is not always the best and is certainly not infallible. On the other hand, what is the alternative? As the evidence in recent years has shown, Congress is too institutionally diffuse and undisciplined to provide foreign policy leadership, even though its consultative and collaborative contributions may often be underestimated. Like it or not, only the chief executive can provide the constancy of leadership and consistency of policy essential for a coherent pursuit of American national security objectives. This goal, admittedly, is not an easy one to realize, even with decisive presidential leadership, but in its absence, achieving it is a virtual impossibility. It is our view that within the framework of the nation's constitutional provisions and political tradition, what is needed for the successful conduct of national security policy is a strong president—not an imperial president but one capable of decisive leadership in world affairs.

This book is organized into three parts. In Part One we cover the many connotations of the concept of national security, discussing in the first chapter the various definitions that have been offered for this often elusive concept. In chapter 2 we describe the nature of the external environment that has made national security concerns such a salient issue since World War II, especially the threats posed by the Cold War and, more recently, by global terrorism. In chapter 3 we survey the internal policy-making process involved in determining national security issues: the pivotal role of the president, the collaborative role of Congress, and the various contributions of the principal executive agencies—the Departments of State and Defense, the CIA, and the National Security Council and its staff.

In Part Two, which represents the book's major focus, we detail the different approaches the presidents have used over the past forty years in the management of national security policy making. We cover the early years of the Cold War, President Truman's responses, and the beginnings of the NSC system in chapter 4 and analyze the Eisenhower administration in chapter 5, paying considerable attention to the development of the NSC as a mechanism for coordinating the policy-making process. Chapter 6 spans the Kennedy and Johnson administrations. In it we focus on the emergence of the assistant for national security affairs as a major policy-making actor in the role of presidential counselor. We deal in chapter 7 with the Nixon administration, when the national security adviser emerged as the president's exclusive agent for the formulation and implementation of international relations. Then, in chapter 8, covering the Carter administration and most of the Reagan years, we show the national security policy-making process in increasing disarray, especially with regard to the always vital relationship between the secretary of state and the national security adviser.

In Part Three we present some general conclusions and speculations based on the past four decades of national security policy making, along with some projections for the 1990s and beyond. In chapter 9 we discuss in detail the insurgency of the NSC staff during the infamous Iran–Contra affair under Reagan, contrasting it with the normal roles national security advisers have played as administrators, coordinators, counselors, or agents and asking if there is a preferred model for presidential–departmental–NSC staff relations. Chapter 10 brings us to the Bush administration, which, though it has adopted more-regularized policy-making procedures, faces substantive policy challenges that may be more difficult than any arising since the beginning of the Cold War. If the Cold War is indeed over, as many observers contend, how should the United States redefine its national security interests?

This book was first conceived in the aftermath of the Iran–Contra affair and was developed over the next three years. During that period we had several opportunities to present some of our thoughts at conferences, in professional journals, and as chapters in books. We would like to acknowledge our gratitude for those opportunities, which allowed us to develop our thinking about many of the matters that concern us here. These writings were as follows: "The National Security Adviser: A Presidential Perspective," in *The Executive Establishment and Executive Leadership,* edited by Colin Campbell and Margaret Wyszomirski (Oxford: Basil Blackwell, forthcoming); "Presidential Management of National Security Policymaking, 1947–87" in *The Managerial Presidency,* edited by James P. Pfiffner (Pacific Grove, Calif.: Brooks/Cole, forthcoming); "What Oliver North Hath Wrought: The Lessons of 'Irangate' for National Security Policymaking," *Journal of Intelligence and CounterIntelligence,* forthcoming; "Presidential Mismanagement of National Security Policymaking: The Lessons of 'Irangate'," a paper presented at the Annual Meeting of the Southern Political Science Association, Charlotte, N.C., November 5–7, 1987; "What Oliver North Hath Wrought: The Implications of 'Irangate' for NSC Staff Organization," a paper presented at the Annual Meetings of the American Political Science Association, Washington, D.C., September 1–5, 1988; "The National Security Adviser: A Presidential Perspective," a paper presented at the Conference on the Executive Establishment and Executive Leadership, Georgetown University, Washington, D.C., September 6–8, 1988; and "Is There a Preferred Role for the National Security Adviser?" a paper presented at the Conference on National Security Strategies for the '90s, National War College, National Defense University, Fort McNair, Washington, D.C., December 8–10, 1988.

No book is written without the help of many people. What follows is a partial list of our most obvious debts; of course, those to whom we are indebted bear no responsibility for our final product. Professor Jerry Sansom of the Department of History of Louisiana State University at Alexandria, who worked on this project as a post-doctoral student, and Michael Vanchiere, who recently graduated from the LBJ School of Public Affairs at the University of Texas and who assisted us as an undergraduate honors-thesis student, both contributed immeasurably in the research phase of this book. Tim McCrary, Kristi Pospicil, David Melancon, Diana Stanford, Steve Richardson, Tim Poché, and Morris Garner, as undergraduate research assistants, provided invaluable help in the preparation and writing of the book. The entire manuscript was typed (and patiently retyped) by Mike Gage, Tonia Chiesa, and Veronica Haynes—our chancellor's undergraduate assistants.

Professor Loch K. Johnson of the University of Georgia provided detailed criticisms and helpful suggestions on an earlier draft of this book. Leo Wiegman first encouraged our writing this book. Cindy Stormer, the political science editor at Brooks/Cole, prodded us to see the project to completion. The various reviewers of the manuscript contributed greatly to its improvement, and we would like to acknowledge their help: A. Stephen Boyan, Jr., University of Maryland, Baltimore County; Grant T. Hammond, Air War College; Joseph Lepgold, University of Wisconsin–Milwaukee; John J. Mearsheimer, University of Chicago; Kenneth Thompson, University of Virginia; and Richard Valcourt, *International Journal of Intelligence and Counterintelligence*. Finally, we owe many thanks to the continuing support of Louisiana State University, the Troy H. Middleton Library, and the staff of the Department of Political Science. With all of these acknowledgments, it should be noted that the finished product is but an approximation of the many helpful suggestions.

Cecil V. Crabb, Jr.
Kevin V. Mulcahy

CONTENTS

Part One
THE MEANING OF NATIONAL SECURITY

CHAPTER 1

National Security:
Basic Concepts and Principles

According to the Preamble to the Constitution of the United States, the Founding Fathers were centrally concerned with the security of the constitutional system that came into existence in 1789. Among the goals that the Founders sought to achieve at Philadelphia were "to provide for the common defense, promote the general Welfare, and secure the Blessings of Liberty to ourselves and to our Posterity." This same preoccupation with the security of the American Republic was reflected in Article II, describing the powers and responsibilities of the president. Before officially assuming his duties as chief executive, every newly elected president takes an oath to "preserve, protect, and defend the Constitution of the United States" (Article II, section 1).

Their recent colonial and revolutionary war experiences had demonstrated to the Founders that the American Republic faced a wide variety of internal and external threats to its security, making its future precarious. For many years, Great Britain appeared to pose the primary external danger—an anxiety reinforced by the eruption of a new war with Britain in 1812 and the burning of the White House in 1814. In time, other threats—from Napoleonic France, the Holy Alliance, and possible expansionism by czarist Russia—presented actual or potential dangers to the security and well-being of the New World. By the end of the nineteenth century, two ominous new threats were emerging: a powerful and ambitious German Empire, determined to achieve naval supremacy; and an increasingly hegemonic and heavily armed Japan, whose leaders in time openly subscribed to a policy of regional dominance and global influence.

Despite such evidence of American concern about national security issues, the concepts of national security and national security policy did not gain wide currency in the United States until after World War II, when the nation's hemispheric isolationism gave way to international leadership. As we shall see, the passage of the National Security Act of 1947 provided tangible evidence that such concepts had come to the forefront of official and public concern within American society. After 1947, this was manifest in the National Security Council's position as the highest-level coordinating mechanism within the federal government for dealing with external issues. By the 1980s, many commentators believed that the National Security Council (NSC) had in fact largely displaced the State Department as the most influential executive agency involved in foreign policy. As we shall see, the NSC's preeminence in regard to foreign policy has been politically controversial and much disputed by other institutional actors.

▌ Definitions and Basic Tenets

An essential point of departure for a detailed examination of our subject is the definition of national security and its principal connotations. A wide range of definitions is available in the now extensive literature on the subject. Yet, even today, informed commentators disagree considerably on the precise meaning and main connotations of national security and on the steps needed to achieve it. What follows is a discussion of the various meanings that have been attached to the term *national security*. As we shall see, many diverse definitions of the term exist.

Many years ago, Walter Lippmann asserted that a nation achieved security to the extent that "it is not in danger of having to sacrifice core values if it wishes to avoid war, and is able, if challenged, to maintain [these values] by victory in such a war."[1] Lippmann's conception emphasized two ideas nearly always present in definitions of national security today: the ability of a nation to deter war or, if deterrence fails, to win a war without losing its national integrity and independence.

Implicit in Lippmann's conception is another idea: that the security of the American nation is in jeopardy if, in the process of relying on the nation's armed forces, the fundamental nature of the American democratic system is changed into a totalitarian or other system that is fundamentally at variance with American beliefs and values. Like many other definitions of national security, Lippmann's conceived of the preservation of American security primarily in military terms.

Other definitions of national security highlight different aspects of the concept. In Arnold Wolfers's view, for example, national security has an objective and a subjective dimension, both of which must be included in any realistic understanding of the concept. Objectively, national security denotes "the absence of threats to acquired values," such as continued national independence, preservation of "the American way of life," democratic freedoms and political processes, and other principles cherished by the American people.[2] Subjectively, in Wolfers's assessment, national security also means "the absence of fear that such values will be attacked."[3] In effect, Wolfers's definition incorporates President Franklin D. Roosevelt's familiar principle of "freedom from fear" as an essential element in the concept of national security.

From a different perspective, Michael H. H. Louw has defined national security to include a nation's "traditional defense policy and also the non-military actions of a state to insure its total capacity to survive as a political entity in order to exert influence and to carry out its internal and international objectives."[4] Besides including the now familiar idea of national survival, or self-preservation, this definition also emphasizes that security must relate to certain "non-military actions" of a nation. Even less in the nuclear era than in earlier periods of history can it be said that national security is exclusively, or even predominantly, a military goal, to be achieved mainly by reliance on armed force.

Louw's definition also underscores another important dimension of national security: Nations have goals or objectives beyond their continued survival. Relatively few Americans or citizens of most other developed countries would be content with survival alone, especially if this were to mean a continual struggle to acquire just the basic necessities of life. For Americans, survival is normally linked to such goals as progress, improvement, evolution, the pursuit of happiness, and achieving "the American way of life"—the common denominator of which is the enrichment or enhancement of life in all its important spheres.

National security, by this definition, clearly has both a negative and a positive dimension. Negatively, it means that Americans want to be protected from internal and external threats to their existence and well-being. Positively, it means that Americans seek such protection for the purpose of pursuing those objectives that they believe contribute to their happiness, well-being, spiritual growth, and individual fulfillment.

Yet another dimension of national security is highlighted by the definition offered by Traeger and Simonie. In their view, "national security is that part of government policy having as its objective the creation of national and international conditions favorable to the protection or extension of vital national values against existing and potential adversaries."[5]

Here, the emphasis is on creating environmental conditions at home and abroad that are conducive to the survival and continued well-being of the nation. "Environmental conditions," of course, refers to more than the physical milieu inside and outside the United States, encompassing the overall political, social, and economic context in which national security decisions are made. The basic idea here is that national security is enhanced to the degree that beneficial changes are made in this milieu—for example, through progress toward achieving arms control between the superpowers; limiting the proliferation of nuclear weapons abroad; promoting the modernization and development of the Third World; and reducing illiteracy, disease, and poverty throughout the world.

Accordingly, national security policy should emphasize identifying and correcting those environmental factors that engender conflict, violence, war, fear, and similar behavior patterns worldwide. In different terms, many commentators differentiate between what are sometimes called the long-range and the short-range causes of war. Nations seeking to enhance their security must be concerned with both categories of threats.

On the one hand, nations must be prepared to respond to immediate threats to their existence—such as a surprise attack by an enemy, denial of access to essential raw materials, or efforts to intimidate a major ally. Concurrently, they must adopt policies and programs designed to help stabilize the global political environment and reduce violence throughout the world while continually seeking effective substitutes for armed force as a means of resolving disputes among the members of the international system. As with the municipal fire department, the ideal is fire prevention: Officials involved in American national security policy succeed to the degree that they effectively prevent developments and conflicts abroad from directly jeopardizing the security of the United States.

Melvin Small conceives of challenges to national security as arising from three general sources: direct military threats, tendencies within the economic system that are inimical to human well-being, and challenges to "national honor."[6] The last category encompasses a variety of psychological tendencies and phenomena that may jeopardize the physical safety or the emotional–psychological well-being of the American people, disturbing their "peace of mind." The concept of a nation's diplomatic credibility rests, in the final analysis, on psychological dimensions of national security. Fundamental to the credibility of America's diplomatic actions, for example, are that the people have confidence in their leaders, that they believe that the government's policies are legitimate and should be supported, and that they perceive some benefit or gain to the nation from pursuing a particular policy abroad. Subtle and intangible as these aspects of national security may be, they are nonetheless vital to the efforts of the United States to protect and maintain its security in an unstable global environment.

The definition employed by Anthony L. Wermuth highlights another important idea: National security is a continually evolving concept, whose meaning must always be reinterpreted and modified in the light of new conditions. Today, no less than in the past, the core meaning of the term may be the protection of a nation "against harm from foreign sources." Yet in an increasingly turbulent and interdependent world, national security must be no less concerned with a number of trends and issues likely to affect the future welfare and destiny of the American society. These include growing competition among the nations of the world for fossil fuels and other raw materials, such as those on the ocean floor; the impact of multinational corporations on political developments abroad; and the rising incidence of international terrorism.[7]

Former Secretary of Defense Robert McNamara has carried the concept of national security a step further. In his view, national security has too long been regarded as mainly (if not sometimes exclusively) "a military problem." For many years, the main goal of national security policy was viewed as protecting the nation from overt military threats to its continued independence. Mc-Namara believes that today, however, especially for nations throughout the Third World, the chief danger to regional and global peace lies in the adverse conditions of continued underdevelopment. It follows that for Third World nations, "security means development."[8] One can, of course, quarrel with McNamara's interpretation of national security. Yet his views appear to accurately reflect official and public thinking within many contemporary Third World countries.

For former Under Secretary of State George Ball, the concept of American national security is relatively simple and easy to comprehend. The American people and their leaders "want, by and large, what other advanced peoples want. We should like to be safe from attack and destruction. We should like to improve our material lot and have happy and interesting individual lives." At home, this means that Americans want to educate their children, reduce the crime rate, achieve social justice, eradicate poverty and disease, and take other steps to prolong and to enrich their lives. Abroad, Americans seek a safer and less violent world—one in which the number of nations friendly to the United States and its ideological values is growing. Yet, on the basis of his diplomatic experience, Ball also concluded, "a rich and powerful country like our own is more likely to be envied and feared than loved and admired."[9]

In his analysis of American national security policy, Bernard Brodie has called attention to the fact that, as has been illustrated time and again since World War II, national security "is a flexible term" whose meaning has expanded to include "something beyond simple self-defense." Since World War II, the United States, in promoting its security, has had "to make its voice heard . . . well beyond its own shores." In other words, the United States has to be able to "project" its power overseas to avert challenges to its security or to confront them far from America's borders.[10]

During World War II, President Franklin D. Roosevelt said that America's strategic frontier had become the Rhine River: Any threat to the security of Europe west of the Rhine endangered the security of the United States directly. If this idea is accepted (and it formally was with the creation of the North Atlantic Treaty Organization in 1949), then it follows that the United States has a security interest in developments that engender military vulnerability, political instability, and economic dislocations in Western Europe. Since World War II, the United States has asserted that interest, as when it, in collaboration with its Western allies, undertook the massive and expensive Marshall Plan (or European Recovery Program) in the late 1940s. Among that program's principal goals (it had several) was, clearly, the bolstering of Western security in the face of Soviet expansionist tendencies and of gains by communist groups on the European continent. This is merely one prominent example in the postwar era—in this case, a highly successful one—of the necessity for the United States to project its power externally to promote its internal security.[11]

Since World War II, concern about its security has led the United States to assume a role of global leadership. In contrast to the earlier isolationist era, American policy makers came to believe that the United States must remain actively and continuously involved in global affairs to prevent threats to national security from emerging or, if prevention fails, to keep such threats at the lowest possible level of intensity and as far from American territory as possible. As Brodie and other commentators have noted, in time this belief gave rise to the kind of "policeman of the world" mentality that led to America's agonizing involvement in the Vietnam War. Paradoxically (and the concept of national security abounds with paradoxes and anomalies), an obsessive preoccupation with national security contributed to the steady escalation of the American commitment to defeat communism in Southeast Asia. The end result of the Vietnam War, of course, was, ironically, widespread feelings of insecurity, uncertainty, and confusion among Americans concerning their nation's proper foreign policy role. Even more broadly, insofar as the Vietnam War weakened America's position of global leadership and its credibility, the outcome may well have heightened insecurity worldwide.

From the foregoing discussion of definitions of national security the concept may seem literally boundless. Indeed, one of the most difficult characteristics of national security policy making is its broad, and often elusive, nature. The very existence of the NSC attests to this fact. As a forum for the expression of different departmental viewpoints, the NSC exists because most national security issues are too broad to be addressed from any one approach. Though these issues usually involve political, military, and economic concerns, they can—and have—also involved concerns such as access to global markets and resources and the interdiction of foreign drugs. Keeping in mind the broadness of the concept, we define American national security as *the promotion of the continued independence and well-being of the American nation in the face of a wide range of continuing external challenges, particularly those involving force or the threat of force.*

▌ National Security and Internationalism

Throughout American history, some groups have believed that national security could best be achieved by reducing military expenditures, cutting military manpower, and subjecting the armed forces to careful scrutiny by Congress, the news media, and citizens' groups. This approach was especially influential in the United States following World War I, when certain leading writers and other prominent figures, including Senator Gerald P. Nye and his investigative committee, contended that the "war profiteers" and "merchants of death" (or what has more recently been called the military-industrial complex) had played a crucial role in persuading Americans to enter World War I. Encouraged by British propagandists, the merchants of death presumably manipulated the American people and their leaders into entering a military conflict that in no way involved their legitimate security interests. This interpretation of World War I seriously misled some segments of American society with regard to the underlying basis of the nation's security and did little to prepare the nation for defending its vital interests against the Axis dictators in World War II.[12]

Better understanding of the isolationist tradition is important in still another significant respect: in comprehending deeply ingrained public attitudes toward the role and purpose of military power within the American democratic system. Many of these same pre–World War II isolationist ideas continue to influence American thought and conduct related to national security issues in the post–World War II era.

From their colonial and revolutionary war experiences, Americans derived a deep suspicion toward, and aversion to, military power—especially toward a "standing army." Many of the American colonies' grievances against Great Britain stemmed from the British practice of quartering (or garrisoning) troops in American homes. Americans also knew that the hated stamp tax and other levies imposed on the colonies by London were intended to pay the cost of Great Britain's recent wars with France and other countries.[13]

For some two centuries, therefore, aversion to the idea of a standing army, or the existence of a large peacetime military establishment, has been a conspicuous feature of the American ethos. This mentality was clearly reflected in the Constitution (Article I, section 8), which prohibits Congress from making appropriations for the Army for more than two years at a time. (Interestingly enough, the Founders did not exhibit the same degree of apprehension about the Navy, which normally operates far from America's own shores.)

As one study of the national ethos has emphasized, Americans have traditionally believed that the "military mind" poses a danger to some of their most cherished values and democratic principles. Americans believe that to a greater or lesser degree, concepts such as equality, freedom, individualism, democracy, progress, and the good life are endangered by the existence of a large and expensive military establishment. Throughout their history, therefore, Americans have been on guard against "the man on horseback," Bonapartism, and other military-based movements they have viewed as detrimental to their way of life.[14]

Many of these traditional American attitudes toward the military establishment have been carried over into the post–World War II era of internationalism. Historically, for example, Americans have exhibited a long-standing aversion to military "preparedness" measures. As a rule, Americans have usually been unwilling to engage in military or contingency planning directed toward preserving their security against possible enemies. When President Woodrow Wilson learned, for example, that certain high-ranking military officers were drawing up plans in anticipation of a possible war with imperial Germany, he was incensed, ordering such planning to be stopped at once and the officers engaged in it to be reassigned. In the view of President Wilson and many of his followers, such military contingency planning greatly increased the likelihood of war.[15]

The antimilitary cast of the American mind has also produced a strong aversion toward military conscription, which in the United States has been resorted to only rarely. Ever since the revolutionary war, for Americans the model has been the "citizen-soldier." When national security is threatened, the ordinary citizen leaves his or her civilian pursuits, assumes military duties, defeats the enemy, and, after the crisis has ended, quickly returns to the normal pursuits of civilian life. Between such crises, as in the period following World War II, the nation's armed forces dwindle rapidly in size, falling to a small fraction of their earlier wartime strength.[16]

A corollary idea is the belief that political or civilian and military decisions constitute separate realms of national policy. To the American mind, war is an abnormal condition, resulting from a failure in political decision making. When civilian leaders are unable to solve global disputes, they turn to military leaders to resolve the conflict on the battlefield. In this latter stage, as President Franklin Roosevelt repeatedly insisted during World War II, civilian officials are expected not to "complicate" the war effort by injecting political controversies or issues into it. Similarly, high-ranking military officials are expected to concentrate on "winning the war" and to leave political questions for later resolution by their civilian superiors.[17]

This is another way of saying that relatively few Americans are familiar with the Prussian General Karl Maria von Clausewitz's celebrated dictum, "War is the continuation of politics by other means." Clausewitz's maxim has many implications for the relationship between political and military decision making. Chief perhaps is that, far from being distinct realms, political and military decision making must be thought of as a continuum: One shades gradually and imperceptibly into the other, with decisions at one end momentously affecting decisions reached at the other. As merely one example of Clausewitz's principle, during World War II Soviet armed forces overran much of Eastern Europe in the final Allied offensive against Nazi Germany. This fact in turn made possible Soviet domination of its satellite system within the region until the late 1980s. Beginning with the emergence and eventual victory of the Solidarity movement in Poland, growing popular resentment against communist misrule in Eastern Europe swept out Marxist-controlled governments and significantly weakened Moscow's influence within the region. The destruction of the infamous Berlin wall symbolized these fundamental changes behind what was once described as the Iron Curtain. The ideas of General Clausewitz have long been known to Soviet officials and approvingly quoted by them. By contrast, most Americans remain ignorant of Clausewitz's teachings and are still reluctant to view military force as an extension or instrument of the political process.

Still another corollary of the historical American distrust of the military establishment has been the nation's reluctance to create and operate an effective intelligence service. Until World War II, American intelligence operations (when they were carried on at all) were conducted on an ad hoc basis, unsystematically, and with little effort to coordinate governmentwide intelligence activities. Even today, many Americans are convinced that intelligence operations per se pose a threat to democratic government. This aversion was expressed by former Secretary of State Henry Stimson, who said during the 1920s that "nice people do not read other people's mail!"

The common denominator to these ideas concerning the role of the military in American life is a concept that for more than two centuries has been viewed as an essential tenet of a democratic system: the principle of civilian supremacy over the military establishment. This principle is reflected in such constitutional provisions as those giving Congress the power to "provide for the common defense" and "declare war," "to raise and support Armies," and "to provide and maintain a Navy" (Article I, section 8). The principle of civilian control over the military is affirmed again in Article II, section 2, which designates the nation's highest elected civilian official—the president—the commander in chief of the armed forces. Further, according to the provisions of the National Security Act of 1947, the president chairs the National Security Council, of which all the statutory (voting) members are also civilians. By long-standing tradition, the Secretary of Defense, along with the operating heads of each of the service arms, are also civilian officials.

As already emphasized, Americans have historically been apprehensive about "the man on horseback," the military leader who might be tempted to usurp civilian authority. Americans want no war lords or militarists, like the Prussian general staff or the Japanese ruling class of the 1930s. To date, the evidence convincingly indicates that for some two centuries U.S. military leaders have fully understood and subscribed to these same traditions. Despite fictionalized accounts (such as the popular novel *Seven Days in May*), the American people have in fact witnessed no serious effort by military leaders to impose a military-dominated government on them. In some measure, the veneration accorded "the father of the country" stemmed from George Washington's retirement from the armed forces and his refusal to exploit his distinguished military record for his own self-aggrandizement. The American people today appear to be no less determined than the Founders to maintain the principle of civilian supremacy in their unique constitutional system.

▌ The National Security Act of 1947

In December 1945, President Harry S Truman called for a reorganization of the nation's military establishment.[18] Not unexpectedly, Truman's proposal aroused intense and prolonged debate inside and outside the government. At the risk of some oversimplification, we may identify two reasonably distinct positions as the most popular in the ensuing debate.

One was identified with the U.S. Army and supported by the Air Force; the other reflected the view of the Navy. By the end of World War II, substantial sentiment existed within the Army favoring the creation of a single unified War Department (consolidating the old War and Navy departments). This department's principal administrative divisions would correspond to the existing military services, each to be headed by a civilian secretary, as would the department as a whole. The Army's plan called for a high degree of cooperation among the services in such activities as weapons development, procurement, and joint military planning. A highly controversial feature of this plan was the idea that a single chief of staff (appointed by the president) would serve as the nation's highest-ranking military commander. (Here, the Army's approach was unquestionably influenced by the highly successful experience of General George C. Marshall, chief of staff during World War II.) In most respects, the Army's plan was also endorsed by the Air Force.[19]

Predictably, spokesmen for the Navy, and organizations sympathetic to its interests, in time offered counterproposals. The "Eberstadt Report" published in late 1945 reflected Navy Secretary James Forrestal's conviction that the Navy's approach must be "positive and constructive." The Eberstadt Report rejected the idea of a single, unified military department in favor of a more decentralized defense organization. As in the past, the three primary service arms (with the Marine Corps administratively part of the Navy) would be retained, with each branch headed by its own civilian secretary, who would hold cabinet rank.

By strong implication at least, advocates of the Navy's plan suggested that the creation of a single, unified military department would weaken civilian control over the armed forces and lead to expanded military influence throughout American life.[20] In addition, several new mechanisms and agencies (such as a Joint Chiefs of Staff and a Central Intelligence Agency) would be established; these would operate under the general supervision of the president and a new National Security Council.

Supporters of the Army's approach were no less active in expressing their views to Congress and to the American people. In late 1945, the "Collins plan" reiterated the Army's insistence that a single, unified defense department be created, headed by a civilian secretary of defense, with a chief of staff serving as the nation's highest-ranking military official and as the principal military adviser to the president.[21]

Although unenthusiastic about a centralization of military operations, most proponents of the Navy's approach to the issue in time came to accept two key realities. One was that after World War II, far-reaching changes in the traditional organization of America's defense were inevitable. By itself, the Navy was not strong enough to stop the momentum toward military reform. The other reality was that implacable opposition to change would likely result in the Navy's having minimal influence in formulating the plan that would ultimately be adopted. For their part, spokesmen for the Army and Air Force also favored compromise, because they knew that in the end their combined views would have a decisive impact on any plan adopted. Over a period of several months, intensive efforts were made to discover common ground within the government for the Navy's and the Army's plans for reorganization. Finally, on July 26, 1947, Congress enacted the most sweeping reorganization in the area of national security policy since World War II.[22]

With the National Security Act of 1947, Congress created a National Military Establishment—later renamed the Department of Defense—headed by a new secretary of defense, who was to be appointed by and responsible to the president. Within this new department were separate departments of the Army, Navy, and Air Force, each administered by a civilian secretary. The act designated the secretary of defense "the principal assistant to the President in all matters relating to the national security" of the United States; the secretary was also made responsible for the overall operations of the Defense Department.

The act also created a new high-level coordinating mechanism—the National Security Council—"to advise the President with respect to the integration of domestic, foreign, and military policies relating to the national security." By law, the president serves as chairman of the National Security Council.

The membership of the NSC has varied over the years. By the late 1980s its statutory, or voting, members comprised the president, the vice president, the secretary of defense, and the secretary of state. The director of central intelligence (DCI) and the chairman of the Joint Chiefs of Staff (JCS) serve as statutory advisers to the NSC. At any time, however, a president is free to (and often does) invite other officials and private citizens to attend NSC meetings and take part in its discussions. A member of the White House staff, rather than a departmental official, has always served as the director of the NSC staff, supervising the overall activities of the agency. As is evident, the membership and procedures of the NSC have from the beginning strongly affirmed the fundamental constitutional principle of civilian supremacy over the military.

The National Security Act of 1947 also created a new intelligence service— called the Central Intelligence Agency (CIA)—to operate under the supervision of the National Security Council. In time, the CIA became the leading member of a large complex of agencies collectively called the "intelligence community," whose members are identified more fully in chapter 3. The CIA is headed by a director, appointed by the president.

Though other executive agencies engage in various kinds of intelligence operations, a major purpose of the CIA, as its name implies, is to centrally coordinate and direct national intelligence activities. Laying the groundwork for what was to prove the most controversial of the CIA's activities, the 1947 act empowered the CIA to perform "such other functions and duties related to intelligence affecting the national security as the National Security Council may from time to time direct." We shall discuss these "special projects" more specifically in chapter 3.

The National Security Act of 1947 also provided for the creation of a new Joint Chiefs of Staff within the Defense Department to plan unified military strategy and to reduce the rivalry and duplication among the armed services in areas such as military procurement, research, and weapons development. As the office has evolved since 1947, the JCS now consists of the chiefs of staff of the Army and the Air Force, the chief of naval operations, the Marine Corps commandant, and a vice chairman and chairman. All members of the JCS, which serves as the principal military adviser to the president and his or her civilian aides, are appointed by the president. Initially, a joint staff for the JCS, consisting of some one hundred officers, was established to assist the members of the JCS in the performance of their duties.

As much as any other provision of the National Security Act, the establishment of the JCS illustrated the degree to which the act reflected a compromise among divergent views on how the national defense was to be organized. For the first time in peacetime, the American military now had a general staff representing all branches of the armed forces. In contrast to the Army's earlier proposals, however, this was a collegial body, rather than a single individual.

As the years passed, however, it became evident that the establishment of the JCS had not resulted in a unified U.S. national defense policy. Instead, in arriving at their decisions members of the JCS routinely engage in bargaining and compromise designed to ensure that none of the service branches gets "left out" in the allocation of military appropriations. In the process, they devote little attention to whether, or to what degree, such interservice negotiations actually promote a more unified and effective national military effort. Meanwhile, critics of the American military establishment believe that rivalries and schisms among the military branches continue—in some respects, perhaps, more acutely than before—and detract from the ability of the United States to respond effectively to external threats.[23]

As envisioned by Congress in the National Security Act of 1947, the members of the Joint Chiefs of Staff continue to "wear two hats," or play two somewhat contradictory roles. In their capacity as members of the nation's highest-level military advisory board to the president and other civilian leaders, they are expected to plan and think nationally—that is, in terms of what is best for the United States as a whole.

But the members of the JCS also serve as the operating heads of their respective military branches. For example, as a naval officer, the chief of naval operations is inevitably identified with naval traditions and viewpoints: His or her professional attainments, friends, lifestyle, and ambitions are all closely tied to a career of faithful and capable service in the United States Navy. In most crucial respects, any candidate for the position on the Joint Chiefs of Staff will be evaluated on the basis of his or her performance as a career naval officer.

After 1947, other changes and modifications in the national security structure were made by formal amendments to the initial act and by executive order. In most instances, these changes were minor. The main substantive changes entailed strengthening the powers of the secretary of defense over both military and civilian rivals in the Pentagon.

From time to time after 1947—as during the 1960s, under Secretary of Defense Robert McNamara—new attempts were made to overcome provincialism and separatist tendencies in the military establishment. McNamara and his "Whiz Kids" did indeed have an impact on the Defense Department. Yet talented as he was, not even McNamara was able to "tame the Pentagon."

More than two decades after McNamara the same complaints are still heard: Little unification exists among the nation's still-separate military "tribes," and their efforts in battle are sometimes seriously impaired because of the feuds and rivalries among their members. Even today, in the allocation of funds for the defense establishment the main consideration appears to be giving each service branch "its share" of an enormous defense budget. Meanwhile, finding a solution to the infinitely more difficult problem—devising a truly unified national strategy to which each of the separate military branches contributes—remains an elusive quest.[24]

One final observation about the National Security Act of 1947 is in order. After leaving the State Department, Secretary of State Dean Rusk used to say that a president is free to consult his barber or his chauffeur in making foreign policy decisions, if he desires! Although no doubt intended facetiously, Rusk's comment calls attention to an important aspect of presidential advisory systems.

Congress may provide for elaborate administrative mechanisms with respect to national security policy and other fields. It may create new executive agencies, reorganize others, and eliminate still others. It may from time to time investigate the operations of the White House staff, the CIA, and other executive agencies, and call for fundamental changes in their organization, personnel, and missions.

Yet it must be remembered that the Constitution (Article II, section 1) provides that "the executive power shall be vested in a President of the United States." In contrast to the legislative and judicial powers of the national government, the executive authority is singular: It is totally vested in one individual—the president. How a particular president actually uses advisers and advisory mechanisms is a matter determined by each occupant of the Oval Office. As our case studies (chapters 4 through 8) clearly demonstrate, since World War II significant differences can be identified with regard to how each chief executive has used his formal and informal advisers; each president has had his own decision-making style or process.

Although presidents have varied widely in their use of advisory mechanisms, we believe that since 1947 four reasonably distinct decision-making patterns or models can be identified. In the case studies that follow, the experiences of particular administrations are examined in detail to illustrate the models and call attention to their main characteristics. (Our treatment makes no attempt to provide a detailed chronological account of developments in American national security policy since World War II.)

First, however, to understand American national security policy more intelligently, we must consider two additional aspects of the problem. One is the external milieu—the international environment—in which decisions are made that affect the national security of the United States. That is the subject of chapter 2. The other, no less crucial aspect is the internal context in which national security decisions are made, examined in chapter 3.

▌ National Security: Axioms and Propositions

To sum up, certain fundamental axioms and propositions about American national security policy can be identified on the basis of our discussion thus far:

- From the earliest days of the Republic, Americans have been concerned about the security of their society.

- Threats to national security can arise both externally and internally, although our discussion must be limited to a consideration of external threats.
- The concept of national security is complex and difficult to define and contains numerous objective and subjective elements, but at its core it appears to refer to a society's perception of external threats and its response to them.
- For most Americans, in addition to mere survival, national security implies the creation and preservation of conditions in which the good life may be pursued.
- Nations must always be prepared to respond to immediate threats to their security, but they should be no less interested in preventive measures that will reduce the likelihood of such threats.
- Since World War II, concern about its security has led the United States to adopt an active interventionist foreign policy involving the projection of American power abroad. A major challenge in the post–Vietnam War era is deciding when and where this power should be used.
- The evidence convincingly indicates that the United States will continue to confront external threats to its security arising from an international system that, in an era of nuclear stalemate, remains unstable, prone to violence, and unpredictable.
- A nation's sense of security (or insecurity) is based heavily on official and popular perceptions. Since World War II, major misperceptions have sometimes been responsible for failures and reverses in national security policy.
- The concept of American national security abounds with contradictions and paradoxes, including the idea that an undue and narrow preoccupation with its own security can threaten the security of the United States and other countries.
- America's long isolationist tradition provided poor preparation for serious thought about national security after World War II. Before the war, certain (usually unrecognized) conditions created a high degree of security for Americans.
- Even today, relatively few Americans understand Clausewitz's teaching regarding the intimate relationship between military power and political outcomes.
- Since World War II, Americans have made a more systematic effort to integrate the political and military aspects of national policy, as exemplified by the National Security Act of 1947, which created new coordinating and advisory mechanisms in the area of national security.
- The Cold War raised a new set of problems and issues related to national security policy, requiring the United States to maintain, and to be prepared to use, a large, modern "peacetime" military establishment to achieve its external goals.
- As most informed commentators are aware, postwar efforts have thus far not ended interservice military rivalries and bureaucratic competi-

tion in the sphere of national security policy; such competition still weakens the nation's efforts to respond to external challenges.

- On the basis of America's actions since 1947, several models or patterns of decision making with regard to national security affairs can be identified. Every incumbent president's decision-making style is to some extent unique; yet it is also possible to apply certain criteria for testing the ultimate value of these individual models in terms of their contribution to the promotion of national security.

NOTES

1. Walter Lippmann's views on national security are quoted in Barry Buzan, *People, States, and Fear: The National Security Problem in International Relations* (Brighton, Sussex, England: Wheatsheaf Books, 1983), p. 216.

2. See Arnold Wolfers, "National Security as an Ambiguous Symbol," *Political Science Quarterly* 67 (December 1952): 481–502.

3. Arnold Wolfers's views are quoted in Buzan, *People, States, and Fear*, pp. 216–217.

4. Michael H. H. Louw's views are quoted in Buzan, *People, States, and Fear*, p. 216.

5. The views of Frank N. Traeger and F. N. Simonie are quoted in Buzan, *People, States, and Fear*, p. 217. A more detailed study emphasizing this idea is Neville Brown, *The Future Global Challenge: A Predictive Study of World Security (1977–1990)* (New York: Crane Russak, 1977).

6. See Melvin Small, "National Security," in *International War: An Anthology*, ed. Melvin Small and J. David Singer, (Homewood, Ill.: Dorsey Press, 1985), pp. 136–137.

7. Anthony L. Wermuth, "The Evolving Domestic Forum for National Security Debates," in *New Dynamics in National Strategy*, the United States Army War College (New York: Thomas Y. Crowell, 1975), pp. 2–3.

8. See the views of Robert McNamara on the concept of national security in Carl W. Borklund, *Men of the Pentagon: From Forrestal to McNamara* (New York: Praeger, 1966), pp. 233–236.

9. See George Ball, *The Discipline of Power: Essentials of a Modern World Structure* (Boston: Little, Brown, 1968), p. 344.

10. Bernard Brodie, *War and Politics* (New York: Macmillan, 1973), pp. 345–365.

11. The momentous transition in American foreign policy during the Truman administration is dealt with more fully in Harry S Truman's memoirs, *Years of Trial and Hope* (Garden City, N.Y.: Doubleday, 1956), especially pp. 93–133; Arthur H. Vandenberg, Jr., ed., *The Private Papers of Senator Vandenberg* (Boston: Houghton Mifflin, 1952), pp. 262–421; and Joseph Jones, *The Fifteen Weeks* (New York: Viking Press, 1955).

12. John E. Wiltz, *In Search of Peace: The Senate Munitions Inquiry, 1934–1936* (Baton Rouge: Louisiana State University Press, 1963).

13. James Clotfelter, *The Military in American Politics* (New York: Harper & Row, 1973), pp. 22–25; and Robert E. Osgood, "The American Approach to War," in *U.S. National Security Policy: A Framework for Analysis,* ed. Daniel J. Kaufman, Jeffrey S. McKitrick, and Thomas J. Leney (Lexington, Mass.: D. C. Heath, 1985), pp. 91–105. For a discussion of traditional American attitudes, see Donald M. Snow, *National Security: Enduring Problems of U.S. Defense Policy* (New York: St. Martin, 1987), pp. 21–43.

14. See the more detailed examination of the antimilitary bias in the American ethos in James Coates and Roland J. Pelligrin, *Military Sociology: A Study of American Military Institutions and Military Life* (University Park, Md.: Social Science Press, 1965), pp. 22–35.

15. The anecdote about President Wilson is recounted in David Rees, *Korea: The Limited War* (Baltimore: Penguin, 1970), pp. x–xi.

16. See Forest C. Pogue, *George C. Marshall: Ordeal and Hope (1939–1942)* (New York: Viking Press, 1966), pp. 3–5; and Eliot A. Cohen, *Citizens and Soldiers: The Dilemmas of Military Service* (Ithaca, N.Y.: Cornell University Press, 1985).

17. See the analyses of public opinion and military questions in Clotfelter, *The Military in American Politics,* pp. 124–127; and Brodie, *War and Politics,* pp. 33–37; and the views of General Maxwell D. Taylor, "National Policy Too Lightly Armed," in *Grand Strategy for the 1980s,* ed. Bruce Palmer (Washington, D.C.: American Enterprise Institute, 1979), p. 1.

18. Truman, *Years of Trial and Hope,* pp. 46–50.

19. For the Army's approach to the problem of defense reorganization after World War II, see C. W. Borklund, *The Department of Defense* (New York: Praeger, 1968), pp. 17–36.

20. The Eberstadt plan was named for Ferdinand Eberstadt, who was requested by Navy Secretary James Forrestal to submit a proposal reflecting the Navy's viewpoints on defense reorganization. See Borklund, *The Department of Defense,* pp. 36–38; and Walter Millis, ed., *The Forrestal Diaries* (New York: Viking Press, 1951), pp. 126–170.

21. The Collins plan is explained more fully in Borklund, *The Department of Defense,* pp. 31–36.

22. For the text of the National Security Act of 1947, see U.S. Congress, *U.S. Statutes at Large,* 80th Cong, 1st sess., 1947, vol. 61, pt. 1, pp. 495–510.

23. The point is the basic theme of the analysis by James Coates and Michael Kilian, *Heavy Losses: The Dangerous Decline of American Defense* (New York: Penguin Books, 1986). See also *Toward A More Effective Defense,* ed. Barry M. Blechman and William J. Lynn (Cambridge, Mass.: Ballinger, 1985); *America's Defense,* ed. Michael Mandelbaum (New York: Holmes & Meier, 1989); Robert S. McNamara, *Out of the Cold: New Thinking for American Foreign and Defense Policy in the 21st Century* (New York: Simon & Schuster, 1989); and *U.S. Defense Policy,* 3rd ed. (Washington, D.C.: Congressional Quarterly Press, 1983) and subsequent volumes in this series.

24. For evaluations of the national defense establishment from various perspectives, see Blechman and Lynn, *Toward a More Effective Defense;* James

Fallows, *National Defense* (New York: Random House, 1982); William Kaufman, *A Reasonable Defense* (Washington, D.C.: Brookings Institution, 1986); Gregg Herken, *Councils of War* (New York: Oxford University Press, 1987); and Edward N. Luttwak, *The Pentagon and the Art of War* (New York: Simon & Schuster, 1985).

CHAPTER 2

National Security:
The External Environment

For more than a century and a half until World War II, the foreign policy of the United States was widely described as isolationist. From the viewpoint of strict accuracy, isolationism defined America's position only toward Europe. Different principles guided American diplomacy toward Asia and Latin America. For example, the United States was willing to pursue interventionism in China to further commercial opportunities (the Open Door policy) and in Latin America to ensure hemispheric hegemony (the Roosevelt corollary to the Monroe Doctrine). Yet, with the exception of Japan after 1900, the most influential global actors—frequently described as the Great Powers—were located in Europe, and it was this region that Americans believed presented the principal threats to their security and well-being.[1]

Pearl Harbor and America's entry into World War II formally ended the long era of U.S. isolationism. Determined not to repeat the lessons of the 1930s, the Roosevelt and Truman administrations took the lead in establishing the United Nations, founded in 1945. For many years thereafter, Americans confidently expected that this second experiment in international organization (the first having been the League of Nations) would relieve the United States of the responsibility for global peacekeeping. As most Americans today are well aware, that hope was unfulfilled.

Through a series of unilateral and multilateral measures beginning during the late 1940s, the United States adopted and implemented a containment policy as its basic response to the threat of Soviet expansionism. By the time of the Korean War, which erupted in June 1950, Americans finally recognized that their new international role made the maintenance of a large, modern peacetime (if the Cold War period could be so described) military establishment essential to preserving national security under a wide variety of conditions abroad.

Meanwhile, American attitudes toward national security after World War II were momentously affected by the long isolationist tradition. The era of isolationism had a profound and lasting impact on official and public attitudes in the United States toward national security issues. It is therefore necessary to examine briefly some of the main characteristics of the isolationist mentality.

▌ The Isolationist Tradition

Before World War II, the American people and their leaders devoted little sustained or systematic thought to the challenge of preserving their national security. For example, why, with rare exceptions, were the European powers content to confine their expansionist activities primarily to regions other than North America? Why did Napoleon not use his control over New Orleans to expand into the American hinterland at the turn of the nineteenth century? Why did czarist Russia (which had a colony in the American Northwest) similarly refrain from expanding its colonial empire in the American West? Toward the end of the nineteenth century, why did an increasingly militant and powerful German nation not attempt to establish colonies in the Western hemisphere?

During the isolationist era, relatively few Americans thought seriously about such questions. Concerned primarily with "building a new nation" and achieving "the American way of life" at home, most citizens simply took the security of their democracy for granted. That the United States enjoyed security from external threats appeared to be another of those favors bestowed by divine providence on a "chosen" American people.[2]

Alternatively, American national security appeared to be a gift from Nature. Certain geographical features presented formidable obstacles to any foreign power with designs on the New World, greatly enhancing its security.

The new and militarily weak American Republic was separated from the Old World by the Atlantic "moat"; the even vaster stretches of the Pacific helped protect it from Asia. An impenetrable Arctic icecap sealed off northern approaches to the New World. As for Canada, its people were usually more concerned about being annexed by the United States than inclined to threaten their more powerful southern neighbor. To the south, after the Mexican War the government of Mexico and most of its Latin American neighbors were too weak and politically unstable to pose a serious threat to the United States. The Monroe Doctrine, issued in 1823, also contained a pointed warning to foreign powers not to intervene in the affairs of the Western hemisphere.

In addition, until World War II, the United States, as much as any other nation in the modern world, was largely self-sufficient in raw materials. For the most part, it could and did meet its own needs for the strategic raw materials required to sustain a relatively small military establishment. By the late 1930s, the United States began to serve as the "arsenal of democracy," sending vast supplies to Great Britain, the Soviet Union, and other allies before and during World War II.

The case for an isolationist foreign policy rested on the pervasive belief that America's democratic ideology and system of government were basically different from those of other nations. As President James Monroe emphasized in his celebrated doctrine in 1823, the political principles of the newly independent nations of North and South America contrasted fundamentally with those prevailing in the Old World, and the people of the United States were determined to preserve these differences. Among other things, this meant avoiding the almost certain contamination of America's democratic political system that would occur if the United States became regularly involved, as a distinctly weaker power, in European wars and political rivalries. (In this sense, America's position before World War II resembled that of new nations throughout the Third World in the postwar period.)

Two other underlying realities enabled America to adhere to an isolationist foreign policy before World War II. Even today, relatively few Americans are aware of the extent to which their nation's security depended on these realities for a century and a half. One crucial factor was the existence of British power—especially British seapower—which played a key role in enforcing the Monroe Doctrine on several occasions after 1823 before the United States emerged as a world power in the early twentieth century. For its own reasons (or as political realists phrase it, pursuing its own "national interests"), Britain supported the Monroe Doctrine and from time to time cautioned other countries not to violate its terms.[3]

Britain's support of the Monroe Doctrine was merely one manifestation of a more general phenomenon that, by the early twentieth century, had become a basic axiom of national security for the United States: the existence of a "special relationship," or underlying identity of interests throughout the world, between the United States and Great Britain. Although the United States had fought Great Britain for independence, British influence on all aspects of American life was extensive and profound. Both nations were (or were becoming) democracies. Both were seapowers and believed in such principles as "freedom of the seas" and unimpeded access to the world's markets. By the 1930s, both nations were also apprehensive about nazism, communism, and other "isms" that posed a threat to the future of democracy. After World War II, it was often said that the United States was required (in regions such as Greece, Turkey, and the Persian Gulf area) to "take over" from Great Britain global obligations and responsibilities that the markedly weaker British government was no longer able to bear. Even then, the special relationship between the United States and Great Britain continued to be a foundation stone of America's national security policy.

The second largely unrecognized factor contributing to America's enjoyment of security before World War II was the dynamics of the balance of power on the European continent. Throughout the nineteenth century, for example, the European powers were too suspicious of one another to combine their power for expansion into the New World. The most serious threat to the Monroe Doctrine in the nineteenth century, for example, was posed by overt French intervention in Mexico during the American Civil War. Napoleon III's

Mexican venture was finally terminated, primarily because of growing French apprehension about an ambitious Germany's intentions on the European continent and elsewhere. Thus, until World War I, the European powers remained too distrustful of one another to become deeply involved in expansionist ventures in the Western hemisphere, especially because Great Britain nearly always opposed such a course.

That Americans devoted little conscious thought to the conditions promoting their security meant that they often erroneously attributed that security to a variety of other, usually extraneous, factors. One erroneous belief was that—since the United States had no desire to intervene in the affairs of other powerful nations—those other nations similarly had no interest in intervening in the New World, or no incentive to do so. Many Americans were also convinced that resounding policy declarations—often dramatically delivered by the president before the assembled Congress—kept predatory powers away from America's shores. Until the present, in fact, such doctrines have played a unique role in American diplomacy. Many Americans believed that their mere issuance from time to time was sufficient to preserve national security. (The crucial role of the British fleet in enforcing the Monroe Doctrine largely escaped the notice of most Americans.)[4]

▌ The Soviet Challenge to American National Security

Since World War II, few Americans have been in doubt concerning the primary danger to the security of the United States: the challenge posed by what Secretary of State John Foster Dulles was to call "international communism," led by the Soviet Union. But in what particular ways or respects did communism jeopardize the security of Americans?[5]

One long-standing cause of American concern (which induced Washington to withhold recognition of the communist government of the USSR until 1933) was that Moscow openly advocated and supported revolutions against established governments. Another cause of deep apprehension in the West—and a factor that became crucial as World War II drew to an end—was that the Kremlin's actions jeopardized the balance of power by threatening to extend Soviet power into the center of Europe. As we have seen, this threat or its potential convinced advocates of realpolitik that Soviet expansionism had to be opposed by the only nation capable of creating and maintaining a power equilibrium—the United States.

Communism could also be, and often was, interpreted as a serious ideological threat to America's national security, insofar as it might endanger the global prospects for the emergence and preservation of democratic governments abroad. President Woodrow Wilson had defined America's goal during World War I as making "the world safe for democracy." To the minds of Wilsonian idealists then and afterward, a clear connection existed between the extension of democracy abroad and the maintenance of global peace and security.

After World War II, the Kremlin engaged in or sponsored several other activities inimical to the security of the United States and its allies and friends abroad. For example, Moscow encouraged and instigated "wars of national liberation" throughout the Third World.[6] Moreover, the Soviet Union and its supporters abroad made concerted efforts to disrupt American-sponsored alliance systems (such as NATO and the Rio Treaty in Latin America). Radio Moscow and other Soviet propaganda agencies conducted extensive broadcasting campaigns against the United States and nations closely associated with it.[7] In addition, the Soviet KGB (or secret police) carried on an ongoing, and in some instances highly successful, campaign of espionage against the United States and its principal military allies (such as Great Britain and West Germany). In recent years also, some Western officials believe that the Kremlin directly instigated or encouraged certain forms of international terrorism.

Each of these aspects of the communist challenge has, of course, over time been answered by the United States alone or in concert with its principal allies. The threat of Soviet military expansionism, for example, has been met with a continuing buildup of strategic and conventional military forces by the United States and its allies. Moscow's intensive propaganda activities have in turn prompted the United States to conduct a worldwide ongoing propaganda and informational campaign of its own, through the United States Information Agency (USIA). The activities of the KGB in the United States and other Western countries have been countered by the growth and activities of the CIA, the FBI, and other members of the U.S. intelligence community.

Just as American foreign policy has undergone fundamental changes, especially since the Vietnam War, so too has the nature of the communist challenge throughout the postwar period. The defection of Yugoslavia from the international communist movement during the late 1940s really began the movement known as polycentrism—a concept later identified with European Marxist groups such as the Italian Communist party. One after another, Marxist organizations outside the Soviet Union challenged the Kremlin's right to serve as the sole authoritative interpreter of Marxist orthodoxy. Such groups also increasingly challenged the relevance of the Soviet model of national development for other societies. Throughout the world, the emergence of several new species of national communism required Moscow and Washington alike to change their policies in dealing with Marxist countries.[8]

Despite the development of polycentrism, until the late 1980s Western officials believed that the danger of overt expansionism by the Soviet Union remained high. Moscow's decision to withdraw its military forces from Afghanistan—together with a reduction in the Soviet military presence on the African continent and the growing independence of Eastern Europe—provided tangible evidence that the Soviet threat had diminished. By 1990, Washington and Moscow were engaged in diplomatic discussions aimed at reducing by substantial numbers American and Soviet military forces on the European continent. Yet, in other settings—and the challenge of formulating an effective policy toward El Salvador and Nicaragua exemplified the problem—the American people and their leaders often seemed genuinely puzzled about the proper role of military force in the achievement of external policy goals.

The Soviet invasion of Afghanistan in late 1979 convinced many Western observers that Moscow would not hesitate to rely on armed forces to gain its objectives in the Third World. For a decade thereafter, American sympathies were with the Afghan rebels resisting Soviet domination. Military aid and other forms of assistance by the United States were crucial in enabling the people of Afghanistan to wage an effective resistance campaign against the Soviet intruder. In assisting rebel forces, however, Washington was always careful to maintain a low profile by avoiding actions in Afghanistan (and elsewhere, such as Eastern Europe) that might provoke the Kremlin. The ultimate withdrawal of Soviet forces from Afghanistan—along with Moscow's overall moderate reaction to the disintegration of its Eastern European satellite system—showed the wisdom of such restrained behavior by the United States.

In addition, the era of national communism witnessed several instances of actual or threatened expansionism by proxies of the Soviet Union. Two noteworthy examples were North Vietnam and North Korea. In the former case, after the Vietnam War the United States relied primarily on the efforts of nations within the region (such as Thailand and China) to restrain North Vietnamese expansionism. In Korea, the United States depended directly on its own power, in close cooperation with the government of South Korea, to contain any new effort by a still-aggressive North Korea to expand its hegemony.[9]

During this era of national communism, the Soviet Union, its proxies, or both also intervened politically from time to time in the affairs of noncommunist nations. For the most part, Moscow preferred to act with or through client states, as in Cuba's massive support of the Marxist regime in Nicaragua and the same country's intervention in Angola.[10] The United States, for its part, also found clients of its own, such as the Contras and other anticommunist groups in Central America. In such cases, both superpowers have usually endeavored to keep their own involvement in the conflict inconspicuous.

In responding to the challenge of national communism, the United States has also relied heavily on pragmatic results to weaken communism's appeal, especially throughout the Third World. On the basis of recent experience, neither the Soviet Union nor any other communist system can claim any noteworthy success in raising production levels and living standards, increasing agricultural output, meeting housing needs, and solving other urgent problems facing most Third World populations. As Communist China's widely publicized abandonment of Mao Tse-tung's rigid version of Marxism indicated, the Chinese in time conceded that an economic system incorporating free-market principles and incentives was simply more productive than a communist system. The people obviously prefer the former to the latter, because they benefit more directly and immediately from it. In this kind of test, the communist model of national development has nearly always lost to an approach based at least in part on free-market concepts and economic enterprise.

Alternatively—and Communist China again provided an example of this approach—the United States has sought to demonstrate the tangible benefits of cooperation with the United States and its allies. By about 1970, policy makers in China had arrived at a twofold conclusion affecting the diplomatic position of their nation: China needed to intensify its drive toward modernization and development, and to achieve that goal, China had to draw on the expertise, technological skill, and capital resources of noncommunist nations, chiefly the United States and Japan. These incentives were crucial in China's decision to normalize relations with the United States under the Nixon administration.[11]

The United States responded positively to Chinese overtures. During the years that followed, China gained American economic and technical assistance to aid in its Four Modernizations program, limited military aid and access to the Western market to buy needed military equipment, infusions of American and other foreign (for example, Japanese) investment capital, access to Western science and medicine, Western assistance in modernizing the Chinese educational system, and numerous other major and minor benefits. Such gains were quite clearly linked to China's gravitation away from ideological and political dependency on the Soviet Union.

The United States has also sought to respond positively to peaceful overtures on the part of the Soviet Union. In the Nixon administration, detente opened the way for the first limitations on strategic weaponry, embodied in the SALT treaty in 1973. More recently, in 1988 the Soviet policy of *glasnost* (or openness) initiated by Mikhail Gorbachev led to the Intermediate Nuclear Force (INF) Treaty, which abolished a whole category of so-called theater nuclear weapons. For President Reagan (as for President Nixon), rapprochement with the Soviet Union reversed long-standing political rhetoric. On the other hand, the easing of tensions between the United States and the Soviet Union was in direct response to changes in the international behavior of the Soviet Union that led the United States to regard it as more responsible and cooperative.

▌ Economic Influences on National Security

Although America's global involvement has been driven more by opposition to communism than by a quest for raw materials, a number of fundamental economic factors also crucially affect the national security of the United States. One such factor is America's continued access to strategic and other raw materials needed for supporting a large, modern military establishment and essential for maintaining a high level of economic activity in the United States.

Without arguing for economic determinism, we assert that few facts more graphically highlight the difference between the old isolationism and the postwar internationalism than the change in America's position with regard to a number of strategic raw materials. Before World War II—and this was another reason for the nation's policy of isolationism—the United States was largely self-sufficient in the key minerals and raw materials needed to support a high level of industrial activity. After Pearl Harbor, for example, the civilian sector of the population was deprived primarily of such commodities as sugar, pineapples, bananas, and coffee. Natural rubber, a major import used mainly for automobile tires, was also in short supply, and, of course, most supplies of metals, such as iron, copper, and aluminum, were used in the war effort.

Since World War II, the nation's position with regard to essential resources has changed dramatically. Domestic supplies of many raw materials have now largely been exhausted or are no longer profitable to mine or extract. Certain (often exotic) raw materials that are needed today (for example, in the manufacture of jet airplanes) can be obtained only from foreign sources. As a result, with each passing year the United States has become increasingly dependent on access to foreign sources of essential materials.

By definition, strategic imports are of such value that a prolonged interruption in the supply of most of these raw materials to the United States would seriously endanger its national security. This is one reason, for example, that the ongoing buildup of the Soviet Navy is viewed with such apprehension by some Western strategists. By the late 1980s, Moscow's submarine strength was already some three times greater than Nazi Germany's in the early 1940s, whose U-boats during the early months of World War II came dangerously close to severing the Atlantic "lifeline" between the United States and its European allies. Although the German effort ultimately failed, it exacted in the process a frightful toll on British and American shipping. No less today than in the past, maintaining communication links and supply lines with the nation's allies by sea remains a vital strategic interest of the United States.

A second economic reality momentously affecting national security is closely related to the first: the growing dependence of the United States on foreign energy sources. As recently as 1957, the United States was still a major petroleum exporter. By the 1960s, however, as homeowners and industry alike shifted to oil as their main source of heat and energy, and as the number of automobiles in the United States continued to increase, Americans began to consume more petroleum products, making the United States increasingly dependent on foreign petroleum sources. (Even so, the United States shipped substantial petroleum supplies from domestic sources to its NATO allies during the 1967 war in the Middle East.) This dependency by the United States and other industrialized nations, such as Western Europe and Japan, was underscored by the boycott imposed by the oil-producing states of the Middle East during the 1973 war. Although the boycott was relatively brief, it lasted long enough to leave little doubt that prolonged deprivation of Middle East oil supplies to the West would cause widespread economic dislocations—in time, almost certainly fueling political unrest—throughout the industrialized world.[12] But the Third World was no less vulnerable: Nearly all Third World nations also imported oil and had to pay the steadily rising price demanded by the Persian Gulf oil producers. This fact in turn jeopardized their national development programs and their financial stability.

After the 1973 oil boycott, President Richard Nixon called upon American society to become self-sufficient in meeting its energy needs by the 1980s.

President Nixon and his successors urged Americans to follow conservationist measures (such as driving smaller, less powerful automobiles and insulating their homes), develop new energy sources (such as nuclear power and solar energy) and better methods of utilizing old ones (such as improved methods of burning coal), and be warmer in summer and cooler in winter. As a result of such measures, American dependence on foreign oil supplies lessened under Presidents Ford and Carter. Yet, with the global demand for oil continuing to increase (as in most countries throughout the Third World) and with the price of oil on the world market at record-low levels, the United States has once again become dangerously dependent on petroleum imports for its prosperity and its national security.[13]

Early in 1980, following the Soviet invasion of Afghanistan, President Jimmy Carter issued a new foreign policy declaration known as the Carter Doctrine. This proclamation explicitly stated that continued access to the oil fields of the Middle East was a vital security interest of the United States, one that would be protected by military force if necessary. Both by word and deed in the years that followed, President Ronald Reagan left little doubt that he fully subscribed to the Carter Doctrine: The buildup of American military power in and around the Persian Gulf area during the late 1980s provided tangible evidence of America's security commitment in the region.[14]

A third economic influence directly affecting national security policy is the nation's growing dependence on access to foreign markets for its economic prosperity. For more than two hundred years, the American nation has been actively involved in international trade. (One cause of the revolutionary war was colonial resentment toward Great Britain for reducing opportunities for commerce with the West Indies and other foreign markets.) Even before 1800, American ships were engaged in "the China trade"—a commercial connection that led, by the end of the nineteenth century, to America's issuance of the Open Door policy toward China. As it came to be interpreted and understood in the years that followed (if not originally), the Open Door meant that the United States became the defender of Chinese territorial integrity—in a word, its independence. This commitment, growing initially out of American trade ties with China, drew the United States more and more onto a collision course with an expansive Japanese Empire.

From early on then, Americans have been interested in foreign commerce. Until the late nineteenth century, many Americans believed that this was the primary mission of the State Department: to promote through its consular services new opportunities for American trade abroad. Furthermore, in both world wars, the United States became increasingly alienated from Germany because, in Washington's view, Germany time and again threatened America's "neutral rights" to trade with Great Britain and other countries. Imperial Germany's refusal to respect these rights was a major factor in the Wilson administration's ultimate declaration of war on the Central Powers.

The dependence of the United States on access to global markets has not diminished since World War II. To the contrary, it has increased, with the United States becoming the largest trading nation in the world.

From the available evidence, the United States will remain highly dependent on expanding sales in foreign markets to maintain its prosperity and standard of living. To cite only a few examples, by the mid-1980s a number of sectors of American agriculture relied heavily on foreign sales to maintain their prosperity (or in some cases, their basic financial stability).[15] A case in point was soybeans: This commodity (extremely high in protein and greatly in demand by Third World societies) was grown widely throughout the United States, and in any given year, 40 percent or more of the crop was sold to foreign consumers. Other agricultural commodities, such as corn, wheat, rice, and animal products, also had heavy sales in foreign markets.[16]

But a high volume of sales abroad has become essential not only for the American agricultural community. In the industrial sector also, exports play a key role in maintaining a high level of production, employment, and income for owners and workers alike. Prevailing misconceptions to the contrary, many segments of American industry are highly competitive in the world market—and are likely to remain so for many years. (America's main quarrel with Japan was that Tokyo refused to allow American firms free access to the highly protected Japanese home market. By contrast, Japanese firms have had virtually unrestricted access to the American consumer market for many years.) A number of major American industrial products—including lumber and lumber products, chemicals, electronics, and aircraft—are in high demand throughout the world. A leading example is civilian aircraft. Hardly a national airline on the globe is not equipped with American planes and is not, because of that fact, heavily dependent on the United States for maintenance, training, and spare parts. Similarly, certain American-made computer components are in demand throughout the world. Other examples might be cited, but these suffice to make the point: In industry, no less than in agriculture, continued access to the world's markets is essential to the economic vitality of the American nation.

As in the past, the United States will firmly resist any attempt to deny Americans access to the world's markets. Expressed negatively, Americans were seldom more insecure than during the Great Depression, beginning with the stock market crash in 1929, and compounded by the notorious Hawley-Smoot Tariff Act of 1930, which erected a high tariff wall, severely limiting American trade with other countries and in turn creating economic and financial hardships throughout the world. Prolonged obstruction of American access to the world market in the future would almost certainly set in motion the same kind of adverse economic forces witnessed during the Great Depression.

▌ The Growing Threat of Global Terrorism

The national security of the United States has been increasingly jeopardized in recent years by the growing incidence of international terrorism, in which American citizens and property have become favorite targets.[17] That the level of terrorist activities throughout the international system is growing cannot be doubted. It is equally clear, however, that what is often described by the single term *terrorism* is in fact an extremely variegated phenomenon. Many individuals and groups identified as terrorists have highly dissimilar objectives. Accordingly, America's response to global terrorism must be similarly varied and resourceful.

For example, one of the groups that often advocates terrorism consists of dissident nationalists or people seeking recognition of their claim to constitute an independent nation. Some of these claims have deep historical roots; others are of relatively recent origin. Examples are the Basques in Spain and France, the Irish, and the Kurds of the Middle East.

Another group that often relies on terrorism to achieve its goals is made up of members of revolutionary political movements. Communist groups come immediately to mind, although, of course, not all revolutionary organizations are communist (as shown by several indigenous revolutionary movements in modern Latin America). In recent years, some of these revolutionary organizations may have become even more prone than Marxist organizations connected with the Soviet Union to pursue their goals through indiscriminate violence.

Still another group often numbered among present-day terrorists are individuals and groups exhibiting a high degree of political angst, alienation, and frustration with "the system." Such groups sometimes commit political assassinations, kidnappings, and other highly publicized acts of violence primarily designed to draw the attention of the news media to the causes of their political discontent. By contrast, the positive goals of such movements (if they have any) are often unclear.

Yet another category of individuals and groups often labeled terrorists today consists of those who continue to nurture a deep sense of historical grievance and who resort to terrorism from time to time to call attention to wrongs they have suffered. A prominent example in recent years has been the Armenians, who still have a strong sense of injustice because of "the Armenian massacres" carried out by Turkey before World War I. Some of the groups that have resorted to terrorism against Israel also fall into this category.

A number of those described as terrorists today also view themselves as "freedom fighters," soldiers engaged in guerrilla warfare who can gain their objectives in no other way except by employing tactics identified with terrorists. This description, for example, would fit most members of the Palestine Liberation Organization (PLO), which became prominent after the 1967 war in the Middle East. After that conflict, it became evident that the Arabs were too weak to defeat Israel in orthodox warfare. Consequently, many of Israel's Arab opponents adopted the same tactics that the Viet Cong used successfully against the Americans, or the Algerian nationalists used against the French army. Most recently, as factionalism has increasingly characterized the PLO, the Arafat-led wing has been less prone to advocate reliance on terrorism to achieve its goals than have more extremist elements within the organization.

Still other groups described as terrorist appear to consist mainly of religious fanatics, such as several groups within what is called "militant Islam" and the Sikhs of India. In some instances, as in the Shiite religious tradition in Iran, the veneration accorded to "martyrs" of the faith—those who have died defending Islam from its enemies—contributes to followers' readiness to use terrorist methods to achieve religious goals.[18]

Finally, today's "terrorists" also no doubt include a fair number of psychotic individuals, who are no longer capable of rational action, such as those who have tried to assassinate the pope or who carry out violence primarily against women and children.

For most of the above groups, a major motivation is to gain maximum publicity for their causes. A related goal (evident, for example, in the strategy of the PLO toward Israel) is to provoke the country being attacked into reacting in a way that will be censured by other countries.

As is evident, modern terrorism is an extremely heterogeneous phenomenon; as such, it calls for a highly varied response by the United States. In recent years, the American response has in fact been diverse and tailored to the circumstances of the cases. It has encompassed a wide range of active and passive measures. In the former category, American military strikes against Libya and against terrorist groups in Lebanon have forcefully conveyed Washington's determination to protect American citizens from terrorist activities. By contrast, the Reagan administration's withdrawal of American armed forces from Lebanon after terrorist attacks against Americans had increased sharply was an essentially passive response to the problem. In Lebanon and other settings (such as Libya), officials in Washington ultimately concluded that the United States could not protect Americans from terrorism as long as they remained in the area.

Other steps taken by authorities in Washington to counteract international terrorism have included issuing pointed warnings to foreign governments and political movements that have been implicated in terrorist activities involving Americans; improving security at international sea- and airports, and international frontiers; gaining the cooperation of other governments in antiterrorist activities and training their armed forces in counterterrorist measures; and seeking (with no very noteworthy success) to reduce the level of publicity accorded to terrorist activities and groups and, in the case of terrorism directed specifically at Israel, to renew the quest for a negotiated settlement of the Arab–Israeli conflict.

Our discussion has emphasized that terrorism today is in reality a highly varied phenomenon. That the world is becoming more dangerous seems undeniable. Around the globe, governments are hard-pressed to protect their citizens from various kinds of threats without, in the process, engaging in what is sometimes another form of terrorism: antiterrorist activities, which in some instances (as in the recent history of Chile and Argentina) may pose a serious threat to the lives and liberties of citizens.

To no small degree, the United States has been—and will likely remain—a preferred target of terrorist activities because of the high visibility that this nation enjoys. The United States is the wealthiest and most powerful nation known to history, and this fact inevitably creates resentment and hostility toward it. Militarily, economically, and in other respects, the gap between the United States and the vast majority of societies throughout the Third World continues to widen in favor of the former—a tendency not likely to be reversed in the near future.

The problem of terrorism in the contemporary international system is not one that will be solved by a panacea or quick fix. As in the past, responding to the challenge will almost certainly entail difficult choices for the American people and their leaders in the years ahead. The best hope for countering certain forms of terrorism is that addressing, however slowly, the underlying causes of conflict and instability in the Middle East will reduce people's incentives to resort to terrorism. As the general public and American leaders must too often be reminded, the instability of the external environment makes the realization of national security elusive and uncertain. No "structure of peace" is ever likely to be permanent or comprehensive. What is certain, however, is that there can be no retreat by the United States from the realities of global politics.

NOTES

1. A brief discussion of the classical doctrine of American isolationism down to World War II may be found in Cecil V. Crabb, Jr., *Policy-Makers and Critics: Conflicting Theories of American Foreign Policy,* 2nd ed. (New York: Praeger, 1986), pp. 1–31. More-detailed treatments are Manfred Jones, *Isolationism in America* (Ithaca, N.Y.: Cornell University Press, 1966); and Selig Adler, *The Isolationist Impulse: Its Twentieth Century Reaction* (New York: Abelard-Schuman, 1957).

2. See, for example, Walter Lippman, *U.S. Foreign Policy: Shield of the Republic* (Boston: Little, Brown, 1943); *George F. Kennan, American Diplomacy 1900–1950* (New York: New American Library, 1951); Nicholas J. Spykman, *America's Strategy in World Affairs* (New York: Harcourt Brace, 1942); and Paul Seabury, *Power, Freedom and Diplomacy: The Foreign Policy of the United States of America* (New York: Random House, 1963).

3. See Gerald W. Johnson, *Our English Heritage* (Philadelphia: Lippincott, 1949); and Henry L. Roberts, *Britain and the United States* (New York: Harper & Row, 1953).

4. The unique role played by diplomatic doctrines in the foreign policy of the United States is examined in detail in Cecil V. Crabb, Jr., *The Doctrines of American Foreign Policy: Their Meaning, Role, and Future* (Baton Rouge: Louisiana State University Press, 1982).

5. For differing approaches to the nature of the Cold War and its origins, see Thomas A. Bailey, *America Faces Russia* (Ithaca, N.Y.: Cornell University Press, 1950); E. Carmen Day, *Soviet Imperialism* (Washington, D.C.: Public Affairs Press, 1950); Bernard S. Morris, *International Communism and American Policy* (New York: Atherton Press, 1966); William A. Williams,

Russian–American Relations: 1781–1947 (New York: Holt, Rinehart & Winston, 1952); Adam B. Ulam, *The Rivals: America and Russia since World War II* (New York: Viking Press, 1971); John Lewis Gaddis, *The United States and the Origins of the Cold War* (New York: Columbia University Press, 1972); Dan Caldwell, *Soviet International Behavior and U.S. Policy Options* (Lexington, Mass.: D. C. Heath, 1985); Richard W. Stevenson, *The Rise and Fall of Detente* (Urbana: University of Illinois Press, 1985); and Joseph L. Nogee and Robert H. Donaldson, *Soviet Foreign Policy since World War II* (New York: Pergamon Press, 1984). The implications of glasnost for future Soviet–American relations are examined in Adam Westoby, *The Evolution of Communism* (New York: The Free Press, 1989); Zbigniew Brzezinski, *The Grand Failure: The Birth and Death of Communism in the Twentieth Century* (New York: The Free Press, 1989); *Central and Eastern Europe: The Opening Curtain,* ed. William E. Griffith (Boulder, Colo.: Westview Press, 1989); *Windows of Opportunity: From Cold War to Competition in U.S.–Soviet Relations,* ed. Graham T. Allison and William L. Ury (Cambridge, Mass.: Ballinger, 1989); and Paul Dukes, *The Last Game: USA Versus USSR* (New York: St. Martin, 1989).

6. Soviet policy toward the Third World is evaluated in *Soviet Policy in the Third World,* ed. Raymond W. Duncan (New York: Pergamon Press, 1980); Stephen T. Hosmer and Thomas Wolfe, *Soviet Policy and Practice Toward Third World Conflicts* (Lexington, Mass.: D. C. Heath, 1975); K. N. Brutents, *National Liberation Revolutions Today* (Moscow: Progress Press, 1977); Rajon Menon, *Soviet Power and the Third World* (New Haven, Conn.: Yale University Press, 1986); and Alex P. Schmid, *Soviet Military Intervention since 1945* (New Brunswick, N. J.: Transaction Books, 1985).

7. More-extended treatment of Soviet and American propaganda activities may be found in Lawrence S. Soley and John S. Nichols, *Clandestine Radio Broadcasting* (New York: Praeger, 1986); Martin Ebon, *The Soviet Propaganda Machine* (New York: McGraw-Hill, 1987); *Western Broadcasting over the Iron Curtain,* ed. K. R. M. Short (New York: St. Martin, 1986); Ladislav Bittman, *The KGB and Soviet Disinformation: An Insider's View* (Washington, D.C.: Pergamon-Brassey, 1985); and The Media Institute, *Voice of America at the Crossroads: Panel Proceedings* (Washington, D.C.: The Media Institute, 1982).

8. See *The United States and Latin America in the 1980s,* ed. Kevin J. Middlebrook and Carlos Rico (Pittsburg, PA.: University of Pittsburg Press, 1986); Michael Oisken, *Trouble in Our Backyard: Central America and the United States in the Eighties* (New York: Pantheon Books, 1984); *United States Policy in Latin America: A Quarter Century of Crisis and Challenge, 1961–1988,* ed. John D. Martz (Lincoln: University of Nebraska Press, 1988); and *Vital Interests: The Soviet Issue in U.S. Central American Policy,* ed. Bruce D. Larkin (Boulder, Colo.: Lynne Rienner, 1988).

9. See Joungwon A. Kim, "Soviet Policy in North Korea," *World Politics* 22 (January 1970): 237–254; *The Soviet Union in East Asia,* ed. Gerald Segal

(London: Heinemann, 1983); and *Soviet Policy in East Asia,* ed. Donald S. Zagoria (New Haven, Conn.: Yale University Press, 1982).

10. For treatments of recent Soviet and Cuban diplomatic activity in Africa, Gerald Chaliand, *The Struggle for Africa: Conflict of the Great Powers* (New York: St. Martin, 1982); Walter F. Hahn and Alvin J. Cottrell, *Soviet Shadow over Africa* (Miami: University of Miami Press, 1976); *The Soviet Impact in Africa,* ed. R. Craig Nation and Mark V. Kauppi (Lexington, Mass.: D. C. Heath, 1984); and David E. Albright, *Communism in Africa* (Bloomington: Indiana University Press, 1980). See also *Arms and the Africans: Military Influences on Africa's International Relations,* ed. William J. Foltz and Henry S. Bienen (New Haven, Conn.: Yale University Press, 1985); Richard Sanbrook, *The Politics of Africa's Economic Stagnation* (New York: Columbia University Press, 1986); Colin Legum, *The Battlefronts of Southern Africa* (New York: Holmes & Meier, 1988); *Africa in the 1990s and Beyond: U.S. Policy Opportunities and Choices,* ed. Robert I. Rotberg (Algonac, Mich.: Reference Publications, 1988); and *Regional Conflict and U.S. Policy: Angola and Mozambique,* ed. Richard J. Bloomfield (Algonac, Mich.: Reference Publications, 1988).

11. *China's Foreign Relations in the 1980s,* ed. Harry Harding (New Haven, Conn.: Yale University Press, 1984); A. Doak Barnett, "Ten Years After Mao," *Foreign Affairs* 65 (Fall 1986): 37–66; Roy Medvedev, *China and the Superpowers* (New York: Basil Blackwell, 1986); and *China and the World: Chinese Foreign Policy in the Post-Mao Era,* ed. Samuel S. Kim (Boulder, Colo.: Westview Press, 1984). The impact of ongoing changes in China's political system on its foreign policy are examined in *China and the World: New Directions in Chinese Foreign Relations,* 2nd ed., ed. Samuel S. Kim (Boulder, Colo.: Westview Press, 1989); and J. Richard Walsh, *Change, Continuity, and Commitment: China's Adaptive Foreign Policy* (Lanham, Md.: University Press of America, 1988); and Jonathan R. Woetzel, *China's Economic Opening to the Outside World* (New York: Praeger, 1989).

12. In 1950 the United States imported some 178 million barrels of oil annually; this figure rose steadily, reaching 483 million barrels in 1970 and 1.2 billion barrels in 1974, and peaking at 2.4 billion barrels in 1977. Following the Arab oil boycott of 1973, and the conservation measures implemented in the United States as a result of it, America's dependence on oil imports declined to 1.6 billion barrels annually in 1981. By the mid-1980s it had fallen to 1.2 billion barrels, or approximately one-fifth of the nation's consumption of petroleum products. See the *Statistical Abstract of the United States: 1987* (Washington, D.C.: Government Printing Office, 1987), pp. 681–682; and *Trade: U.S. Policy since 1945* (Washington, D.C.: Congressional Quarterly, 1984); Howard Buckness, *Energy and National Defense* (Lexington: University of Kentucky Press, 1983); and *The Middle East,* 6th ed. (Washington, D.C.: Congressional Quarterly, 1986), pp. 97–118.

13. See Uri Ra'anan and C. M. Perry, *Strategic Minerals and International Security* (New York: Pergamon-Brassey, 1985); Howard Bucknell, *Energy and*

National Defense (Lexington: University of Kentucky Press, 1983). For more general discussions of the importance of economic aspects of external policy, see Stephen D. Cohen, *The Making of United States International Economic Policy: Principles, Problems, and Proposals for Reform*, 2nd ed. (New York: Praeger, 1984); Raymond Vernon and Debora Spar, *Beyond Globalism: Remaking American Foreign Economic Policy* (New York: The Free Press, 1988); and C. Michael Aho and Marc Levinson, *After Reagan: Confronting the Changed World Economy* (New York: Council on Foreign Relations, 1988).

14. The Carter Doctrine, committing the United States to preserve the security of the Persian Gulf area, is discussed more fully in Cecil V. Crabb, Jr., *The Doctrines of American Foreign Policy: Their Meaning, Role, and Future* (Baton Rouge: Louisiana State University Press, 1982), pp. 325–371.

15. See Ibid., pp. 56–107.

16. See Nick Butler, *The International Grain Trade* (New York: St. Martin, 1986); William P. Browne and Don F. Hadwiger, *World Food Policies: Toward Agricultural Interdependence* (Boulder, Colo.: Lynne Rienner, 1986); and Robert L. Paarlberg, *Food, Trade, and Foreign Policy: India, the Soviet Union, and the United States* (Ithaca, N.Y.: Cornell University Press, 1985). More recent studies are *U.S. Agriculture and Third World Development: The Critical Linkage*, ed. Randall Purcell and Elizabeth Morrison (Boulder, Colo.: Lynne Rienner, 1987); Peter F. Drucker, *The New Realities* (New York: Harper & Row, 1989); and C. Fred Bergsten, *America in the World Economy: A Strategy for the 1990s* (Washington, D.C.: Institute for International Economics, 1988).

17. See Abraham D. Sofaer, "Terrorism and the Law," *Foreign Affairs* 64 (Summer 1986): 907–923; Walter Laqueur, "Reflections on Terrorism," *Foreign Affairs* 65 (Fall 1986): 86–101; Christopher H. Pyle, "Defining Terrorism," *Foreign Affairs* 64 (Fall 1986): 63–79; *Fighting Back: Winning the War against Terrorism*, ed. Neil C. Livingston and Terrell E. Arnold (Lexington, Mass.: D. C. Heath, 1986); and the symposium on "Terrorism," ed. Neil C. Livingston, *World Politics* 146 (Summer 1983): 1–116. Among the more recent studies of terrorism are *Multidimensional Terrorism*, ed. Martin Slann and Bernard Schechterman (Boulder, Colo.: Lynne Rienner, 1987); Antonio Cassese, *Terrorism, Politics and the Law* (Princeton, N.J.: Princeton University Press, 1989); and Andrew Seth, *Against Every Human Law: The Terrorist Threat to Democracy* (Canberra: Australian National University, 1988).

18. The concept of martyrdom in the Shiite branch of Islam is explained in detail in Shaul Bakhash, *The Reign of the Ayatollahs* (New York: Basic Books, 1984); Cheryl Benard and Zalmany Khalilzad, *"The Government of God": Iran's Islamic Republic* (New York: Columbia University Press, 1984); and *Shiism and Social Protest*, ed. Juan R. I. Cole and Nikki R. Keddie (New Haven, Conn.: Yale University Press, 1986).

CHAPTER 3

National Security: The Internal Policy Process

In the United States, decision making in the field of national security policy occurs in a distinctive constitutional setting. The decision-making environment of every nation is no doubt to some degree unique, but America's contains a number of novel features affecting both how decisions in national security affairs are reached and their substance. In this chapter, we shall note five features that are especially significant for national security policy.

∎ The American Constitutional System

First, there is the American constitutional principle of checks and balances. On the national level, power is divided or shared among three coordinate branches of the government. In reality, in the fields of national defense and foreign policy, the Supreme Court plays a very limited role. For the most part, it is confined to keeping the executive and legislative branches within their proper constitutional orbits.[1]

Second, after some two hundred years of constitutional experience, it is clear that the distribution of powers between the president and Congress in external policy is not equal. Whatever the intentions of the Founding Fathers (who were known to favor legislative over executive power), two centuries of constitutional practice and evolution has resulted in the president's dominating the decision-making process. We shall examine the reasons for this later.

Third, a fundamental principle of the American constitutional system, one that influences decision making in national security policy at all stages, is the concept of civilian supremacy over the military establishment. As noted in chapter 1, the nation's highest civilian official—the president—also serves as the commander in chief of its armed forces; the same principle of civilian supremacy is observed at lower levels (with civilians heading the Department of Defense and each of the separate branches of the military establishment, for example). Further, in 1947, Congress by law designated the president the chairman of the National Security Council, the highest executive committee involved in national security policy. All of the statutory (or voting) members of the NSC are also civilians.

Fourth, key features of the American constitutional system are that it has evolved since 1787 and continues to evolve in the light of experience. Americans frequently refer to their "living Constitution" and view it as an "organic" system of government. As such, it has proved itself to be a highly flexible and adaptable instrument—capable of accommodating such momentous changes, for example, as occurred in America's shift from isolationism to internationalism.

Fifth, the U.S. constitutional system has been greatly affected by key individuals. Nowhere is this fact better illustrated than in the presidential advisory system created to assist the president and his subordinates in deciding matters of national security. As our case studies in chapters 4 through 8 will show, several patterns of decision making have emerged in the United States since the late 1940s. These different patterns represent a broad repertory of presidential approaches to national security policy.

▌ Constitutional Powers of the President

The president of the United States is required by the oath of office to "preserve, protect, and defend the Constitution of the United States" (Article II, section 1). Another constitutional provision (Article II, section 3) requires the president to "take care that the laws be faithfully executed." Among the laws that the president is required to execute are treaties and international law (Article VI).

Yet, among the direct sources of constitutional power, none has proved to be more crucial than the designation of the president as the commander in chief of the military establishment (Article II, section 2). Throughout American history, two totally different interpretations of this provision have competed.[2]

The "symbolic theory" holds that the Founding Fathers, who were, of course, intensely suspicious of executive power, intended for the president to serve as essentially a ceremonial head of the nation's armed services, such as is currently the case with the British sovereign. Actual strategic and tactical decisions were presumably to be made by the high command and by congressional committees, as was done during the revolutionary war. Though the president's role as commander in chief may never have been seriously interpreted as being completely passive, a strong sentiment persists today in many circles for a more delimited presidential role in war making—that is, one that would be more subject to congressional direction.

The other interpretation, and the one that has come to be routinely accepted today, conceives of the president's authority over the military establishment as dynamic and active. According to this interpretation, the title "commander in chief" exactly describes the chief executive's role: The president actually commands the armed forces of the United States. In practice, this means that the chief executive either personally makes or delegates a broad range of decisions affecting the armed forces, although the president must retain congressional support for both political backing and continuing appropriations. Thus, if the president as commander in chief is not simply a congressional agent, he is also not a generalissimo beyond public accountability.

Abraham Lincoln's administration during the Civil War went far toward establishing this conception of the presidential office. In later years, President Woodrow Wilson's actions during World War I, followed by those of President Franklin D. Roosevelt in World War II, strengthened this view of executive power. Though even today critics occasionally lament the tendency, it seems beyond serious dispute that a substantial majority of the American people now expect the chief executive to exhibit firm and decisive leadership in protecting national security. Although they may be suspicious of the "imperial presidency," few Americans today call for a return to the concept of a weak and immobilized presidency as exemplified by James Buchanan. Indeed, the public's perception, correct or not, of a vacillating foreign policy under Jimmy Carter was one of the principal reasons for his defeat in 1980. In October 1989, President George Bush was widely criticized on Capitol Hill and in the news media for his initial failure to use armed force to oust the regime of General Manuel Noriega in Panama. In addition to operating an internally oppressive regime, Noriega was unquestionably implicated in drug trafficking. As political opposition to Noriega steadily increased within Panama, and after Noriega declared war against the United States, President Bush finally ordered the armed forces to intervene within the country. As a result, Noriega's regime was ousted. The Panamanian dictator was arrested by American authorities and sent to the United States, where he faced trial for violations of federal law. By mid-February of 1990, the U.S. expeditionary force that had been sent to Panama was withdrawn. The response on Capitol Hill and among the American people to President Bush's action left little doubt that his reliance on armed force in the Panamanian case enjoyed overwhelming congressional and public approval.

What may an American chief executive actually do in his capacity as commander in chief of the armed forces? The list of specific prerogatives generally associated with legitimate presidential power today is long and impressive, if not always constitutionally orthodox. For example, the president may send troops into a strife-torn country (such as Lebanon) and may order them home. He may, and every incumbent president routinely does, "show the flag" or order a forceful demonstration of American military power in an area where American interests are endangered.

The commander in chief may direct U.S. Navy and Air Force units to strike suspected terrorist bases, as President Reagan did in dealing with Libya, or order the armed forces to rescue Americans being held captive in other countries. Under presidential order American military supplies and arms aid (including large sums of money) may be channeled to anticommunist groups abroad (such as the Afghan rebels or the Contras in Central America). As commander in chief, the president may send pointed warnings to other governments to refrain from actions detrimental to American security. President Eisenhower, for example, after his election in 1952, warned the government of Communist China not to renew the Korean War, or it would risk compelling the United States to use its nuclear arsenal. On several occasions since World War II, incumbent presidents have placed the armed forces of the United States on alert—an unmistakable signal to possible adversaries, such as the Kremlin, not to jeopardize American vital interests. In 1962, during the Cuban missile crisis, President Kennedy dramatically warned Moscow against the consequences of introducing Soviet missiles into the Western hemisphere and ultimately ordered the U.S. Navy to intercept Soviet cargo vessels suspected of carrying missiles to Cuba.

Occasionally since World War II, presidents have gone over the brink by involving U.S. armed forces in military hostilities without a declaration of war by Congress. The last "declared" war in American history was World War II—and it could well be the last military conflict to fall into that category. All other actual or potential conflicts involving American forces—from the defense of the Allied position in Berlin in the late 1940s, through the Korean and Vietnam wars, to the Reagan administration's intervention in Lebanon—have been undeclared conflicts.[3] America's initial involvement in them, as well as the decision to terminate the nation's role in these conflicts, were ultimately presidential decisions. Inevitably, as the Vietnam war dramatized, such decisions were crucially influenced by forces such as American public opinion. Nonetheless, in the end it was a decision by President Johnson, and one later by President Nixon, that resulted in the withdrawal of American forces from Southeast Asia. (Congress "ordered" the withdrawal of American forces from Southeast Asia after the Nixon White House had already announced their impending evacuation.)[4]

▌ Informal Methods of Presidential Leadership

In addition to the powers that presidents have accrued through expansive readings of the Constitution, chief executives have acquired numerous informal, or extraconstitutional, powers that give them dominance in the sphere of national security policy.

There is, for example, the president's unrivaled control over information. No other official in the U.S. government—or, for that matter, anywhere in the world—can really compete with the president of the United States on this front. Two specific presidential powers regarding news and information are involved here. One is the president's unequaled newsworthiness: No other political figure in the contemporary world comes close to rivaling the president in commanding the attention of the press, and the media of radio and television. The main international evening news programs routinely begin by focusing on the most recent activities or statements of the president of the United States.

The other side of the coin of the president's control over information is the ability of the White House to gain access to news and intelligence not available to the ordinary citizen. As we shall see, the chief executive can call upon the resources of the intelligence community, as well as having information supplied by the State Department, the Defense Department, and all other executive agencies. Presidents can control the flow of such information, or, as President Lyndon B. Johnson was frequently accused of doing, can manipulate the news to gain support for the administration's policies.[5]

The president serves as the nation's chief budget officer. Routine as that power might sound, the budget submitted early in the year by the White House to Congress contains the president's detailed requests for funds to operate the entire executive branch of the national government. Congress depends heavily on this document as a guide to its own budgetary deliberations and actions, and with rare exceptions, it provides the White House a substantial portion of the requested funds. Conversely, rarely does Congress independently propose, authorize, and appropriate funds for important projects not recommended by the White House.[6]

Over the course of American history, the president has also emerged (contrary to the constitutional principle of checks and balances) as what may be called the nation's "legislator-in-chief." Although Congress does legislate today on its own initiative, without regard for the wishes of the White House, especially in domestic affairs, in nearly all major legislation affecting national security policy, Congress acts on bills that have been drafted in the executive branch, sponsored by the White House, and guided through the legislative labyrinth by the president's supporters at both ends of Pennsylvania Avenue.

The national defense budget, for example, is drafted in the Pentagon, in collaboration with the president's budgetary assistants. This document serves as the framework for congressional actions on the national defense budget. Predictably, Congress will amend certain items in it, maybe delete a few altogether, and sometimes increase spending in certain categories. Despite such changes, however, in the end it will still be recognizable as the president's budget, and the chances are that congressional cuts in defense spending will be a relatively small part of the total funds ultimately made available to the armed forces.

Another informal power of the president that affects national security policy is the chief executive's ability to publicly commit the nation to a course of action that critics will find very difficult to change. Time and again, President Reagan proved himself extremely gifted in using this technique. In the diplomacy toward Central America, for example, Reagan took the position that critics of his Latin American policies were jeopardizing hemispheric and international security—intentionally or not, he said, they were aiding the communist cause in Central America, and if they prevailed, he insisted, they alone would bear the responsibility for a major diplomatic defeat by the United States, with serious consequences for national security.

The Reagan White House took basically the same approach to the issue of arms competition with the Soviet Union in Europe, confronting groups on both sides of the Atlantic that opposed the administration's policy of strengthening NATO's nuclear arsenal with the charge that a rigid and polemical antinuclear position severely weakened Western security during a period of ongoing Soviet military expansion. As became evident, few members of Congress really wanted to have to defend themselves against the charge of directly or indirectly aiding a threat to the security interests of the United States.

This informal presidential power is in turn heavily dependent on another, which, in the final analysis, may well be the most important single source of presidential influence on national security policy: the degree of confidence or trust exhibited by the people toward the president vis-à-vis his critics on Capitol Hill or in the news media. Since the New Deal at least, the American people have displayed great expectations and a high level of confidence in the occupant of the Oval Office.

As was demonstrated time and again during the presidency of Ronald Reagan, the American people tend to give the president the benefit of the doubt, holding his advisers and subordinates, rather than the chief executive himself, primarily responsible for major policy failures. In fact, after a dramatic policy setback (such as the Bay of Pigs episode during the Kennedy administration or President Carter's failure to rescue American hostages in Iran), the president's popularity with the American people has in fact risen. The American people appear extremely reluctant to withdraw their confidence even from a chief executive whose policies have miscarried.

Nor is there any discernible inclination by the people to look to Congress or other sources for leadership in meeting serious challenges to national security. Even after the Watergate scandal and the Iran–Contra affair, the American people still look to the White House for leadership in solving national security and other problems at home and overseas. The public assumption apparently is that even after such episodes, the best prospect for recovering from them, and for meeting new internal and external challenges successfully, is to rely on a "reformed" and reinvigorated presidency![7]

The reason for this fascinating phenomenon may lie in one or more of the following explanations. The president of the United States (along with the vice president, of course) is the only official of the United States government who is elected by the entire body of citizens. In that sense, the president symbolizes the national interest better than any other figure within the government. Another possible explanation is that when Americans ask the familiar question—"Who's in charge here?"—they expect to find a single individual, not a faceless bureaucracy or anonymous congressional committees. Increasingly, Americans vote in presidential elections for the individual candidate, rather than according to a political ideology or program; they place their confidence in a person. Even less in the sphere of national security policy than in other realms are citizens enthusiastic about "government by committee." For these reasons, they continue to look to the White House for dynamic and effective leadership—and they are likely to give low marks to any incumbent president who does not, or who is not widely perceived as able to, provide it.

▌ The Presidential Advisory System

All incumbent presidents rely on advisers and aides in arriving at major policy decisions. Two points about the presidential advisory system should be remembered from the outset. In the first place, a president is free to use his advisers in any way he chooses in arriving at decisions in foreign and domestic affairs. (This also implies that the chief executive may choose not to rely on advisers in making decisions, or to use them to a very limited degree.) As our case studies will clearly demonstrate, each president has had his own administrative style, preferences, and idiosyncrasies. Congress may create advisory mechanisms, such as the National Security Council, but Congress cannot specify exactly how a particular occupant of the Oval Office will in fact use these and other devices in the decision-making process.

A second point to remember is that under the U.S. Constitution, executive power is vested in a single person: the president of the United States. The National Security Council, the executive departments, the members of the intelligence community, and other executive units merely recommend and propose courses of action to the president. The national security policy of the United States is not determined by a majority vote of the National Security Council, nor is it necessarily the result of a consensus among the president's chief aides. Whether offered individually or collectively, the viewpoints of presidential assistants are nothing more than recommendations. Within the executive branch, the only "vote" that ultimately counts is the president's alone. Naturally, chief executives tend to follow the advice of their principal aides in most instances; if they do not do so regularly, then they need new advisers! In the end, however, it is the president's decision that determines the national security policy of the United States, as when President Truman ordered American forces in the Far East to defend South Korea in 1950, or when President Kennedy determined that Soviet missiles must be removed from Cuba, or when President Johnson stated time and again that the United States must defend Southeast Asia from communism. In these and other cases, it was also the president who decided that the external crisis had passed or that the time had come to negotiate an end to the crisis abroad.

▌ The Department of State

The oldest and best-known advisory body to the president is the Department of State. Created in 1789, with Thomas Jefferson as its first head, the State Department is, of course, directed by the secretary of state (America's foreign minister), the highest-ranking member of the president's cabinet.

The traditional province of the State Department is political relations between the United States and foreign governments. Until World War II, however, this dimension of American policy was extremely limited. Before Pearl Harbor, many Americans believed that the primary function of the State Department was (or ought to be) consular—promoting commerce abroad, assisting American tourists with problems, and undertaking similar routine assignments.

As emphasized in chapter 1, Americans have traditionally distrusted diplomacy, an enterprise they associated with Old World political intrigue, monarchy, aristocracy, war, and other concepts viewed as antithetical to democracy. Some Americans even believed that, as the governments of the world gradually became democratized, there would be no need for diplomacy, and it would be abandoned as unnecessary! At any rate, not until passage of the Rogers Act in 1924 did the United States establish a professional diplomatic service, with appointment to the Foreign Service based on merit, rather than on social background, personal connections, or other extraneous factors.[8] It should be noted that the position of ambassador or minister (who is in charge of the American diplomatic establishment within a foreign nation) is still often filled by the president on the basis of political, social, personal, or other considerations having little to do with merit. Yet during some administrations, three-quarters or more of the individuals selected to fill these high-level positions came from the Foreign Service. A major reason that some ambassadorial appointments (such as London, Paris, Bonn, and Rome) are still made outside the Foreign Service is that after two hundred years, Congress is still unwilling to provide the funds necessary for adequate operations of the larger and more prestigious embassies abroad. Customarily, therefore, the individual who serves as U.S. ambassador in these posts (primarily in Western Europe) is expected to subsidize certain embassy expenses (especially entertainment) from private funds. This anachronism provides still further evidence of the deeply ingrained American skepticism toward diplomacy.

By the mid-1980s, the Department of State supervised relations with more than 160 independent nations throughout the world. In any given year, American officials participated in some 800 international conferences, and the United States belonged to more than fifty international organizations. Yet, even with the steady expansion in its responsibilities, the Department of State remains one of the smallest of the executive departments. In 1987, for example, the cost of operating the State Department amounted to some four-tenths of 1 percent of the entire federal budget.[9] The cost of one modern Trident submarine would pay the total salaries and expenses of all State Department officials at home and abroad for a year with some funds unspent!

Or consider another indicator of the State Department's relatively low priority: For fiscal year 1988, the Reagan administration requested a total of $3.6 billion to operate all international programs. This total was approximately 1 percent of the Defense Department's budget for the same year. Even after the United States emerged as an international superpower, Americans still did not, as judged by such budgetary criteria, place a high value on acquiring skill in negotiation, accurate reporting of developments abroad, and other activities normally assigned to the State Department.[10]

Since World War II, presidents have routinely designated the secretary of state their principal foreign policy adviser and have made this official responsible for coordinating the activities of all executive agencies involved in foreign affairs. Yet, as we shall see, even though presidents have periodically expressed great confidence in their secretaries of state, in reality most chief executives have increasingly relied on other advisory mechanisms in arriving at foreign policy decisions. Indeed, as we shall see in chapter 7, during the Nixon presidency a rival State Department (headed by the national security adviser, Henry Kissinger) was created in the White House, a development that could only have occurred with President Nixon's active encouragement and cooperation.

As a result, since World War II a number of commentators and former diplomatic officials have referred to the "decline of the State Department" in the overall foreign policy process.[11] Before the war, the State Department, as the agency that was clearly "in charge" of American foreign policy under the president's direction, seldom faced effective competition from bureaucratic rivals. Yet developments before and during World War II—when President Franklin D. Roosevelt routinely bypassed the State Department in making foreign policy decisions—clearly presaged a change in the department's once preeminent position in dealing with external problems.[12]

Since 1945, at some stage nearly every president has complained about the State Department's lack of "creativity" and leadership in responding to new challenges abroad. To many of its critics, the State Department epitomizes an entrenched bureaucracy, with all the defects that term implies concerning resistance to change, attachment to traditional procedures, and zealous protection of its own bureaucratic interests. For another group of critics, State Department attitudes since World War II have reflected those of the American foreign policy "establishment," traditionally identified with a European-oriented, East Coast, Ivy League elite.

In different terms, State Department officials have sometimes epitomized the militantly anticommunist "Cold Warriors," who have largely dictated America's approach to foreign affairs since World War II. Paradoxically, according to other critics—usually found on the extreme right-wing politically—during and after World War II the State Department was infiltrated by communists and other left-wing elements that were part of a "communist global conspiracy." Thus, at times, groups on both the political right and left have criticized the State Department's performance. As a result, the department has often been hard-pressed to find supporters and allies in its efforts to preserve its premier position in the foreign policy process.[13]

Yet the primary reason for the decline of the State Department is illustrated by the subject of our study: In realms such as national security policy, several other governmental agencies are, and must be, involved in decision making. Expressed differently, national security policy is not a "traditional" subject and cannot be dealt with by traditional organizational methods. For example, it may involve decisions relating to the commitment of the armed forces abroad (the responsibility of the Defense Department), the intentions and capabilities of the Soviet Union and other possible adversaries (the province of members of the intelligence community); and the respective impact of Soviet and American propaganda on foreign opinion (the sphere of the United States

Information Agency). A persuasive case can be made for the contention that, despite the changes in the nature of international relations since World War II, the political component of external policy—which has traditionally been the domain of the State Department—is (or should be) paramount. In recent years, however, it has proved extremely difficult for the State Department to gain converts to that viewpoint among the widening circle of federal agencies involved in making and administering national security policy.

▌ The National Defense Establishment

Another executive department that is a major actor in the realm of national security is the Department of Defense, created, as explained in chapter 1, by the National Security Act of 1947. The Defense Department both plays a crucial advisory role and bears major responsibility for implementing national security decisions.[14]

For fiscal year 1988, for example, the Reagan administration proposed a national defense budget totaling $1 trillion over the next three years, or an average of about $333.3 billion annually. The Reagan administration experienced behavior typical of Congress in dealing with the national defense budget in recent years. Although the president's political opponents on Capitol Hill have typically accused the White House of inflating the nation's defense needs and have complained about "Pentagon waste," in the end Congress nearly always provides the vast preponderance of the funds requested by the president for the military establishment. This is another way of saying that, as a rule, the debate within Congress on the national defense budget is usually confined to relatively few (often highly newsworthy) items, representing only a small fraction of the total outlay requested by the White House.

By the late 1980s, the armed forces of the United States comprised 1.6 million personnel. The Army was the largest branch of the service (with more than 778,000 personnel), the Air Force was next (with more than 600,000), the Navy was third, and the Marine Corps was the smallest. These forces were stationed around the globe: 1.6 million in the United States; more than 350,000 in Europe; more than 120,000 in East Asia and the Pacific; and the remainder in Africa, south Asia, the Western hemisphere, and other regions. Their missions ranged from deterring global war to protecting the continental United States from enemy missile attack, preserving access to the Persian Gulf oil fields, and maintaining the security of the Pacific region in the post-Vietnam War era.[15]

As explained earlier, the president is the commander in chief of the nation's armed forces. By tradition, the secretary of defense and the secretaries of the military services are also civilians. The secretary of defense represents the military viewpoint on the National Security Council, although the president may (and frequently does) invite members of the Joint Chiefs of Staff to participate in NSC meetings and sometimes to advise him privately, as well. Retired military officers may also be called upon from time to time to advise the president on national security questions.

Within the Defense Department, the Office of International Security Affairs (ISA) was established specifically to provide a direct link between the Defense and State departments. Sometimes called "the Pentagon's State Department," ISA's organizational structure parallels the State Department's so civilian and military aspects of particular policies or programs may be smoothly coordinated. During the 1980s, the head of ISA in the Pentagon, Richard Perle, was one of the Reagan administration's most forceful and articulate spokesmen on foreign affairs, especially concerning strategic weapons.[16]

At the risk of oversimplifying a complex relationship, we can say that the military establishment's primary responsibility is to provide the means (or, at least, the military means) to achieve goals defined by civilian policy makers. For example, once the president has determined, after consultation with his advisers, that continued American access to the Persian Gulf area is vital to the preservation of national security, the Pentagon is expected to provide the military strength, together with the appropriate military strategy, needed to achieve the objective. (Ultimately, as will be explained more fully below, the Pentagon's ability to supply the military strength required to achieve any national security goal depends, of course, on the willingness of Congress to furnish the military personnel, the weapons, the funds, and whatever other resources are needed to attain the objective. In this sense, civilian policy makers actually determine both the goals and the means of national security policy.) At the same time, in practice military officials are often consulted in determining whether a given goal—such as trying to stabilize Lebanon politically or counter international terrorism—is "worth" the cost it would entail in lives and resources. Military viewpoints are important, in other words, in defining the nation's vital interests, as well as in defending them.

The military contribution to national security policy exemplifies the old public administration adage, "Experts should be on tap, but never on top." Faced with a crisis overseas, every chief executive wants professional advice from the nation's military leaders on how to respond. President Dwight D. Eisenhower was one of the few chief executives who was a military expert in his own right; most occupants of the Oval Office are not. Yet in the end, the president decides American policy toward a variety of crises and other developments overseas. In many cases, these presidential decisions include such military matters as the strategy to be employed against the Axis powers in World War II, the use of the atomic bomb against Japan, the decision to defend South Korea from aggression, and the nature of the conflict to be waged in Southeast Asia.

▌ The Intelligence Community

Sound policy making depends on having, and being able to evaluate objectively, information bearing on the decision to be made. Although nearly all departments and agencies of the federal governments are to some degree involved in the process, the collection, distribution, and evaluation of such information is the special province of those agencies comprising what has come to be called the intelligence community.

The concept of the intelligence community is somewhat subjective and dynamic, changing from one period to another. The principal members are the CIA; the National Security Agency (NSA), which monitors communications by foreign governments, radar signals, and the like; the National Reconnaissance Office, which operates space satellite surveillance programs; the Defense Intelligence Agency, along with the more specialized intelligence arms of the Army, Navy, Air Force, and Marine Corps; the FBI, which conducts counterintelligence operations against foreign espionage activities; and the departments of the Treasury and Energy, along with the Drug Enforcement Administration.[17]

The best known member of the intelligence community is the Central Intelligence Agency, established by the National Security Act of 1947. The CIA may be thought of as the hub of the intelligence wheel. As its name implies, the CIA is expected to direct and coordinate the intelligence operations of the entire government. For example, the CIA takes data gathered by its own personnel and agents, together with information supplied by other agencies involved in intelligence activities, collates it, organizes it, and prepares intelligence reports for the president and his principal advisers.

During the 1970s, for example, the CIA prepared a detailed study of Soviet defense spending that became the basis for the Carter and the Reagan administrations' defense budget requests to Congress; this same study weighed heavily in the provision by Congress of most of the funds requested. How strong are communist military forces in Europe vis-à-vis those of the Western alliance? What are the prospects for improvement in Soviet economic performance? What are the chances of a new war between the Arab states and Israel in the Middle East? How stable is the government of Libya? What kind of new government is likely to emerge in Afghanistan? These analyses are typical of the kinds of intelligence reports prepared for the president and other officials involved in making foreign policy decisions.

Another, and considerably more controversial, aspect of intelligence operations relates to what are sometimes described as "special projects" or, in the language of the media, "dirty tricks," carried out by American intelligence agencies. These encompass a wide range of usually covert activities, most of which in time become overt, well-publicized throughout the world.

As noted in chapter 1, the National Security Act provides that the Central Intelligence Agency may undertake such special projects or missions as may be assigned to it from time to time by the National Security Council, operating under the president's ultimate direction. Since 1947, such activities have included efforts to counteract growing communist influence in Western Europe in the early postwar period; the overthrow of an allegedly anti-Western regime in Iran, followed by the installation of the Shah as the ruler of that country; intervention to oust a supposedly procommunist government in Guatemala during the 1950s; large-scale support for Cuban refugees in an ill-fated attempt to overthrow Castro's regime in 1961; the assumption of a prominent role in America's attempt to prevent the communization of Southeast Asia; intervention by the Nixon Administration to oust a pro-Marxist regime in Chile; and extensive aid to anti-Marxist groups on the African continent, to Islamic rebels in Afghanistan, to the Contras in Nicaragua, and to other groups in different settings under the Reagan administration. Most recently, the CIA has played an active role in U.S. efforts to counteract the rising incidence of international terrorism.

In time, some of these covert actions by the CIA and other members of the intelligence community have proved to be highly divisive sources of ongoing contention between the White House and Congress—especially when certain secret intelligence operations were exposed by the news media. Yet several points about this more controversial aspect of intelligence operations must be borne in mind.

In the first place, in the vast majority of cases, these covert intelligence operations were authorized by the president, as the law requires. With a few exceptions (as in the Iran–Contra affair under the Reagan administration), the evidence indicates that the CIA has not been out of control or engaged in unauthorized or illegal activities.

In the second place, after numerous investigations of intelligence activities, Congress has thus far refrained from declaring most such activities illegal or prohibiting the CIA from engaging in them. At least tacitly, Congress has acknowledged that under certain circumstances, covert activities by American agencies represent a calculated risk the United States must sometimes assume. By definition, such a policy may fail, but the consequences of not assuming such risks at all may sometimes entail an even greater risk to national security. For example, what danger would ultimately have been posed to American—and, more broadly, to Western—security if France and Italy had come under communist control shortly after World War II? Alternatively, what kind of threat to regional security—and ultimately to world peace—would now exist if the Soviet Union had been permitted to acquire a strong and dangerous base of operations in Central America?

In the third place, as became obvious from the Iran–Contra affair during the late 1980s, the American people and their leaders are still endeavoring to formulate a set of guiding principles for the conduct of covert interventionist activities. On the basis of several recent cases, some forms of such interventionism appear to be acceptable to the American people, whereas others are clearly not. By what standard then can interventionist conduct be judged in particular cases? As with other aspects of post–World War II American diplomacy, guidelines for answering that question are rudimentary and formative. For the most part the answers are given pragmatically, in the light of experience and of prevailing circumstances.

For all the occasional negative consequences, there appears to be no alternative to intelligence operations by the CIA and other members of the intelligence community. It would be difficult to support the proposition that American policy abroad would be more successful—or that national security would be better protected—without essential information on which to base national policy. In many cases, covert activities by intelligence agencies—even when there is a risk they will become overt—must be viewed as part of the effort to prevent or counteract serious risks to the security of individual Americans and of the American society as a whole.[18]

▌ Propaganda and Informational Activities

Another important dimension of national security policy that has come to the fore since World War II is the propaganda, or psychological warfare, programs operated by the United States government. After World War I, the Axis powers, especially the Nazi regime in Germany and the communist government of the Soviet Union, used propaganda as a major instrument of diplomacy. Hitler's minister of propaganda, Joseph Goebbels, was an expert in using information and disinformation to achieve Germany's goals at home and abroad. Since 1917, Moscow has similarly emphasized propaganda and informational dimensions of foreign affairs, as illustrated by the unequalled worldwide broadcasting activities of Radio Moscow.[19]

Propaganda was used by both sides in World War I. However, it was not until World War II that it became a major component of American policy. When this global conflict was soon followed by the Cold War, the United States found itself involved in what was sometimes described as "a battle for the minds of men" against a resourceful and determined communist adversary. Ultimately, American officials concluded that overt and covert propaganda must be used systematically and in an organized manner in the nation's foreign relations. After certain tentative and sporadic efforts in this direction, the Eisenhower administration established the United States Information Agency (USIA) in 1953 as America's overt, or official, propaganda arm.[20] Though it is organizationally separate and has its own director, the USIA takes its policy guidance from the State Department. Covert, or officially unacknowledged, propaganda activities are coordinated by the Central Intelligence Agency.

Broadly construed, USIA's mission is to cultivate abroad as favorable an image for American society as possible and to gain maximum support overseas for the policies of the United States. USIA's activities are aimed specifically at influencing public opinion abroad, especially the attitudes of political elites and opinion makers, such as labor and business leaders and intellectuals. The Voice of America—a global shortwave radio broadcasting service—is the USIA's best-known program. Other activities include operating student and faculty exchange programs between the United States and other countries; arranging for cultural and scientific exchanges (such as visits by the Boston Symphony Orchestra to the Soviet Union and by the Bolshoi Ballet to the United States); sponsoring lectures, exhibits (such as those featuring America's exploits in space), and films on various aspects of American life; and preparing press releases and providing other services to foreign news media. In many countries, the USIA's best known activity is the operation of an American cultural center, usually located prominently in the capital city, making it an inviting target for anti-American groups abroad. Frequently, these centers comprise the largest collection of Americana available to scholars, students, and others interested in various aspects of American life.

How successful or effective are the USIA's efforts in promoting American foreign policy goals? The question is extremely difficult to answer with assurance. Informed students of propaganda have long known that words and rhetoric alone—no matter how skillfully packaged and disseminated—do little to achieve a nation's diplomatic objectives. As President John F. Kennedy and other chief executives recognized, in the final analysis the most influential "voice of America" is the nation's diplomatic behavior. For good or for ill, that provides a more eloquent message about the United States than any of the USIA's activities. At best, skillful propaganda serves as an auxiliary instrument of diplomacy and is an activity that essentially reinforces sound national security policy.[21]

■ Other Executive Agencies and National Security

Among students of American foreign relations today, it has become commonplace to observe that the traditional line between domestic and foreign affairs in the United States has largely disappeared. This has meant that a large number of executive departments—including those not traditionally thought of as having a foreign affairs component—have played a role in forming or implementing national security policy. Here, we can do no more than allude briefly to this phenomenon.

The Commerce Department, for example, is involved in national security policy, since the maintenance of a sound and prosperous economic base is a prerequisite for a secure nation. As our earlier discussion emphasized, access to markets and raw materials overseas will continue indefinitely to be a major objective of national security policy; this is also traditionally a goal of the Commerce Department. Similarly, the Treasury Department, which is keenly interested in maintaining the soundness of the dollar in international currency markets, is also directly involved in such problems as efforts by Third World nations to pay off or successfully "manage" their staggering burdens of external debt—an international problem that has major domestic ramifications for the American nation.

The Department of Agriculture plays a key role in America's Food for Peace program (Public Law 480), inaugurated in 1954. By 1985, almost $40 billion in American farm commodities had been made available to other countries under this program, whose operation and future were a concern of the Department of Agriculture.[22] The Department of Energy, on the other hand, is involved in such problems as the future supply and consumption of various kinds of energy sources to and by the United States and other countries.

Executive departments such as Commerce and Agriculture are admittedly relatively minor actors in the drama of formulating and administering national security policy. Yet even their limited influence illustrates the extent to which the process has become more and more bureaucratically diffuse, complex, and subject to the interplay of a wide range of narrowly focused bureaucratic interests.

▌ Congress and National Security Policy

Our emphasis in this chapter on the roles of the president and of executive departments and agencies in determining national security policy should not obscure the fact that Congress also contributes substantially to the preservation of national security. Admittedly, the congressional role is subordinate, in the sense that for the most part legislators respond to presidential initiatives in the field of national security.[23]

As the United States entered its third century under the Constitution, members of the House and Senate expect the president to take the lead in the sphere of national security. To use a familiar figure of speech, if the president serves as the captain of the American ship of state as it attempts to navigate in often stormy international waters, Congress serves in a number of other capacities. For example, legislators are the shipbuilders: Congress constructs the vessel the president commands, and at intervals, Congress must renovate and refit the ship of state. The legislative branch also serves as the quartermaster, providing the stores, equipment, and ammunition needed for a successful voyage. And from time to time, Congress also carries out inspections, or investigations, to see how well the captain and the crew are performing their duties; on the basis of such investigations, Congress may demand changes in the ship's personnel, its routines and operating procedures, and other matters related to the voyage.

In terms of constitutional prerogatives and responsibilities with respect to national security policy, the Senate has two responsibilities not shared with the House of Representatives. One is to give its "advice and consent" to treaties between the United States and other nations, such as the Rio Treaty, NATO, and the U.S.–Korean and the U.S.–Japanese mutual-defense treaties. The assumption of such formal defense obligations is carefully scrutinized by the Senate after the agreement has been negotiated by executive officials. Senate approval by a two-thirds vote, followed by the president's signing and proclamation of the treaty, makes such a defense agreement part of the law of the land. The Senate's role in treaty ratification also gives it a keen interest in the implementation of the agreement, as well as in possible changes in its provisions in the years ahead.

Another special Senate prerogative in national security policy lies in its duty to confirm presidential appointments. Presidential appointees for high office (by tradition, from the rank of assistant secretaries of departments to the level of cabinet officers) are subject to senatorial confirmation. The Senate must also confirm the appointments or promotions of high-ranking military officers. In the main, such senatorial scrutiny of presidential appointments tends to be nominal. (The Senate normally operates on the principle that every president is entitled to have advisers in whom he has confidence and with whom he can work harmoniously.) Occasionally, however, the Senate does use its confirmation power to express its viewpoints forcefully, for example, refusing for a time to approve President Jimmy Carter's nominee for ambassador to Communist China, Leonard Woodcock. The Woodcock appointment was finally confirmed, but not before the Senate had unmistakably conveyed its belief—widely prevalent on Capitol Hill—that in recognizing Communist China, the White House must not abandon the nation's long-time ally, Taiwan.

The House and Senate jointly exercise a number of important powers affecting national security policy. Under the Constitution (Article I, section 8), Congress is required to "provide for the common defense," to define and specify the punishment for piracy and other crimes committed on the high seas (and, today, in the air) and other offenses against international law, to declare war, to "raise and support Armies" (although no appropriation for the Army may extend for more than two years), to "provide and maintain a Navy" (and, by extension today, an Air Force), and to make rules governing the armed forces (called the Articles of War).

In other words, constitutionally the president can command only such armed forces as Congress places at his disposal. Specifically, this means that Congress determines such important national security questions as the nature and composition of the American military establishment (for example, the proportion of Army, Navy, and Air Force units to the total); the condition or state of readiness of the armed forces; the quality and quantity of weapons available to the military establishment; the size of the armed forces at any given time; the way in which the nation's military personnel needs are met (for example, conscription versus reliance on volunteers); and the kinds of new weapons systems being developed for future use by the American military (military research and development).

As in the exercise of its law-making powers generally, Congress has general legislative authority over national security policy. It is also empowered to investigate problems related to legislation in the realm of national security policy.[24] Its general authority means that Congress may, and, of course, from time to time does, reorganize the Pentagon, redefine the duties of officials such as the secretary of defense and the civilian secretaries of each of the service branches, create new agencies (such as the CIA) and define their missions, and provide the operating funds for these agencies, in the form of annual budgetary appropriations.

According to some commentators, the legislative power to investigate (nowhere specifically mentioned in the Constitution) may be the most powerful instrument Congress has for influencing national security policy. During World War II, Senator Harry S Truman of Missouri headed a Senate committee established to carry on a kind of continuing review of the war effort.[25] Since the war, innumerable legislative investigations have been conducted into various aspects of national security policy. A joint investigation by the Senate Armed Services–Foreign Relations Committee, for example, inquired into President Truman's dismissal of General Douglas MacArthur during the Korean War. The Senate Foreign Relations Committee investigated at length the Johnson administration's intervention in the Dominican Republic in 1965; in the months that followed, the same committee examined the conduct of the Vietnam War. Both of these latter investigations contributed to a decline in public confidence in the Johnson administration's diplomacy.

During the Reagan administration, committees of the House and Senate investigated such diverse issues as American policy toward Central America, the development of new missile systems and a new long-range bomber for the armed forces, the Soviet–American military balance, and the operations of the National Security Council with regard to American policy toward Iran and Central America. In the Iran–Contra affair especially, congressional exposure of several problems involving the presidential advisory system—together with personnel and procedural changes demanded by legislators—gave Congress enhanced influence in national security affairs.[26]

▌ An "Invitation to Struggle"

An eminent constitutional authority, Edward S. Corwin, once said that the constitutional doctrine of checks and balances is "an invitation to struggle" between the president and Congress, especially in regard to their respective prerogatives over the armed forces. On one hand, the Constitution vests in Congress such powers as the right to declare war and to raise and support the military establishment. On the other hand, it designates the president commander in chief of the armed forces and permits the chief executive (with the confirmation of the Senate) to appoint high-ranking military and civilian leaders in the Pentagon. Until the Vietnam War, there appeared little doubt how this "invitation to struggle" was going: In the twentieth century, successive presidents had unquestionably strengthened their positions vis-à-vis Congress in controlling the military establishment.[27]

The effects of the Vietnam War were far-reaching in many respects, not least with regard to the constitutional distribution of power within the federal government over use of the armed forces. For many legislative critics of the war, the nation's failure in Vietnam could be attributed mainly to the emergence of what came to be called the "imperial presidency," exemplified by the presidencies of Lyndon B. Johnson and Richard M. Nixon. Although no two critics would define the imperial presidency in exactly the same way, in general terms it denoted a chief executive who recognized few, if any, limits on executive power in foreign affairs; who seldom sought advice outside of his own closed circle, whose members routinely supported his policies; and who manipulated Congress and public opinion to achieve his goals.

For those holding this view, it was perhaps inevitable that after the Vietnam War serious efforts would be made to limit the powers of the president to use the armed forces for foreign policy ends. This movement culminated in the passage of the War Powers Resolution on November 7, 1973, over President Richard Nixon's veto. With this resolution legislators attempted to impose strict limits on the president's authority to use the armed forces abroad without the explicit approval of Congress. For example, the resolution prohibits future presidents from following the example of LBJ, who during the Vietnam War interpreted annual congressional passage of the Defense Department budget as giving de facto legislative approval to the steady buildup of American forces in Southeast Asia. The resolution requires that in future conflicts involving American forces overseas, the president must withdraw the forces within sixty days (in certain cases, ninety days), unless Congress has declared war or specifically authorized their presence in the crisis zone for longer than sixty days or extended the sixty-day timetable, or unless Congress is physically unable to meet. In other words, according to the resolution, a president must have explicit and unambiguous authorization from both houses of Congress before maintaining American forces in overseas combat zones for any extended period of time. Congress recognized in the War Powers Resolution that, for periods shorter than sixty days, the president could use the armed forces, provided the chief executive reported that fact to Congress within forty-eight hours after deploying American forces abroad. [28]

The view of most informed commentators is that the attempt in 1973 to resolve the old constitutional dispute between the president and Congress over control of the armed forces has not been a notable success. The attempt bears many of the earmarks of an earlier effort by Congress to prevent America's entry into World War II by passing "neutrality legislation" in the 1930s. President Roosevelt's complaint then was comparable to that of President Nixon and other chief executives after 1973: The actual result of such attempts by Congress was to shackle the president, significantly reducing his ability to protect the nation's diplomatic and security interests during international crises. In reality, as illustrated by the Reagan presidency, the War Powers Resolution did little to inhibit the White House from intervening (on two separate occasions) in Lebanon; from using armed force to overthrow a procommunist regime in Grenada; from supplying large quantities of arms aid, equipment, money, and other forms of support to the Contras and other anticommunist forces in Central America; from carrying out an air strike against Libya, which was accused of sponsoring terrorist attacks against Americans; and from using naval power to preserve Western access to the Persian Gulf. In none of the above cases did the War Powers Resolution appear to constrain the president's actions.

Several reasons can be offered for the inability of the War Powers Resolution to resolve the problem of the distribution of power between the White House and Congress regarding the armed forces. It has been pointed out, for example, that the resolution provides no sanctions—other than the extreme step of impeaching the president—against a chief executive who violates its provisions. In addition, a number of provisions in the resolution are unclear and ambiguous, leaving ample scope for widely differing interpretations.

In the final analysis, however, the resolution has failed to achieve its purpose primarily for two reasons. One was identified earlier, in our discussion of informal presidential powers: Few legislators want to be accused—or to defend themselves against the charge—of being responsible for a major foreign policy failure. Much as they might take issue, for example, with the

Reagan administration's diplomacy in Central America, legislative critics of the president did not want to be blamed for "losing Central America to communism."

A second reason for the failure of the War Powers Resolution was that its authors and supporters misjudged the mood of the American people in the post–Vietnam War era. Even after Vietnam and Watergate, for example, there was no discernible public demand in favor of severely limiting the powers of the chief executive in foreign or domestic affairs. All presidents, of course, are expected to obey the law and to observe the principles of the U.S. Constitution. Within these limits, since the New Deal the American people have expected— and continue to expect—the White House to provide vigorous leadership in responding to challenges at home and abroad. At the end of the 1980s, no such unified and dynamic national leadership appeared to be forthcoming from Congress. On the other hand, there has been no evidence of public support for any military interventionism that would involve American forces in a protracted land war. President Reagan's failure to gain broad support for the Contras in Nicaragua indicates that the American public is still leery of becoming embroiled in "another Vietnam."

▌ Coordinating National Security Policy

The emergence of national security policy as a central concern of the nation's leaders—coupled with the involvement of a steadily widening circle of executive agencies in the decision-making process—places a high premium on the successful coordination of governmental activities in the national security field. As was emphasized in chapter 1, such coordination was either totally lacking before World War II or provided only sporadically by dominant personalities such as President Franklin D. Roosevelt. FDR's untimely death meant, of course, that his successor, Harry S Truman, faced the difficult challenge of imposing order on the chaotic New Deal administration. Since Truman, successive administrations have relied on a wide variety of techniques and mechanisms to coordinate governmentwide national security efforts. For convenience, these may be divided into two broad categories: formal methods and informal modes.

In the category of formal methods of coordination, there is, of course, the oldest coordinating mechanism in the federal government: the president's cabinet. During certain periods of American history, as during George Washington's administration, the president has relied heavily on the cabinet for this purpose.[29]

Throughout the course of American history, however, the influence of the cabinet in the decision-making process has steadily declined—until, by the post–World War II period, its role as a coordinating device was minimal. Although calls for the revival of the president's cabinet are heard from time to time, no evidence exists that such a revival is imminent. One after another, postwar presidents have expressed the view that little is gained by having prolonged cabinet consideration of national security issues. Most cabinet officials have little to offer by way of informed background or expertise related to national security policy. Successive presidents have allowed the Cabinet to decline as an advisory body in national security affairs primarily because they have not found it to be a useful forum in this policy-making sphere.

The decline of the cabinet has coincided with the rise of the National Security Council as the chief formal mechanism for coordinating executive efforts in national security affairs. As established by Congress, the NSC is intended to function as the highest-level committee within the federal government with regard to national security issues. It is expected to blend civilian and military components of national policy into an integrated national security policy that all agencies of the government understand and cooperate in implementing.

The chairman of the National Security Council is the president, who convenes NSC meetings and presides over its discussions when he is present. All the statutory members of the NSC are civilians, in accordance with the tradition of civilian supremacy in decision making. Moreover, as we have emphasized, the NSC serves the president as an advisory body. The president's assistant for national security affairs (ANSA)—that is, the national security advisor—is a White House aide who directs the work of the NSC staff as its executive secretary. The size of the staff has varied from well over a hundred to fewer than twenty, depending on the importance the president has attached to the NSC's role in the decision-making process.

As the material presented in our case studies (chapters 4 through 8) will clearly demonstrate, the way in which particular presidents have used the National Security Council has varied widely since 1947. President Truman, for example, had little interest in the NSC and (when he convened it at all) used it mainly to ratify decisions he had already reached. By contrast, President Nixon, who was highly suspicious of the State Department, relied heavily on Henry Kissinger, his ANSA, creating in effect a rival State Department in the White House. Other presidents have used the NSC and its staff in still different ways in the decision-making process.

Along with formal mechanisms such as the cabinet and the National Security Council, modern presidents have relied on a number of informal methods for coordinating national security policy. Such procedures are almost infinitely varied, reflecting the particular administrative style and personal preferences of successive chief executives. FDR, for example, deliberately dispersed responsibility for particular programs among several of his subordinates—thereby enabling him to play off one official or agency against another, leaving himself free to serve as referee among bureaucratic rivals. Other chief executives (Lyndon Johnson was a leading example) have preferred to consult with small groups of trusted individuals, rather than with large collective bodies like the National Security Council. LBJ and other presidents have also from time to time sought the advice of individuals outside the government on domestic and foreign policy questions.

During the Cuban missile crisis of 1962, President John F. Kennedy formed an ad hoc group of advisers called the Executive Committee of the National Security Council (ExComm). We shall examine this committee's role more fully in chapter 6.

Meanwhile, it suffices to observe here that ExComm functioned very effectively to avert possible war between the United States and the Soviet Union. The Kennedy administration's mode of decision making during the Cuban missile crisis has in fact been widely cited as a model of prudent statesmanship. Among its other accomplishments, it did achieve a high level of coordination among the departments and agencies involved in the Cuban crisis.

As already indicated, President Lyndon B. Johnson preferred informal advisers. During the Vietnam War, for example, the "Tuesday Lunch Group" served as his most influential advisory body, largely displacing the National Security Council in this respect. LBJ also leaned heavily on a group of distinguished former public servants called "the Wise Men."[30] This group, for example, played a key role in convincing President Johnson that the United States could not achieve its objectives in the Vietnam War. The role of these and other advisory groups during the Johnson administration is examined more fully in chapter 6.

NOTES

1. In dealing with foreign policy issues, the Supreme Court has in most cases ruled that such issues are "political questions." In the words of one study, this means that such issues are "more suitable for resolution by legislators or executive officials" than by judges. It is very difficult to know precisely what a "political question" is, since in practice it is "whatever a court says it is." Most foreign policy issues fall into the category of political questions. See Robert J. Janosik, ed., *Encyclopedia of the American Judicial System* (New York: Scribner's, 1987), vol. 2, pp. 830–831; and the Supreme Court's decision in *Luther v. Borden,* 7 Howard 1 (1849). Or, as the Supreme Court held in a later case dealing with the president's power to "recognize" another government, the question of who is sovereign over a territory "is not a judicial question, but one the determination of which by the political department [i.e., the executive or legislative branches] conclusively binds the courts." See *United States v. Belmont,* 301 U.S. 324 (1937).

2. Since the Vietnam War, a debate has continued over the scope of the president's constitutional authority in foreign affairs, especially over the armed forces. An invaluable reference, providing a wealth of historical insights and precedents on the subject, is Edward S. Corwin, ed., *The Constitution of the United States of America: Analysis and Interpretation.* (Washington, D.C.: Library of Congress, 1953). See also Corwin's classic work *The President's Control of Foreign Relations* (Princeton, N.J.: Princeton University Press, 1917). Other studies, focusing on World War II and the postwar era, are Charles Fairman, "The President As Commander-in-Chief," in the symposium on *The*

Presidency in Transition (Gainesville: University of Florida Press, 1949); Clinton Rossiter, *The Supreme Court and the Commander in Chief* (Ithaca, N.Y.: Cornell University Press, 1951); Henry Paolucci, *War, Peace, and the Presidency* (New York: McGraw-Hill, 1968); Richard Neustadt, *Presidential Power: The Politics of Leadership from FDR to Carter* (New York: Wiley, 1980); Ernest R. May, *The Ultimate Decision—The President as Commander in Chief* (New York: Braziller, 1960); Sidney Warren, *The President as World Leader* (New York: McGraw-Hill, 1967); Michael Nelson, ed., *The Presidency and the Political System* (Washington, D.C.: Congressional Quarterly Press, 1984); Samuel Kernell, *New Strategies of Presidential Leadership* (Washington, D.C.: Congressional Quarterly Press, 1986); Jacob K. Javits, *Who Makes War: The President Versus Congress* (New York: Morrow, 1973).

3. Because there is sometimes widespread public confusion and uncertainty about the matter, the reader is reminded that well over a century ago, the Supreme Court held, in connection with the Civil War, that a war does not have to be declared to be a constitutional exercise of power by the national government. In other words, President Abraham Lincoln's broad exercise of executive authority in responding to the attack on Fort Sumter was constitutional. Many of Lincoln's actions were in fact later supported or reinforced by acts of Congress. Many times before and after the Civil War, the Supreme Court has ruled that the United States may be legally at war and that the wartime actions of the government are consequently legal, without a formal declaration of that fact by Congress. See *The Prize Cases*, 2 Black 635 (1863). It may be argued that this precedent really dealt only with civil, as distinct from international, war; however, this has been a dissenting viewpoint. In *The Prize Cases*, the Supreme Court relied on precedents applying to war generally, and not merely to insurrections. This broad interpretation of presidential war-making powers did not distinguish one set of principles for internal war and another for external wars.

4. An informative study of the use of presidential power in using the armed forces to achieve diplomatic goals is Herbert K. Tilleman, *Appeal to Force: American Military Intervention in the Era of Containment* (New York: Thomas Y. Crowell, 1973). A more recent treatment of the same subject may be found in Cecil V. Crabb, Jr., and Pat Holt, *Invitation to Struggle: Congress, the President and Foreign Policy*, 2nd ed. (Washington, D.C.: Congressional Quarterly Press, 1984), pp. 129–161. Recent studies of presidential leadership in the foreign policy field are Samuel Kernell, *Going Public: New Strategies in Presidential Leadership* (Washington, D.C.: Congressional Quarterly Press, 1986); Gerald F. Warburg, *Conflict and Consensus: The Struggle Between Congress and the President Over Foreign Policymaking* (New York: Harper & Row, 1989); and *National Security and the U.S. Constitution*, ed. George C. Edwards III and Wallace E. Walker (Baltimore: The Johns Hopkins University Press, 1988).

5. For studies of the president's control of, and impact on, the news media, see Kathleen J. Turner, *Lyndon Johnson's Dual War: Vietnam and the Press* (Chicago: University of Chicago Press, 1985); Michael T. Grossman and

Martha J. Kumar, *Portraying the President: The White House and the News Media* (Baltimore: Johns Hopkins University Press, 1981); John M. Orman, *Presidential Secrecy and Deception: Beyond the Power to Persuade* (Westport, Conn.: Greenwood Press, 1980); and Montague Kern, Patricia M. Levering, and Ralph D. Levering, *The Kennedy Crisis: The Press, the Presidency, and Foreign Policy* (Chapel Hill: University of North Carolina Press, 1983).

6. For an analysis of the national defense effort from a budgetary perspective, see Richard A. Stubbing and Richard A. Mendel, *The Defense Game* (New York: Harper & Row, 1986). See also George F. Hudson and Joseph Kruzel, eds., *American Defense Annual: 1985–86* (Lexington, Mass.: D. C. Heath, 1986), and later volumes in this series; *America's Defense*, ed. Michael Mandelbaum (New York: Holmes & Meier, 1989); Scott D. Sagan, *Moving Targets: Nuclear Strategy and National Security* (Princeton, N.J.: Princeton University Press, 1989); and Mark Perry, *Four Stars: The Inside Story of the Forty-Year Battle Between the Joint Chiefs of Staff and America's Civilian Leaders* (Boston: Houghton Mifflin, 1989). Current information on U.S. defense spending is available in *The United States Budget in Brief: 1987* (Washington, D.C.: Government Printing Office, 1986), pp. 34–35, and in later volumes in this series.

7. For a number of examples of rising presidential popularity following major and minor diplomatic reverses, see Cecil V. Crabb, Jr., *The Doctrines of American Foreign Policy: Their Meaning, Role, and Future* (Baton Rouge: Louisiana State University Press, 1982); see also John E. Mueller, *War, Presidents and Public Opinion* (New York: Wiley, 1973).

8. For a historical account of the establishment and evolution of the American diplomatic service, see Graham H. Stuart, *The Department of State* (New York: Macmillan, 1949). Other studies are Bertram D. Hulen, *Inside the Department of State* (New York: Whittlesley House, 1939); George F. Kennan, "The Future of Our Professional Diplomacy," *Foreign Affairs* 33 (July 1955): 566–587; James L. McCamy, *The Administration of American Foreign Affairs* (New York: Knopf, 1950); Elmer Plischke, *The Conduct of American Diplomacy* (Princeton, N.J.: Van Nostrand, 1950); and Barry Rubin, *Secrets of State: The State Department and the Struggle Over U.S. Foreign Policy* (New York: Oxford University Press, 1985).

9. Several examples of Americans' ingrained distaste for diplomacy and association of it with Old World political intrigue may be found in Norman A. Graebner, ed., *Ideas and Diplomacy: Readings in the Intellectual Tradition of American Foreign Policy* (New York: Oxford University Press, 1964).

10. See the statement by Secretary of State George Shultz, "International Affairs: FY 1987 Budget," Department of State, *Current Policy* No. 795 (February 19, 1986), pp. 1–8. In mid–1986, Senator Charles Mathias (R.-Md.) observed that the proposed $1.5 billion operating budget for the Department of State constituted some 0.25 percent of the total federal budget—and some legislators wanted to cut even this by 10 percent! In his view, this step would mean a critical curtailment of the agency that serves as America's first line of defense in the continuing effort to see that force does not have to be used to

protect the nation's vital interests abroad. See the *New York Times*, June 26, 1986.

11. See, for example, the analysis by former Secretary of State Dean Acheson in his memoirs, *Present at the Creation: My Years in the State Department* (New York: Norton, 1969); Smith Simpson, *Anatomy of the State Department* (Boston: Houghton Mifflin, 1967); John M. Cabot, *First Line of Defense: Forty Years' Experience of a Career Diplomat* (Washington, D.C.: Foreign Service School, Georgetown University, 1979); Lawrence H. Silberman, "Toward Presidential Control of the State Department," *Foreign Affairs* 57 (Spring 1979): 872–893; and Martin F. Herz, ed., *The Modern Ambassador: The Challenge and the Search* (Lanham, Md.: University Press of America, 1983).

12. See Robert Dallek, *Franklin D. Roosevelt and American Foreign Policy: 1932–1945* (New York: Oxford University Press, 1979); a briefer treatment may be found in Cecil V. Crabb, Jr., and Kevin V. Mulcahy, *Presidents and Foreign Policy Making: FDR to Reagan* (Baton Rouge: Louisiana State University Press, 1986), pp. 82–122.

13. See the criticisms of the State Department in Crabb and Mulcahy, *Presidents and Foreign Policy Making,* pp. 55–62. President John F. Kennedy's criticisms of the State Department's performance are recounted in Theodore Sorensen, *Kennedy* (New York: Harper & Row, 1965), pp. 270–272 and 287–290.

14. For recent studies of the Defense Department, see Stephen J. Cimbala, ed., *The Reagan Defense Program: An Interim Assessment* (Wilmington, Del.: Scholarly Resources, 1986); Christopher Coker, *U.S. Military Power in the 1980s* (Salem, Mass.: Salem House, 1983); James Fallows, *National Defense* (New York: Random House, 1982); Edward Luttwak, *The Meaning of Victory* (New York: Simon & Schuster, 1987); and Joshua M. Epstein, *The 1988 Defense Budget* (Washington, D.C.: Brookings Institution, 1987).

15. See the *World Almanac: 1986* (New York: Newspaper Enterprise Association, 1987), pp. 327–331.

16. See the discussion of Assistant Secretary of Defense for International Security Affairs Richard Perle's role in shaping the Reagan administration's position on arms control in *Newsweek*, March 23, 1987, p. 27. Perle was described as "the effective architect of arms-control policy" who was in some respects even more influential in the councils of the Reagan administration than his administrative superior, Defense Secretary Caspar Weinberger.

17. More-detailed analyses of the intelligence activities of the United States government are available in Scott D. Breckinridge, *The CIA and the U.S. Intelligence System* (Boulder, Colo.: Westview Press, 1986); Stansfield Turner, *Secrecy and Democracy: The CIA in Transition* (Boston: Houghton Mifflin, 1985); *Intelligence Requirements for the 1980s*, 2 vols., ed. Roy Godson (Lexington, Mass.: D. C. Heath, 1986); John Ranelagh, *The Agency: The Rise and Fall of the CIA* (New York: Simon & Schuster, 1986); Robert J. Lamphere and Tom Shachtman, *The FBI–KGB War* (New York: Random House, 1986); William E. Burrows, *Deep Black: Space Espionage and National Security* (New

York: Random House, 1987); *Intelligence Requirements for the 1990s*, ed. Roy Godson (Lexington, Mass.: Lexington Books, 1989); and Loch K. Johnson, *America's Secret Weapon: The CIA in a Democratic Society* (New York: Oxford University Press, 1989).

18. Congressional efforts to supervise the activities of intelligence agencies are described more fully in Loch Johnson, *A Season of Inquiry: The Senate Intelligence Investigation* (Lexington, Ky.: University of Kentucky Press, 1985); and in Crabb and Holt, *Invitation to Struggle*, pp. 161–187.

19. Useful studies of propaganda as an instrument of diplomacy are John Henderson, *The United States Information Agency* (New York: Praeger, 1969); Leo Bogart, *Premises for Propaganda* (New York: Free Press, 1976); the symposium on *The Voice of America at the Crossroads* (Washington, D.C.: The Media Institute, 1982); and Frederick C. Barghoorn, *Soviet Foreign Propaganda* (Princeton, N. J.: Princeton University Press, 1964). For a recent discussion of overt and covert propaganda, see Loch Johnson, *America's Secret Weapon: The CIA in a Democratic Society* (New York: Oxford University Press, 1989), pp. 22–26.

20. Overseas, the USIA is called the United States Information Service (USIS). During the Carter administration, the USIA was called the International Communications Agency, but early in the Reagan administration that name was dropped in favor of the more familiar title, USIA.

21. Examples of American foreign propaganda programs are provided in Robert E. Elder, *The United States Information Agency and American Foreign Policy* (Syracuse, N.Y.: Syracuse University Press, 1968); and Chalmers M. Roberts, "New Image for Voice of America," *New York Times Magazine*, April 13, 1982, pp. 107–114. See also, Johnson, *America's Secret Weapon*, pp. 190–91 and 196–98.

22. For detailed discussions of agricultural aspects of recent American foreign policy, see Donald F. McHenry and Kai Bird, "Food Bungle in Bangladesh," *Foreign Policy* 27 (Summer 1977): pp. 72–89; Raymond F. Hopkins, "How to Make Food Aid Work," *Foreign Policy* 27 (Summer 1977): pp. 89–109; *Trade: U. S. Policy since 1945* (Washington, D.C.: Congressional Quarterly Press, 1984); *The Washington Lobby*, 4th ed. (Washington, D.C.: Congressional Quarterly Press, 1982); D. Gale Johnson, *World Food Problems and Prospects* (Lanham, Md.: University Press of America, 1975); and *Food and Agricultural Policy for the Nineteen Eighties,* ed. D. Gale Johnson (Lanham, Md.: University Press of America, 1981); D. Gale Johnson, Kenzo Hemmi, and Pierre Landinois, *Agricultural Policy and Trade: Adjusting Domestic Programs in an International Framework* (New York: New York University Press, 1986); and *U.S. Agricultural and Third World Development: The Critical Linkage*, ed. Randall Purcell and Elizabeth Morrison (Boulder, Colo.: Lynne Rienner, 1987).

23. More detailed analyses of legislative activities in the foreign policy field are available in Crabb and Holt, *Invitation to Struggle*; Francis D. Wormuth and Edwin B. Firmage, *To Chain The Dogs of War: The War Powers of Congress in History and Law* (Dallas: Southern Methodist University Press,

1986); Phil Williams, *The Senate and U.S. Troops in Europe* (New York: St. Martin, 1985); G. Rystad, ed., *Congress and American Foreign Policy* (Atlantic Highlands, N.J.: Humanities Press, 1982).

24. A comprehensive source on the investigative activities of Congress is Arthur M. Schlesinger, Jr., and Roger Burns, ed., *Congress Investigates: A Documented History, 1792–1974*, 5 vols. (New York Chelsea House, 1975).

25. The official name of the Truman committee was the Special Senate Committee Investigating the National Defense Program, chaired by Senator Harry Truman, Democrat from Missouri.

26. In 1987 Congress undertook a thorough investigation of the Iran–Contra affair. During the months that followed, Oliver North, Robert Mc-Farland, John Poindexter, and other members of the NSC staff under the Reagan administration were tried in the federal courts for numerous violations of the law, such as illegal expenditure of funds, obstruction of Congress, perjury, and other serious offenses. In some instances, as of early 1990 the conviction of these individuals was under appeal. To date, no formal accusation of wrongdoing or violations of federal law in the Iran–Contra affair had been brought against former President Ronald Reagan. Nor had Congress enacted new laws (such as making the appointment of the president's national security adviser subject to senatorial confirmation) designed to prevent another usurpation of authority as had occurred in the Iran–Contra episode.

27. For recent examples of executive–legislative conflict in foreign affairs, see Crabb and Holt, *Invitation to Struggle*; Warren Christopher, "Ceasefire Between the Branches: A Compact in Foreign Affairs" *Foreign Affairs* 60 (Summer 1982): 989–1006; Sen. J. William Fulbright, "The Legislator as Educator," *Foreign Affairs* 57 (Spring 1979): pp. 723–729; and Sen. John Tower, "Congress versus the President: The Formulation and Implementation of American Foreign Policy," *Foreign Affairs* 60 (Winter 1982): 229–247.

28. See Pat M. Holt, *The War Powers Resolution: The Role of Congress in U.S. Armed Intervention* (Washington, D.C.: American Enterprise Institute, 1978); and the analysis of the War Powers Resolution in Crabb and Holt, *Invitation to Struggle,* pp. 143–152.

29. See, for example, the views of President John F. Kennedy on the cabinet as an advisory mechanism, in Sorensen, *Kennedy,* pp. 281–283; a more general assessment may be found in Crabb and Mulcahy, *Presidents and Foreign Policy,* pp. 74–75.

30. The "Tuesday Lunch Group" consisted of President Johnson, Secretary of State Dean Rusk, Secretary of Defense Robert McNamara, the director of the CIA, the national security adviser, the White House press secretary, and sometimes the members of the Joint Chiefs of Staff. The "Wise Men" comprised a group of former public servants and policy makers including Dean Acheson, W. Averell Harriman, Robert Lovett, John J. McCloy, and two of the nation's Kremlinologists, George F. Kennan and Charles E. Bohlen.

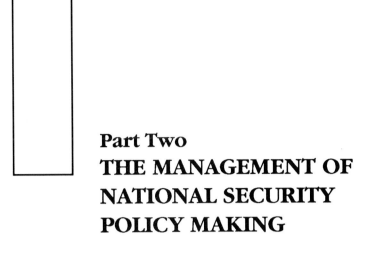

Part Two
THE MANAGEMENT OF NATIONAL SECURITY POLICY MAKING

CHAPTER 4
Laying the Foundations: The Truman Administration and National Security Policy

The concept of national security policy first came into wide currency during the Truman administration (1945–1952). Under President Truman, executive officials became aware of the need to blend civilian and military components of national policy into a unified approach to external challenges; for the first time also, policy makers possessed the institutional machinery and procedures needed for achieving that goal.

As is nearly always the case in domestic and foreign affairs, major policy innovations came about as the United States had to respond to challenges at home and abroad. In this chapter, we shall focus on the external and internal contexts of national security policy during this formative period. We may conveniently summarize the legacy of the Truman administration by discussing the following challenges: the termination and aftermath of World War II, the transition from isolationism to internationalism, the inauguration of the Cold War and America's adoption of a strategy of containment, and major developments in the internal policy-making context, especially the creation of the National Security Council.

▌ From Allied Unity to Cold War

President Franklin D. Roosevelt died suddenly on April 12, 1945—less than a month before Nazi Germany surrendered to the Allies on May 7. Japan finally surrendered on August 15. As FDR's successor, therefore, Harry S Truman's most pressing duty was to prosecute the war to a victorious conclusion. This in turn required the maintenance of the allied coalition, the nucleus of which was Soviet–American cooperation. Though some commentators believe that FDR's death was a severe blow to cooperative Soviet–American relations, the Truman White House did manage to hold the coalition together. The last of the wartime summit conferences was held at Potsdam, Germany, in July 1945. Although results of the conference were minimal, allied unity was preserved at least until after the defeat of Japan.[1]

Immediately upon taking office, President Truman was familiarized with the Manhattan Project—the secret wartime program for the development of the atomic bomb. As chief executive, Truman made three key decisions affecting nuclear weapons. The first was to continue the intensive efforts begun by the Roosevelt administration to perfect the atomic bomb. The second was to use nuclear weapons against Japan (on August 6 and August 9). The third was the administration's comprehensive nuclear disarmament proposal, known as the Baruch Plan. As we shall see, this plan set forth the American approach to strategic arms control; its central feature was an emphasis on effective inspection and control of national compliance with any arms control agreement reached. The Soviet Union rejected the Baruch Plan in favor of its own Gromyko Plan, which Washington in turn dismissed as unacceptable.[2]

A related decision by the Truman administration that directly affected national security was the president's determination to reduce the nation's conventional (or nonnuclear) arsenal after the war. From the end of World War II until early 1947, the total strength of U.S. armed forces declined from 12 million to 1.6 million troops. Correctly or not (and well-informed students of Soviet affairs are divided on the question), Western political leaders believed that, despite America's nuclear monopoly, the military balance in the early postwar period strongly favored Moscow and encouraged the Kremlin to embark on expansionist foreign policy ventures.[3]

The end of World War II confronted the United States with another novel challenge: the creation and operation of allied occupation zones for Germany and the administration of occupation policy for the defeated Axis nations. In accordance with Clausewitz's teachings (see chapter 1), the postwar political division of Germany reflected existing military realities. East Germany became, and until 1990 remained, closely dependent on the Soviet Union, and most of Berlin and its environs were incorporated into the Soviet zone of occupation. The United States, Great Britain, and France shared the responsibility for administering the western zone of Germany. To the American mind, the "artificial division" of the German nation became a major source of Cold War controversy.[4]

The occupation of defeated Germany and Japan had basically similar objectives. In both instances, the goal was to effect a sweeping transformation of the society's economic and political life, to eliminate all traces of the previous totalitarian political system, to implant democratic institutions and processes, and to ensure that neither nation was again in a position to embark on an aggressive course.

The continued division of the German nation—along with the deepening suspicions that characterized Soviet–American relations—meant that these goals could not be achieved for Germany as a whole. The Western allies did, however, successfully implement them in West Germany, whose democratic system appears stable and strongly rooted.

In Japan, the United States continually resisted Moscow's efforts to gain a voice in occupation policy. Directed by General Douglas MacArthur, the occupation regime carried out sweeping changes in all aspects of Japanese society, including, of course, the political system. In 1947, Japan received a new constitution; on September 8, 1951, most of the countries that had fought against Japan (with the notable exception of the Soviet Union) signed a peace treaty restoring Japanese sovereignty. Japan is still prohibited by the terms of its constitution from maintaining anything other than internal police and self-defense forces.[5]

The Truman administration inherited a number of problems arising from World War II. Besides the division of Germany (and of Korea and Indochina, as well), a major problem was Moscow's overt political intervention in Eastern Europe. In Washington's view, Moscow's creation of "people's democracies"—imposed on Eastern Europeans by the might of the Red Army—flagrantly violated allied wartime agreements calling for the democratization of the region after the war. Moreover, the Kremlin's conduct provided what appeared to be irrefutable proof of aggressive and untrustworthy Soviet behavior. Reluctantly, Americans widely came to believe that, like Hitler before him, Stalin could not be trusted; with other dictators, Stalin viewed treaties and other international agreements as mere "scraps of paper."[6]

This leads to another major dimension of the Truman administration's external policies: Soviet–American relations in the early postwar period. Though to discuss the historic development of relations between the United States and the Soviet Union up until 1917 would distract from our purpose here, that early period had a significant impact on the course of their later diplomatic interaction. We must necessarily confine our discussion to World War II and the years that followed.[7]

During the war, President Roosevelt made a concerted effort to win and retain the goodwill of Stalin's government. As a master practitioner of the political art, FDR was convinced that he could handle "Uncle Joe" and could preserve a high level of Soviet–American unity after the war.[8] Yet, on the eve of his death, after returning from the Yalta Conference, even FDR expressed real doubts about whether Soviet–American friendship would in fact endure after the war. During the war, such questions as the timing of the "second front" (the Allied landing in France on D day) and the nature and extent of American wartime aid to the USSR engendered sharp controversy among the Allies.

As the new president, Truman soon revealed his belief in two propositions: that Soviet–American relations were rapidly deteriorating and that the primary responsibility for that condition rested with Soviet leadership. The deterioration stemmed mainly from Moscow's unwillingness to carry out its international commitments in good faith and its determination to exploit postwar conditions of economic dislocation and political instability to its own advantage.[9]

President Truman of course was not alone in reaching these conclusions. From his position in the American embassy in Moscow, for example, George F. Kennan repeatedly warned Washington about Soviet intentions in the postwar period, especially in areas subject to Soviet military power. Time and again, Kennan called attention to two factors—the ideological incompatibility between Soviet communism and Western democracy, and the reassertion of certain historical goals of the Russian state in global affairs—to account for the growing distrust between the two superpowers. Other commentators (such as Walter Lippmann) believed that what came to be called the Cold War derived chiefly from realpolitik considerations—specifically, from Moscow's threat to the postwar balance of power in Europe.[10]

As always, American attitudes and policies abroad were strongly influenced by Soviet actions, which, in the early postwar era, appeared to convincingly demonstrate expansionist tendencies. Moscow's creation of a zone of political satellites in Eastern Europe; its insistence on playing a role in the Japanese occupation; Stalin's expressed interest in inheriting Italy's former colony in Libya; overt Soviet political intervention in Iran, involving efforts to raise the local Communist (or Tudeh) party to a dominant position; a series of militant ideological statements, in which communist spokesmen predicted economic, followed by political, crises in the West; the activities of the communist parties of Western Europe during the early postwar era—all these developments caused genuine apprehension among officials of the Truman administration. The common denominator of these geographically diverse activities appeared to be that Moscow was determined to fill any postwar power vacuum with Soviet power.

President Truman and his diplomatic aides had no doubt that the Soviet threat was real and that it was directed chiefly at the Western Europe–Mediterranean area. A series of developments supported that belief. After World War II, for example, there was what the administration believed to be irrefutable evidence of external support for the communist-led Greek force (called the National Liberation Front, or EAM), the military arm of which (the People's Liberation Army, or ELAS) used force in the effort to overthrow the pro-Western Greek monarchy. The Greek civil war was waged for several months following Germany's surrender. Its outcome was finally determined by two principal factors. One crucial development was Yugoslavia's "defection" from the Kremlin in 1948. Marshall Tito's refusal to follow Stalin's orders was the first example of national communism after World War II. Tito's break with the Kremlin led to the closing of the Greek–Yugoslav border, and this meant that procommunist rebel forces in Greece were thereafter denied a sanctuary in Yugoslavia where they could regroup, be resupplied by the Soviet Union and other communist nations, and return to carry out new subversive activities in Greece.[11]

The other momentous development was congressional passage of the Greek–Turkish Aid Program, requested by President Truman in his epochal address to Congress on March 12, 1947. In this speech—ranking among the most influential in American diplomatic history—the president announced what came to be called the Truman Doctrine or the containment strategy. The key idea of the doctrine was the president's assertion that the United States must "support free peoples who are resisting attempted subjugation by armed minorities or by outside pressures." The United States, Truman declared, must "assist free peoples to work out their own destinies in their own way."[12]

The strategy of containment enunciated by President Truman has generally remained the underlying principle governing American relations with the Soviet Union for more than forty years (although the early Reagan Doctrine arguably went beyond mere containment). Reflecting the ideas of George F. Kennan and other presidential advisers, the containment concept symbolized the fundamental transition in American foreign policy from isolationism to internationalism (or as the latter was sometimes called by critics, interventionism). The basic idea was that the United States must confront Soviet expansionism with what George Kennan called effective "counterforce." The successful containment of Moscow's expansionist tendencies was expected in turn to lead to a mellowing in Soviet policy, resulting in a more stable and peaceful international system. In the view of some commentators, the era of *glasnost* identified with Soviet Premier Mikhail Gorbachev represents the kind of mellowing of Soviet internal and external policy that Kennan had anticipated would follow from successful application of the containment strategy.

The Greek–Turkish Aid Program, involving an allocation of $400 million in American aid to these countries, is usually viewed as the Truman administration's initial application of the containment strategy. (Although at the time the request was undoubtedly traumatic for many legislators, this modest sum was less than one-tenth of the foreign aid that Israel alone hoped to secure from Congress in the mid-1980s.) The Greek–Turkish Aid Program was the hallmark of the profound change that occurred in American diplomacy after World War II, symbolizing what is sometimes called the revolution in the nation's foreign policy. Most of the funds were allocated for economic assistance to these countries.

Concurrently with the crisis in Greece and with Soviet pressures against Turkey, officials in Washington were also concerned about communist political activity in Western Europe. In two nations particularly—France and Italy—communists and their supporters sought to exploit the postwar economic and social chaos, and for several months, it appeared the communists would achieve their objective.[13]

Then, early in 1948, another ominous event occurred, confirming the Truman administration's worst fears about Soviet diplomatic ambitions. This was the Berlin blockade, in which the Kremlin sought to force the Western Allies out of the historic German capital by denying them use of the land routes through Soviet controlled Germany. If the Berlin blockade had succeeded, the results would have been devastating for America's position in Western Europe and for NATO's subsequent defense efforts.

Typically, President Truman left no doubt about his intention to maintain Allied access to Berlin. The ingenious and successful method decided on was an around-the-clock airlift of vital supplies into beleaguered Berlin. Finally, in September 1949, Stalin's government concluded that the Soviet blockade had failed; Western nations were again permitted to use land routes to Berlin. On the basis of the outcome, the Truman administration could justifiably conclude that one of its diplomatic maxims—"patience and firmness" in responding to Soviet moves abroad—had achieved positive results.[14]

The impact of these developments on official and public opinion in the United States was momentous. Congress had barely finished providing aid to Greece and Turkey before the Truman White House proposed an infinitely more ambitious and costly overseas spending program: the European Recovery Program (ERP) or Marshall Plan, as it was popularly called in honor of Secretary of State George C. Marshall. Over a four-year period, the ERP ultimately entailed some $13 billion in American aid for European reconstruction. The European participants, it must be emphasized, drew up the ERP plan, implemented it, and provided some 90 percent of the funds and other resources needed to achieve its goals. By many criteria, the Marshall Plan was perhaps the best "investment" of American funds abroad witnessed since World War II. For example, in the years that followed European reconstruction, the "disarray" or disunity often seen within the NATO alliance, and the evident unwillingness of the European allies to follow Washington's diplomatic lead toward a number of global issues, could largely be explained by the fact that an increasingly prosperous and politically stable Western Europe had substantially reduced its earlier dependence on the United States. The phenomenon was also in part an outgrowth of the European conviction that over the years the Soviet threat to Western security had significantly declined.[15]

The Berlin blockade graphically underscored the military vulnerability of Western Europe. Experienced political leaders, such as Winston Churchill, had said for many months that only the American nuclear arsenal deterred a Soviet military incursion into a debilitated Western Europe. (Moscow, of course, was in the process of breaking the American nuclear monopoly and succeeded in doing so in 1949.) Many members of Congress questioned the point of providing large-scale economic assistance to Europe, when the region remained militarily vulnerable. In fact, many thought, an economically prosperous Western Europe might well tempt Moscow to launch a military intrusion into the West.

As a result of such concerns, Western officials focused intensely on the problem of regional security in the late 1940s. These efforts culminated in the establishment of the North Atlantic Treaty Organization (NATO) on August 24, 1949.[16] Article 5 of the treaty obligates the signatories to treat an attack against one as an attack against all. The Kremlin, in other words, would not be permitted to use "salami tactics" against the weaker European allies; it could not slice off a portion of West Germany and keep it without fear of response by the alliance as a whole. Throughout the years that followed, events left no doubt that NATO was America's most important alliance system.

The Truman administration took another step to strengthen the security of the West. With the failure of the wartime allies to agree on a peace treaty with Germany, the United States took the lead in restoring West Germany to the society of nations. On May 23, 1949, the Federal Republic of Germany came into existence, with a new constitution providing for a parliamentary system of government. In May 1955, West Germany became fully independent. From the beginning, except for America's own contribution, West Germany has provided the largest contingent of troops to the common NATO defense effort. The ultimate political reunification of the German nation has remained a paramount goal of American foreign policy since the end of World War II. For example, as the Soviet-dominated satellite system in Eastern Europe disintegrated, President George Bush and his advisers reiterated Washington's long-standing support for the idea of German reunification. They insisted, however, that—to safeguard against a resurgence of German expansionism at the expense of its neighbors—a unified Germany's military power must continue to be closely integrated into, and controlled by, the NATO alliance. Whether this idea would be acceptable to Moscow, or for that matter to the Germans themselves, of course remained an uncertain issue.

■ The Korean War and Its Aftermath

Perhaps the best-known development in external policy under the Truman administration was the Korean War.[17] On June 25, 1950, North Korean troops crossed the border into South Korea, in an evident attempt to "liberate" the latter from its pro-American government and unite the whole of Korea politically into a new "people's democracy." Some forty-eight hours later, President Truman ordered American air and naval forces to defend South Korea; soon thereafter, he directed General Douglas MacArthur to defend South Korea with ground forces as well. The Truman White House also succeeded in having the defense of South Korea brought under the jurisdiction of the United Nations, with some fifty nations in time contributing to that undertaking.

Though peace talks began in 1951, two years passed before an armistice agreement was reached and fighting ended (in July 1953). During the course of the Korean War, the United States fought directly against Chinese forces, as well as those of North Korea. Even before the war ended, a partisan storm was precipitated in the United States between the followers of General MacArthur and the Truman administration. Because of MacArthur's failure to follow White House directives, President Truman relieved him of his command. This action came close to destroying the administration's political credibility, although in time most Americans came to realize that on most grounds, Truman's actions were justified and defensible—especially his determination to avoid a superpower confrontation in Asia.[18]

Yet, as one of the earliest postwar examples of "limited war," the Korean conflict continues to elicit highly divergent responses from the American people and their leaders. Did the United States win or lose that contest? Alternatively, precisely what did it win or lose? Such questions still evoke fundamentally different answers from informed Americans.[19] Many of the frustrations and dilemmas reflected in American thinking toward the Korean War have continued to characterize public and congressional attitudes toward the use of armed forces abroad since the early 1950s.

Another long-range consequence of the Korean conflict is related to the president's control of foreign relations and, more specifically, to the chief executive's authority over the armed forces. The Korean War was widely described (especially by critics) as "Mr. Truman's war." President Truman neither asked for nor received a declaration of war by Congress. The nation's participation in the Korean conflict resulted from decisions made ultimately by the president, after consultation with his foreign policy advisers. The Truman administration's "consultations" with Congress (when they occurred at all) usually amounted to informing selected legislators about moves the White House either had already made or was in the process of making. Nevertheless, relatively little objection to this procedure was heard on Capitol Hill at the time. As was also true of the Vietnam War later, much of the criticism directed at the Truman White House for its decisions in Korea stemmed from the fact that, in the view of perhaps a majority of citizens, the United States had lost—or at any rate, had not won—this encounter with communism in Asia.[20]

▮ International Organization and Global Community

In most aspects of its foreign policy, the Truman administration continued with the diplomacy of the Roosevelt administration—nowhere more so than in efforts to establish successful new international and regional institutions. President Roosevelt and his advisers were determined to avoid the mistakes of the Wilson administration. Planning for the second attempt at international organization—the United Nations—began early in World War II on a bipartisan basis, and it continued throughout the conflict.[21] President Truman maintained this momentum, deciding that the scheduled San Francisco conference on international organization (April 25–June 25, 1945), at which the UN was established, must be held as planned. Truman was equally determined that America's participation in this assembly would be a bipartisan undertaking, with members of the House and Senate and spokesmen for both political parties taking part in both the planning and the San Francisco conference. At that meeting, the United Nations Charter was drafted; it was subsequently approved by the U.S. Senate by the decisive vote of 89–2 and ratified by some fifty original signatory nations on October 15, 1945. Headquartered in New York City, the UN owed its existence largely to American initiative, and after 1945 the United States remained the largest contributor to the organization's budget and programs.

America's longtime interest in international organization and the concept of global community was not confined to the United Nations. Under the

Roosevelt administration—and again, the Truman White House maintained this commitment—the United States was at the forefront in efforts to create new international financial institutions and agreements, such as the International Monetary Fund and the World Bank. On the European continent, Washington also encouraged the tendency toward regional economic and political cooperation, culminating in the creation of the European Community (EC). For example, the Truman administration favored the establishment of the Benelux (Belgium, the Netherlands, and Luxembourg) customs union in the early postwar period and the even more far-reaching European Coal and Steel Community (ECSC) agreement between France and Germany. ECSC became one of the major antecedents of the even more ambitious European Community.[22]

In Latin America, the Roosevelt administration had committed the United States to the Good Neighbor policy and had taken several other steps to improve inter-American relations. Under the Truman administration, the Organization of American States (OAS) was created in 1948. Officials in Washington hoped that the OAS would assume mounting responsibility for solving hemispheric problems. The Rio Treaty of regional defense was negotiated and ratified in 1947 (two years before NATO was created).[23]

The Truman White House also sought to arrive at an acceptable arms control agreement with the Soviet Union, initially covering nuclear armaments. Presented to the United Nations in June 1946, the American-sponsored Baruch Plan called for establishment of an International Atomic Development Authority (IADA) under the auspices of the United Nations. In effect, the IADA would supervise the production of nuclear materials throughout the world, ensuring that they would be used only for peaceful purposes. The new agency would have the power—and in the American view, this was the crux of the proposal—to inspect the nuclear activities of all nations. After an effective inspection and control system had been established and successfully demonstrated, Washington would turn over its nuclear technology to the international community.

The Soviet Union rejected the Baruch Plan at the time, and for many years thereafter, because it called for an international system of inspection and control. Moscow's counterproposal (the Gromyko Plan) in effect left the matter of inspection and control to be conducted and certified by the national governments concerned. This in turn was totally unacceptable to the United States. As a result, the early postwar deadlock on nuclear arms control characterized Soviet–American disarmament negotiations for some forty years.[24]

▌ The Internal Policy Environment

The diplomatic record of the Truman administration was memorable for another reason: because of the significant changes made in the internal policy-making environment. Since we have already looked at some of these, they will be mentioned here only briefly.

The diplomacy of the Truman administration exhibited two contrary tendencies. On one side, the Truman White House succeeded in achieving perhaps the highest level of bipartisanship in American diplomatic experience. From wartime and postwar planning for the United Nations, to negotiation of the minor Axis peace treaties, to the Greek–Turkish Aid Program, to the Marshall Plan, and to NATO—these landmark undertakings were characterized by an impressive degree of bipartisan collaboration in the making of foreign policy.[25]

On the other side, the Truman diplomatic record was also paradoxically one of the most partisan ever in the saga of American diplomacy! Except perhaps for the controversy surrounding American membership in the League of Nations or the final stage of the Vietnam War, it would be difficult to recall an era when a comparable degree of partisan strife existed over international questions. Two developments in particular illustrated this tendency: the political conflict that erupted over the administration's conduct of the Korean War (with some critics calling for Truman's resignation, if not his impeachment) and the phenomenon known as McCarthyism.[26]

McCarthyism—named for Joseph R. McCarthy, a junior (Republican) senator from Wisconsin—was a particularly freewheeling and virulent form of right-wing political opposition that left in its wake broken careers, unproven accusations and insinuations, shattered morale in the State Department, and a confused public opinion. Beginning early in 1950, Senator McCarthy attracted a wide following, and gained extensive media coverage through frequent, irresponsible accusations that the policies of the Roosevelt and Truman administrations had been dictated by officials who were part of a "communist global conspiracy." At one point, Senator McCarthy even accused General George C. Marshall of being an agent (one of McCarthy's favorite phrases was "an unwilling dupe") of the Kremlin. On several occasions, McCarthy accused the State Department of being infiltrated by communists and their sympathizers.[27]

One of McCarthyism's most serious legacies was the implication that whenever the United States was unable to achieve its foreign policy objectives the underlying reason was "betrayal" by the nation's leaders and public servants. For McCarthyites, the fact that evidence of such betrayal was difficult to discover proved only how insidious and deep-seated the "communist conspiracy" in America had become! During the Truman period and afterward, such self-delusion (concerning, for example, why the United States "lost China" to communism) made the always difficult task of gaining informed public support in America for necessary policies abroad even more difficult.

Two other specific developments affected the American foreign policy process under the Truman administration. The first has already been described in some detail: passage of the National Security Act of 1947. To recapitulate briefly, this act established a new Department of Defense, the Central Intelligence Agency, and the National Security Council. During the Truman and successive administrations, these became key agencies in the formulation and administration of national security policy.

The other noteworthy development entailed organizational changes within the Department of State: After conducting a detailed study of the department (along with other executive agencies), the Hoover Commission (1947–1949) issued a comprehensive report designed to modernize the department and equip it administratively for its new responsibilities in the post–World War II era.

The most noteworthy change in the State Department's organizational machinery occurred while General George C. Marshall was secretary of state (1947–1949). A long-standing complaint about the department—still heard, almost a half-century later—was that the United States lacked an overall diplomatic strategy, capable of integrating its separate moves in Latin America, Western Europe, East Asia, and elsewhere. Under Secretary of State Marshall, a new bureau, called the Policy Planning Staff (later renamed the Policy Planning Council), was created within the State Department; it was expected to function as a kind of diplomatic general staff, providing civilian officials with long-range plans and projections. Its first director was the noted Kremlinologist George F. Kennan.

Whatever its theoretical merits and goals, however, the Policy Planning Staff has never achieved its intended objective. Staffed by some of the most distinguished and experienced members of the diplomatic service, the agency has perhaps inevitably been diverted by the need to solve urgent, day-to-day diplomatic problems.

An even more fundamental question about policy planning from World War II to the present has been whether the president, the secretary of state, and other high-level policy makers—supported by American public opinion—really value long-range diplomatic planning and want to encourage it. The evidence to date affords few grounds for optimism on the subject. Today, as in the past, the American approach to foreign policy remains characterized by an "incremental" or pragmatic mentality, by a tendency to engage in "crisis diplomacy," and by a preference for concentrating on immediate problems requiring urgent solutions.[28]

▋ President Truman's Administrative Style

From a consideration of the numerous and important external challenges confronting the Truman administration shortly after World War II, we turn to an examination of the national security policy-making process under the Truman White House. How were decisions in the national security field actually reached under Truman? What were the roles of the National Security Council, the president's national security adviser, the secretary of state, and other major actors in the decision-making process?

Our inquiry begins with a brief examination of an all-important aspect of the subject: President Truman's administrative style and modus operandi as chief executive. On that topic, several points seem noteworthy. One was Truman's lack of background and preparation in foreign affairs.[29] As vice president, Truman had typically played little or no role in decision making in the Roosevelt White House. Like most of FDR's advisers (including his secretary of state), Truman had little familiarity with Roosevelt's diplomatic moves, commitments, and plans.

Truman's lack of formal training or expertise in foreign affairs, however, was in some measure compensated by certain other qualities.[30] One of these was his keen and ongoing interest in history and (after he entered the Oval Office) his place in it. In his knowledge of history and applicable precedents, Truman ranked high among chief executives.

Another compensatory factor was Truman's own awareness of his lack of background in foreign affairs, and, in light of that fact, his willingness to rely upon the advice of those who were better informed than he was on the subject. As chief executive, Truman exhibited little "ego stress" in office: He freely sought advice from others, even if (as in the case of American policy toward Israel) he did not always follow it.

Still another hallmark of Truman's administrative style was his decisiveness. President Truman, Secretary of State Dean Acheson said, was a "creature of instinct." Truman's approach to decision making was intuitive, rather than coldly rational. Normally, Truman did not require a prolonged process of discussion and soul searching before deciding on a course of action. (Both President Truman and Secretary Acheson viewed the wartime chief of staff, General George C. Marshall, as a role model. After reasonable discussion, General Marshall used to tell his subordinates not to "fight the issue" any longer but to "decide it.")[31] Prolonged deliberations among Truman's advisers sometimes did occur, but as in Truman's response to the communist attack on South Korea, such discussions often appeared to be pro forma and ritualistic. It seemed clear that Truman had made up his mind early on that the United States must assist South Korea in resisting aggression. (On other occasions, however—as in Truman's removal of General Douglas MacArthur—the president carefully considered the opinions of his aides and was influenced by them.)[32]

President Truman's decisiveness and his tendency to make decisions instinctively were especially pronounced qualities in his dealings with the Soviet Union and with questions involving democracy versus communism. As Soviet leaders quickly became aware, the transition from the Roosevelt to the Truman administration was marked: Truman seldom bothered to conceal his abhorrence of communism and his determination to resist it. Though he seldom criticized his predecessor's diplomatic decisions, he nevertheless made clear that the era of unilateral American concessions to win and retain Soviet goodwill had ended. As Truman demonstrated in his celebrated interview with Soviet Foreign Minister Molotov, the president was convinced that all the Kremlin really "understood" and responded to was American firmness.[33] Much as Stalin's government might dislike such an American posture, in Truman's view at least, the Kremlin understood and respected it. Or, as one commentator on the Cold War observed, the Truman administration's containment policy quite possibly provoked the Kremlin but in the right way—into being more restrained and less aggressive in its international behavior.[34]

Administratively, the Truman White House exhibited another significant quality. President Truman believed in what can be called a classical mode of decision making. Truman clearly viewed the decision-making process as hierarchical, with the chief executive at the apex of the pyramid. Truman's widely quoted motto—"The buck stops here"—reflected his firm conviction that the president was in charge of American foreign policy and served as the ultimate decision maker. In Truman's case, he nearly always did so in consultation with his chief advisers. But as his dramatic removal of Secretary of State James F. Byrnes in 1945 clearly indicated, the president did not want subordinates who were in doubt about where the ultimate authority to make foreign policy resided.[35]

Truman's classical model of decision making included another component. Like nearly every other modern chief executive, Truman designated the secretary of state as his principal deputy and spokesman in external affairs—but in contrast to other presidents, Truman operated on that principle. This was illustrated time and again by the president's defense of Secretary of State Dean Acheson in the face of attacks by the McCarthyites and by his repeated refusal to fire Acheson, as McCarthy and other critics demanded.[36]

Moreover, Truman did not permit other officials or administrative procedures to come between the president and the secretary of state. In contrast to Secretary of State Alexander Haig during the Reagan administration, Secretary Acheson did not find his access to the Oval Office blocked by the president's national security adviser or other White House aides. Acheson conferred freely and regularly with President Truman; recognized, as Secretary Byrnes had not, where the final decision-making power resided; and invariably carried out and defended whatever decision President Truman finally made.[37]

By the same token, President Truman was zealous in safeguarding presidential prerogatives in foreign affairs. Some commentators believe, for example, that President Truman viewed the establishment of the National Security Council as part of an effort by advocates of greater legislative influence in the foreign policy process to expand their power at presidential expense.[38] Still other commentators have noted that some of the president's executive advisers (notably, certain officials in the Defense Department) sought to use the NSC to curb the chief executive's power and to gain a greater voice in decision making.[39]

In brief, President Truman's approach to decision making in external policy was relatively simple. Truman believed that in the American constitutional system, the president was ultimately in charge of foreign affairs. A wise chief executive chose advisers in whom he had confidence and whose viewpoints he considered. Truman gave his department heads and other advisers a free hand to run their departments or agencies, under his supervision. Truman expected complete loyalty from his aides and an awareness at all times that the final decision-making power resided in the Oval Office.

For his part, Truman defended his subordinates against critics inside and outside the government, and he took full responsibility for the policies of the United States. Our discussion implies, of course, as our later treatment will show, that President Truman did not as a rule rely heavily on coordinating mechanisms such as the National Security Council, nor did he permit the White House assistant for national security affairs to play an active or influential role in national decision making.

Implicit in our analysis thus far has been an idea that may have been the Truman presidency's most important contribution to the foundations of American national security policy. This was Truman's conviction that the National Security Council's function is strictly advisory. Truman repeatedly insisted that congressionally created mechanisms like the NSC could not alter the president's ultimate responsibility for decision making in external affairs. As President Truman's actions repeatedly demonstrated, in the end the chief executive was free to accept or reject the NSC's recommendations, as he determined were in the best interests of the United States.

▌ Truman and National Security Policy

President Truman's strong preference for a classical, or departmentally centered, mode of decision making was further indicated by the history of the National Security Council during his administration.[40] Both Truman's choice of individuals to direct the NSC and his use of the mechanism in making major policy decisions provide evidence of the president's state of mind.

The first presidential assistant for national security affairs was Admiral Sidney W. Souers, who had the title of executive secretary to the National Security Council. (The national security adviser has had several official designations, noted in the text; however, we have used the acronym ANSA [assistant for national security affairs] to refer to all such presidential advisers. This has been the designation used since the Nixon administration.) Admiral Souers exemplified the old public administration description of staff officers as individuals who exhibit "a passion for anonymity." He has been described as a "shadowy figure" within the Truman administration, whose role as a presidential aide was to serve as a "quiet manager," as a "facilitator," and as "the perfect coordinator of an interdepartmental council."

Admiral Souers's own training and interests were primarily in the intelligence field. He had extensive contacts throughout the government, and he was extremely gifted in the art of achieving compromise among rival bureaucratic positions. Appropriately, Admiral Souers shared President Truman's belief in the primacy of the State Department in foreign affairs; he carefully avoided converting—or even the appearance of converting—the NSC into what it became under the Nixon administration: a rival State Department (see chapter 7). Admiral Souers, in other words, did not aspire to become "another Kissinger."[41] Indeed, while Admiral Souers served as ANSA, many NSC papers originated within the State Department. In turn, the NSC staff served as a kind of administrative secretariat by preparing and circulating drafts of important policy papers and by getting the responses of a wide range of governmental agencies to them.

Admiral Souers once described his position as that of a "neutral coordinator" who carefully avoided exerting independent policy initiatives of his own or attempting to get the president to accept a particular point of view. In marked contrast to Henry Kissinger in the Nixon administration, Souers did not emerge as the administration's principal diplomatic spokesman or (next to the president) the most visible member of the president's foreign policy team. While Truman remained in office, either he or his secretary of state stood as the visible symbol of the administration's foreign policy. Nor did Admiral Souers play any noteworthy role in promoting bipartisanship among executive and legislative officials involved in making foreign policy decisions.[42]

Throughout most of his tenure in the White House, President Truman relied minimally on the National Security Council as a decision-making instrument. Until the Korean War erupted in June 1950, Truman made most important national security decisions outside the formal NSC structure. (In common with other postwar chief executives, such as Lyndon B. Johnson, Truman continued to rely on interdepartmental committees and other formal and informal devices for coordinating external policy.)[43] Even when Truman relied on the NSC, the evidence strongly suggests that the outcome was often predictable: The NSC reached conclusions that conformed with the president's known desires and ideological inclinations.[44]

Before the Korean War, Truman refused to attend most NSC meetings, on the twofold theory that his presence would inhibit frank discussion among NSC members and that his attendance would suggest that national policies were being made by (or in) the council. As we have emphasized, Truman emphatically rejected the latter notion of the NSC's role. If the number of NSC meetings increased after the Korean War, and if the president attended these meetings more frequently, Truman's basic position remained unchanged. In the final analysis—irrespective of whether the decision was made inside or outside the formal NSC structure—the president remained what has been called "the ultimate decider" in the sphere of national security policy.

It is instructive to note what did not happen in this formative stage of national security policy under the Truman administration. As we have emphasized, throughout his tenure in office Truman insisted that the National Security Council was an advisory organ to the president. To Truman's mind, this meant that the council should not be viewed (as some advocates of the agency were prone to do) as a kind of "supercabinet" or American equivalent of the British cabinet. Nor did Truman believe that the ANSA was a director, with authority over established departments and agencies. Moreover (in contrast to his successor, President Dwight D. Eisenhower), Truman was unwilling to give the ANSA and the NSC staff authority to supervise policy implementation by the State Department and other departments. Under Truman, the number of participants in NSC meetings was also kept sharply limited, by restricting the number of aides and assistants who were permitted to accompany NSC members. Truman's NSC also avoided what Secretary of State Dean Acheson called the "illusion of policy": the tendency to adopt "agreed [or unanimous] recommendations," necessarily entailing language so general and ambiguous that successful implementation of the decisions often proved impossible.

In our typology of national security decision-making systems since World War II, we have identified the Truman model as exemplifying the concept of the ANSA as administrator. Alternatively, Admiral Souers functioned as what Alexander George has called a "Custodian-Manager."[45] As these terms suggest, and as the evidence presented in this chapter indicates, this conception implies several things about the process of national security policy making in its formative stage.

Initially, officials in the Truman White House and on Capitol Hill clearly recognized that a new era was necessary in the field of national security policy. Indeed, the concept of national security policy was first adopted and became widely accepted within the United States during the Truman era. And the formal mechanism needed to produce a unified national security policy was designed, installed, and began to operate during the Truman presidency.

Yet the legacy of the Truman administration in the field of national security policy was strangely ambivalent. On the one hand were the accomplishments we have identified thus far—and in many respects, they were noteworthy. On the other hand, the Truman administration's record in external policy making left unresolved a number of problems—some of which were to plague national security policy makers in the years ahead. Among these, three deserve specific mention.

One was the question of the relationship of military force to diplomatic decisions. Despite the steps taken by the Truman administration to unify the nation's military efforts and to establish the National Security Council, it cannot really be said that significant progress was made in deepening the American understanding of Clausewitz's celebrated principle. The Korean War illustrated convincingly, for example, that officials and citizens alike in the United States continued to experience difficulty with concepts such as "limited war," which, by definition, must entail limited political goals and limited public expectations. Ironically, the Truman administration—the presidency that was responsible for bringing the National Security Council into existence—was almost destroyed politically because of this pervasive American failure to understand such concepts.

A second problem—one that is extremely difficult to comprehend—was the Truman administration's failure to include economic and financial dimensions in national security policy. No provision was made under the Truman White House to include the Treasury and Commerce departments in making national security decisions; yet the cost of national security programs and projects is always a crucial aspect of them.[46]

Third, the concept of national security policy inherently perhaps involves a delicate balance between two contrary tendencies or forces within the executive branch. One of these is the tendency toward what we have called classical, or departmentally centered, decision making, as exemplified by the Truman administration. The other is the tendency toward creating what the authors have described as a "rival State Department," or a White House–centered model of decision making, as represented by the Nixon–Kissinger era (described more fully in chapter 7).

To develop a unified national security policy, these contrary forces must be maintained in rough equilibrium. Yet, to employ a term often used by physicists, such a balance is at best an "unstable equilibrium"—extremely precarious and easily upset (as when a coin is balanced on its edge). In most instances in the Truman period, when the balance was destroyed the influence of the State Department was enhanced vis-à-vis the National Security Council and other executive departments. Though this kind of classical pattern of decision making may have appealed to President Truman and to officials such as Secretary of State Dean Acheson, it may be seriously questioned whether the resulting imbalance facilitated the achievement of a national security policy and whether in the long run it really contributed to maximum unity and lasting coordination among executive officials on national security issues.

NOTES

1. The last of the great wartime conferences was held in Potsdam, Germany, July 17–August 1, 1945. See Harry S Truman, *Year of Decisions* (Garden City, N.Y.: Doubleday, 1955), pp. 332–412; James M. Byrnes, *Speaking Frankly* (New York: Harper & Row, 1947), pp. 67–91; and Herbert Feis, *Between War and Peace: The Potsdam Conference* (Princeton, N.J.: Princeton University Press, 1960).

2. Harry S Truman, *Years of Trial and Hope* (Garden City, N.Y.: Doubleday, 1956), pp. 7–12.

3. See the discussion of the role of military power in postwar Soviet policy in John L. Gaddis, *The United States and the Origins of the Cold War, 1941–1947* (New York: Columbia University Press, 1972), pp. 319–322. As an illustration of the rapid decline in American military power, in May 1945, the United States had an army of 3.5 million troops (68 divisions) stationed in Western Europe; ten months later, this figure had fallen to some 400,000 troops—approximately one-tenth the wartime level. See John Spanier, *American Foreign Policy since World War II*, 9th ed. (New York: Holt, Rinehart & Winston, 1983), pp. 23–24. For widely differing assessments of the Soviet–American military equation, see William T. Lee and Richard F. Staar, *Soviet Military Policy since World War II* (Stanford, Calif.: Hoover Institution Press, 1986); and Tom Gervasi, *The Myth of Soviet Military Supremacy* (New York: Harper & Row, 1986).

4. See Truman, *Year of Decisions,* pp. 305–307; and Dean Acheson, *Present at the Creation: My Years in the State Department* (New York: Norton, 1969), pp. 258–263.

5. See Bernard C. Cohen, *The Political Process and Foreign Policy: The Making of the Japanese Peace Settlement* (Princeton, N.J.: Princeton University Press, 1957); and John Foster Dulles, *A Peace Treaty in the Making* (San Francisco: Japanese Peace Conference, 1951).

6. See Truman, *Year of Decisions,* pp. 14–17; and W. Averell Harriman and Elie Abel, *Special Envoy to Churchill and Stalin: 1941–1946* (New York: Random House, 1975), pp. 413–454.

7. Russian–American relations before 1917 are discussed more fully in Thomas A. Bailey, *America Faces Russia* (Ithaca, N.Y.: Cornell University Press, 1950); Robert P. Browder, *The Origins of Soviet–American Diplomacy* (Princeton, N.J.: Princeton University Press, 1953); and William A. Williams, *American–Russian Relations: 1781–1947* (New York: Holt, Rinehart & Winston, 1952).

8. See the discussion of FDR's assessment of the prospects for postwar peace and security in Daniel Yergin, *Shattered Peace: The Origins of the Cold War and the National Security State* (Boston: Houghton Mifflin, 1978), pp. 65–68; and James E. Dougherty and Robert L. Pfaltzgraff, Jr., *American Foreign Policy: FDR to Reagan* (New York: Harper & Row, 1986), pp. 40–41.

9. See the account of President Truman's meeting with Soviet Foreign Minister V. M. Molotov in late April 1945, in Truman, *Year of Decisions,* pp. 74–77. See also Herbert Druks, *Harry S Truman and the Russians, 1945–1953* (New York: Robert Speller, 1966).

10. Walter Lippmann, *The Cold War* (New York: Harper & Row, 1947).

11. Fuller discussions of Titoism and its implications may be found in Hugh Seton-Watson, *The East European Revolution,* 3rd ed. (New York: Praeger, 1956), pp. 157–162, 219–226, and 339–347; and Robert H. McNeal, *International Relations among Communists* (Englewood Cliffs, N.J.: Prentice-Hall, 1967), pp. 58–72.

12. The Greek–Turkish Aid Program and Truman Doctrine are dealt with at greater length in Truman, *Years of Trial and Hope,* pp. 93–109; Arthur H. Vandenberg, Jr., ed., *The Private Papers of Senator Vandenberg* (Boston: Houghton Mifflin, 1952), pp. 337–372; Joseph M. Jones, *The Fifteen Weeks* (New York: Viking Press, 1955); and Cecil V. Crabb, Jr., *The Doctrines of American Foreign Policy: Their Meaning, Role, and Future* (Baton Rouge: Louisiana State University Press, 1982), pp. 107–152.

13. See Truman, *Year of Decisions,* pp. 236–237 and 496–500; and Gaddis, *The United States and the Origins of the Cold War,* pp. 296–298.

14. President Truman believed that the Soviet-instigated Berlin blockade was a deliberate test of "our firmness and our patience." In his view, it was part of the Kremlin's strategy of attempting to make the postwar reconstruction of Europe, as envisioned by the Marshall Plan, fail. See his *Years of Trial and Hope,* pp. 120–131, 247, and 357–362.

15. The planning and implementation of the Marshall Plan are analyzed in greater detail in Truman, *Years of Trial and Hope,* pp. 110–131; Vandenberg, *The Private Papers of Senator Vandenberg,* pp. 373–399; and Acheson, *Present at the Creation,* pp. 226–236.

16. The origins of the North Atlantic Treaty are explained in Vandenberg, *The Private Papers of Senator Vandenberg,* pp. 339–421; Acheson, *Present at the Creation,* pp. 276–285; and Truman, *Years of Trial and Hope,* pp. 240–261.

17. Several studies of the Korean War are available. See, for example, David Rees, *Korea: The Limited War* (New York: St. Martin, 1964); Matthew B. Ridgway, *The Korean War* (Garden City, N.Y.: Doubleday, 1967); and Rosemary Foot, *The Wrong War: American Policy and Dimensions of the Korean Conflict, 1950–1953* (Ithaca, N.Y.: Cornell University Press, 1985).

18. See John Spanier, *The Truman–MacArthur Controversy and the Korean War* (Cambridge, Mass.: Belknap Press, Harvard University, 1959).

19. The concept of limited war is examined in Rees, *Korea*; Foot, *The Wrong War*; Glenn D. Paige, *The Korean Decision* (New York: Free Press, 1968); Michael Walzer, *Just and Unjust Wars* (New York: Basic Books, 1967); James M. Gavin, *War and Peace in the Space Age* (New York: Harper & Row, 1958); and Bernard Brodie, *War and Politics* (New York: Macmillan, 1973).

20. See the account of the congressional hearings on President Truman's dismissal of General MacArthur, in Spanier, *The Truman–MacArthur Controversy and the Korean War,* pp. 211–257.

21. Wartime and early postwar planning for the United States is discussed more fully in Vandenberg, *The Private Papers of Senator Vandenberg,* pp. 172–220; Truman, *Year of Decisions,* pp. 26–28, 48–49, 59–73, and 277–293; W. A. Scott and Stephen B. Withey, *The United States and the United Nations: The Public View, 1945–1955* (New York: Manhattan, 1958); and Francis O. Wilcox and H. Field Haviland, *The United States and the United Nations* (Baltimore: Johns Hopkins University Press, 1961).

22. See, for example, Emile Benoit, *Europe at Sixes and Sevens: The Common Market, the Free Trade Association and the United States* (New York: Columbia University Press, 1961); Vera M. Dean, *Europe and the United States* (New York: Knopf, 1950); and D. D. Humphrey, *The United States and the Common Market: A Background Study* (New York: Praeger, 1962).

23. For the evolution of U.S. policy toward Latin America, see Donald Dozer, *Are We Good Neighbors? Three Decades of Inter-American Relations, 1930–1960* (Gainesville: University of Florida Press, 1959); and O. C. Stoetzer, *The Organization of American States: An Introduction* (New York: Praeger, 1965), pp. 1–74.

24. Documentary materials and the texts of official statements on arms control during the early postwar period are available in the Senate Foreign Relations Committee, *A Decade of American Foreign Policy, 1940–1949,* 81st Cong., 2nd sess., Washington, D.C., 1950, pp. 1076–1143; and the same committee's publication, *Disarmament and Security: A Collection of Documents, 1919–1955,* Committee Print, 84th Cong., 2nd sess., Washington, D.C., 1956. Useful interpretive studies are Elis Biorklund, *International Atomic Policy during a Decade* (Princeton, N.J.: Van Nostrand, 1956); and William R. Frye, *Disarmament: Atoms into Plowshares* (New York: Foreign Policy Association, Headline Books, 1955).

25. The concept of bipartisanship as it evolved during the Roosevelt and Truman periods is analyzed more fully in Cecil V. Crabb, Jr., *Bipartisan Foreign Policy: Myth or Reality?* (New York: Harper & Row, 1957). See also H. Bradford

Westerfield, *Foreign Policy and Party Politics: Pearl Harbor to Korea* (New Haven, Conn.: Yale University Press, 1955); Robert A. Dahl, *Congress and Foreign Policy* (New York: Harcourt Brace, 1950); and Vandenberg, *The Private Papers of Senator Vandenberg,* pp. 1–446.

26. The political movement called McCarthyism during the Truman–Eisenhower era is discussed more fully in Richard M. Freeland, *The Truman Doctrine and the Origins of McCarthyism: Foreign Policy, Domestic Politics, and Internal Security, 1945–1948* (New York: Knopf, 1972); Ross Y. Koen, *The China Lobby in American Politics* (New York: Macmillan, 1960); Daniel Bell, ed., *The New American Right* (New York: Criterion Books, 1955); James Rorty and Moshe Decter, *McCarthy and the Communists* (Boston: Beacon Press, 1954); and Morris H. Rubin, ed., *The McCarthy Record* (New York: Anglobooks, 1952).

27. See, for example, Acheson, *Present at the Creation,* pp. 354–371.

28. The concept of policy planning in the State Department is examined in greater detail in Acheson, *Present at the Creation,* pp. 214, 228, and 345–371; I. M. Destler, *Presidents, Bureaucrats and Foreign Policy* (Princeton, N.J.: Princeton University Press, 1972), pp. 224–252; and the Introduction by Dean Acheson in Louis J. Halle, *Civilization and Foreign Policy: An Inquiry for Americans* (New York: Harper & Row, 1955), pp. xvii–xxii.

29. President Truman's formal education was limited to graduation from high school and some night school courses taken as an adult. After Roosevelt's death, he said that a million people were better qualified to be president than he was! Truman had traveled to Europe only once—as a soldier in World War I. See Robert J. Donovan, *Conflict and Crisis: The Presidency of Harry S Truman, 1945–1948,* (New York: Norton, 1977), pp. xiii–xvii.

30. Truman was well aware of the inadequacy of his knowledge of many aspects of foreign policy questions. As president, he was energetic and conscientious in endeavoring to inform himself about complex foreign policy issues. See Truman, *Year of Decisions,* pp. 13–17; and Acheson, *Present at the Creation,* pp. 730–731.

31. See the discussion of President Truman's support of Israel, in Walter Isaacson and Evan Thomas, *The Wise Men: Six Friends and the World They Made* (New York: Simon & Schuster, 1986), pp. 451–452; and Dean Acheson's reflections on Truman's decision-making style, in *Acheson, Present at the Creation,* pp. 729–734.

32. See Acheson, *Present at the Creation,* pp. 506–508; and the discussion of the Truman administration's decision to proceed with the manufacture of the hydrogen (or H-) bomb early in 1950 in Barton J. Bernstein, "The H-Bomb Decisions: Were They Inevitable?" in *National Security and International Stability,* ed. Bernard Brodie and Michael D. Intriligator (Cambridge, Mass.: Oelgeschlager, Gunn & Hain, 1983), pp. 327–357; and Merlo J. Pusey, *The Way We Go to War* (Boston: Houghton Mifflin, 1971), pp. 87–88.

33. As a senator in 1941, Truman had publicly expressed the view that Hitler's Germany and Stalin's Russia should be allowed to fight to the point of mutual exhaustion—then the United States would be left as the arbiter of the

European continent! For these and other examples of Truman's anticommunism, see Gaddis, *The United States and the Origins of the Cold War,* pp. 198–243 and 284–315. Truman and his advisers were heavily influenced in their attitudes toward the Soviet Union by the "lessons" derived from earlier experience dealing with the Axis dictators. See Les K. Adler and Thomas G. Paterson, " 'Red Fascism' and the Development of the Cold War," in *America and Russia: From Cold War Confrontation to Coexistence,* ed. Gary R. Hess (New York: Thomas Y. Crowell, 1973), pp. 62–77.

34. See the views of Adam Ulam and others on the containment strategy, as presented in Crabb, *The Doctrines of American Foreign Policy,* pp. 151–152.

35. Secretary of State James F. Byrnes apparently regarded himself as a kind of "assistant president" for foreign affairs—a fact increasingly resented by President Truman. See Robert L. Messer, *The End of an Alliance: James F. Byrnes, Roosevelt, Truman and the Origins of the Cold War* (Chapel Hill: University of North Carolina Press, 1982), p. 3. See also Donovan, *Conflict and Crisis,* pp. 155–156, and 266–267; and I. M. Destler, "National Security Advice to U.S. Presidents: Some Lessons from Thirty Years," in *U.S. National Security: A Framework for Analysis,* ed. Daniel J. Kaufman, et al. (Lexington, MA.: Lexington Books, 1985) p. 552.

36. See the discussion of President Truman's decision-making style in Dougherty and Pfaltzgraff, *American Foreign Policy,* pp. 91–92; and Acheson, *Present at the Creation,* p. 731.

37. Acheson, *Present at the Creation,* pp. 734–737.

38. See Keith C. Clark and Laurence J. Legere, eds., *The President and the Management of National Security* (New York: Praeger, 1969), pp. 58–59; and Stephen Hess, *Organizing for the Presidency* (Washington, D.C.: Brookings Institution, 1976), pp. 56–57.

39. See the discussion of the conception of the NSC by some of Truman's executive advisers in Destler, "National Security Advice to U.S. Presidents," pp. 554–555.

40. The original members of the National Security Council were the president (as chairman); the secretary of state; the secretary of defense; the secretaries of Army, Navy, and Air Force; the chairman of the National Security Resources Board (an agency that later became part of the Office of Defense Mobilization); and such officials as the president might appoint to the NSC. Later amendments to the National Security Act of 1947 added the vice president to the NSC membership and dropped the three civilian secretaries of the armed services. By the late 1980s, by law the president, vice president, and secretaries of state and defense were voting members of the NSC, and the chairman of the Joint Chiefs of Staff and the director of the Central Intelligence Agency were statutory advisers. The president was free to (and does) invite others to attend NSC meetings.

41. See Anna K. Nelson, "President Truman and the Evolution of the National Security Council," *The Journal of American History* 72 (September 1985): 360–378; and the views of President Truman in *Years of Trial and Hope,* pp. 58–60.

42. See Bernstein, "The H-Bomb Decisions," pp. 327–357; Acheson, *Present at the Creation,* pp. 732–734; Dougherty and Pfaltzgraff, *American Foreign Policy,* pp. 90–92; Destler, "National Security Advice to U.S. Presidents," pp. 554–555; Pusey, *The Way We Go to War,* pp. 87–89; and Isaacson and Thomas, *The Wise Men,* pp. 506–508.

43. Destler, "National Security Advice to U.S. Presidents," pp. 554–555.

44. Acheson, *Present at the Creation,* p. 733.

45. See the views of Alexander George, as cited in Lincoln P. Bloomfield, *The Foreign Policy Process: A Modern Primer* (Englewood Cliffs, N.J.: Prentice-Hall, 1982), p. 46. I. M. Destler's view is that President Truman expected his assistants for national security policy to exhibit "neutral competence" in performing their duties. See his "National Security Advice to U.S. Presidents," p. 186.

46. President Truman believed that the NSC must take full account of the nation's resources in formulating and implementing national security policy. See his *Years of Trial and Hope,* p. 59. Yet some commentators believe that this dimension was neglected in national security planning. See Arthur Cyr, "How Important is National Security Structure to National Security Policy?" in James M. McCormick, *A Reader in American Foreign Policy* (Itasca, Ill.: F. E. Peacock, 1986), p. 270.

CHAPTER 5

The Eisenhower Administration: The NSC and Policy Coordination

One of the many ironies of American politics is that Dwight Eisenhower was perceived as a part-time president and laissez-faire leader, a perception completely at odds with his administrative and policy-making record. Much of the journalism of the time characterized Eisenhower as a golf-playing, semiretired chief executive, but not a chief operating officer, who left most decision-making responsibilities to cabinet officials and White House staff aides.[1]

Recent scholarly work, especially by Fred Greenstein of Princeton University, has largely dispelled the myth of Eisenhower as an uninterested and uninvolved president. Part of Eisenhower's "image problem" was that, compared to his predecessors (and successors), Eisenhower espoused a more moderate (or "Whigish") conception of presidential powers, including, for example, a greater respect for the separation of powers and for cabinet government. However, the appearance of presidential noninvolvement was also largely a calculated stance designed to enhance Eisenhower's political fortunes. Greenstein has termed this political behavior Eisenhower's "hidden-hand presidency" and argues that, appearances to the contrary, Eisenhower was politically astute and informed, actively engaged in putting his personal stamp on public policy and applying a carefully thought out conception of leadership in the conduct of his presidency.[2]

Eisenhower's approach to presidential management can be characterized as "cabinet government." Though presidents since (and before) have taken office pledged to administer through their cabinet secretaries, Eisenhower actually worked to make this pledge a reality. Foreign policy making, in particular, was the exclusive preserve of the president and the secretary of state, John Foster Dulles. Other executive-branch officials were aware that Dulles spoke for Eisenhower and that the secretary's policies had explicit presidential approval. Any notion—whatever the conventional wisdom at the time—that Eisenhower was dominated by Dulles or that Ike administered foreign affairs by remote control is not borne out by the facts. Indeed, unlike most presidents, Eisenhower had substantial prior experience in the management of complex organizations, especially the inter-Allied command in Europe. The citizen-soldier of campaign hagiography was both a skillful bureaucratic politician and a consummate coordinator of organizational resources.

Eisenhower demonstrated his desire for administrative orderliness in the way he organized both the domestic and the national security advisory processes. Both were more structured and had a more explicit chain of command than had been the case under Truman or FDR.[3] For example, a cabinet secretariat was created in 1954 to prepare agendas for the weekly meetings and to circulate background papers. Furthermore, a Record of Action detailing Eisenhower's decisions was kept and Status of Action reports were compiled every three months to monitor implementation. Overseeing the cabinet secretariat and domestic policy making generally was White House Chief of Staff Sherman Adams, the assistant to the president.[4]

▎ The Great Partnership

For all his powers, Sherman Adams, unlike subsequent White House chiefs of staff, had no doubt about who was responsible for making foreign policy. Eisenhower "delegated to Dulles the responsibility of developing the specific policy, including the decision about where the Administration would stand and what course of action would be followed in each international crisis."[5] Adams reflected as follows:

> As I watched Eisenhower and Dulles weather this first trying crisis they faced together, it seemed to me that the President was shouldering a heavier responsibility in their close partnership than most of the people around them realized. Although Eisenhower depended on Dulles to make the invariably decisive recommendation of what should be done . . . , I noticed that Dulles . . . placed great reliance upon Eisenhower to sense what the effect of doing it would be.[6]

This was the essence of a great partnership. Eisenhower was happy to give the impression that Dulles was the man in charge. Much of this perception came about because Ike left Dulles "in full command of day-to-day operations," while "reserving himself for the judicial role of weighing and deciding only transcendent issues."[7] This division of labor stood Eisenhower in good stead during the Formosa Strait crisis in 1955, when the Nationalist Chinese of Taiwan appealed to the United States to help defend them against raids by mainland China on Taiwan's offshore islands. (The Nationalists saw the air raids as precursors to raids on Taiwan itself.) As the tensions mounted, there were press reports of serious official differences over U.S. policy in the Formosa Strait. Opinion was divided between "a 'White House faction' favoring minimum commitment and 'a Pentagon–Capitol Hill faction' favoring maximum commitment."[8] Dulles wanted to use atomic weapons if Peking attacked the offshore islands of Quemoy and Matsu.[9]

This is an instance where Eisenhower stepped in, weighed the alternatives, and then told his secretary of state to take a diplomatic route in solving the problem. A diplomatic solution was indeed reached after Dulles realized that Ike would not approve military intervention. According to Townsend Hoopes, "Eisenhower, in his relative detachment and deceptive passivity, saw the issues in a larger frame, maintained a superb sense of proportion, and managed to retain control of the U.S. government, including those powerful factors within it who did not share, but sought to fail, the President's peaceful purposes."[10]

In sum, the decision maker was Eisenhower, while Dulles saw himself as the president's attorney for foreign affairs and his job as one of providing advice and counsel. Dulles was "a maximalist secretary of state," because he had the ability to win the president's unlimited confidence. The keys to his access to the president were his "detailed knowledge, decisiveness, and objective discussion."[11] Ike "trusted his secretary of state to represent his interests faithfully and zealously and with the firm conviction that Dulles understood that, while he might propose, Eisenhower disposed."[12]

Despite Dulles's dominance in the making of foreign policy, the State Department suffered as an institution during his tenure as secretary. Though Dulles may have been one of the greatest secretaries of state in the postwar period (along with Dean Acheson and Henry Kissinger), this period saw "the beginning of a dramatic decline" in the department's "influence and professional prestige."[13] Dulles made himself "the sole intellectual wellspring of conception and action in foreign policy during his period in office."[14] As a result, the policy planning staff—the creative center of Acheson's State Department—fell progressively into disuse. Townsend Hoopes described Dulles's mindset as follows: "His own ideas being largely self-developed, he needed facts, and relished debate with those he considered informed and tough enough to defend their position, but the purpose of the process was to produce, at most, minor refinements of his handiwork."[15]

It needs to be emphasized that Dulles could function as a strong secretary of state because he realized that the fundamental basis of his power lay in maintaining Eisenhower's confidence in him. Dulles carefully cultivated his relationship with Eisenhower and allowed no encroachments on his role as the president's principal adviser on foreign policy. Various presidential staffers whose domains overlapped Dulles's discovered how skilled the secretary of state could be in protecting his suzerainty over foreign policy. Consider the sharp tone of the following cable from Dulles to Harold Stassen, the cabinet-level assistant to the president for mutual security and disarmament, concerning an unauthorized communication by the presidential assistant with the Soviet ambassador.

With the personal approval of the President I send you the following instructions: You will notify Mr. Zorin at the earliest possible moment that the memorandum you submitted to him was not only informal and unofficial, but had no approval in its submitted form either by the President or the State Department, and that there were some aspects of the memorandum to which the government cannot agree at this moment. Therefore, you will request that Mr. Zorin return the memorandum.[16]

Stassen was not the only White House staffer whom Dulles rebuked over turf conflicts. C. D. Jackson (a specialist on Cold War psychology), Lewis Strauss (an adviser on atomic energy affairs), the various assistants to the president for national security affairs (who will be discussed presently), and even the redoubtable Sherman Adams were careful to avoid incurring the secretary's wrath.

The effect was very little sniping between the State Department and the White House during Dulles's tenure in office. Indeed, Stassen's continued forays into diplomacy led Dulles to demand (and receive) his dismissal by Eisenhower. Nor did the special assistant for national security affairs seek to challenge the secretary of state's paramount position. This would be a later development in the administration of American foreign policy.

Despite what seemed to some to be presidential passivity (what we now better understand to have been a "hidden-hand presidency"), in reality Eisenhower maintained a firm grasp on the making of foreign policy decisions. For example, Sherman Adams reported that during the Suez crisis of 1956, Eisenhower stood firmly behind Dulles and that "every action taken by the Secretary of State in the Middle East negotiations had the personal approval of the President 'from top to bottom.'"[17] The president trusted his secretary of state as an adviser and confidant; but he did not abdicate his paramount role. As Eisenhower put it,

> He would not deliver an important speech or statement until after I had read, edited, and approved it; he guarded constantly against the possibility that any misunderstanding could rise between us. It was the mutual trust and understanding, thus engendered, that enabled me, with complete confidence, to delegate to him an unusual degree of flexibility as my representative in international conferences, well knowing that he would not in the slightest degree operate outside the limits previously agreed between us.[18]

Whatever the differences between Dulles and Eisenhower, they spoke with one voice with regard to American foreign policy. Dulles was the unquestioned spokesman for the administration in foreign affairs. He was never pushed aside when the president personally conducted foreign policy, nor was he locked in warfare with the White House staff, let alone superseded by the president's assistant for national security affairs—though these would be the fates of future secretaries of state as the locus of foreign policy making shifted to the west wing of the White House.

▮ The Eisenhower NSC

According to Eisenhower, "organization cannot make a genius out of an incompetent" but "disorganization can scarcely fail to result in inefficiency and can easily lead to disaster."[19] National security policy especially was to benefit from orderly decision-making procedures.

During the 1952 presidential campaign, Eisenhower pledged that "if elected he would elevate the Council to the position originally planned for it under the National Security Act and use it as his principal arm in formulating policy on military, international, and internal security affairs."[20] Upon his election Eisenhower commissioned a study of national security policy making by Robert Cutler, a Boston banker and occasional consultant to the Truman NSC who was to serve as the first special assistant for national security affairs (until 1955 and again in 1957–1958). Cutler's recommendations became the standard operating procedures for Eisenhower's NSC.[21] The heart of this system was a regular meeting (on Thursdays) of the council, whose statutory members were the president, vice president, the secretaries of state and defense, and the director of the Office of Civil and Defense Mobilization (although a large number of informal participants also attended regularly in various capacities).

In the Eisenhower administration, the National Security Council was established as the chief forum for the formulation and implementation of national security policy.[22] Eisenhower's basic concept of the NSC was as follows:

> The Council is a corporate body, composed of individuals advising the President in their own right, rather than as representatives of their respective departments and agencies. Their function should be to seek, with their background of experience, the most statesmanlike solution to the problem of national security, rather than to reach solutions which represent merely a compromise of departmental positions.[23]

The NSC was designed to function as a presidential advisory body—that is, to provide the chief executive with the information and perspective necessary to make complex foreign policy decisions: "It prepares advice for the President as his Cabinet level committee on national security."[24] For Eisenhower, the NSC was to foreign policy what the cabinet was to domestic policy: a forum for the exchange of views among the relevant departments and a mechanism for ensuring governmentwide coordination of policy. Indeed, Eisenhower gave the Thursday council meetings more time and attention than he did the less highly regarded cabinet meetings, which tended to be ritualized and informational.

In accordance with his views on the NSC, Eisenhower (and Cutler) instituted major changes in the overall NSC organization and in the processes by which the council handled matters. These will be discussed in greater detail. However, before doing so, certain general observations need to be made. Overall, Eisenhower gave the National Security Council what might be best expressed as a sense of purpose. Wanting to use the NSC as a coordinating and policy-making body, Eisenhower institutionalized it as his main tool for formulating national security policy. Meeting at least weekly, the NSC considered all major policy issues and all proposed procedures and included a financial appendix with each policy paper. In general, the NSC system Eisenhower established had the council at the top, with a highly formalized set of procedures established for bringing policy issues to the council.

Eisenhower believed that top-level decision-making bodies should provide general direction and guidance; accordingly, "the Council dealt with strategies, not tactics."[25] For example, in each year of the Eisenhower administration, the NSC conducted a review of the basic national security policy (BNSP) that set forth a national strategy for achieving U.S. objectives through political, economic, and military means.[26] Fred Greenstein also maintains that the structure and conduct of these NSC meetings "refutes the premise of Eisenhower's critics that formalized advisory procedures stultify vigorous exchanges of views among advisers."[27]

Under Eisenhower, the procedure by which NSC decisions were debated became institutionalized as part of the foreign policy-making process.

> The characteristics of the pattern are regular attendance and participation by the President at NSC meetings; regular meetings which held top priority with members of the Council; detailed agendas; and a much broader view of Council functions. In short, the NSC under Eisenhower was a full partner involved in all aspects of national security policy from policy formulation (the Planning Board) to implementation and evaluation (the OCB).[28]

NSC agendas were set in sessions of the newly created NSC Planning Board, which consisted of senior policy-making officers from each department represented on the council. (The board was thus very similar to Truman's senior staff.) The special assistant for national security affairs (SANSA), most prominently Robert Cutler, chaired Planning Board sessions and supervised its staff. Eisenhower directed Cutler to ensure that all differences of opinion received serious consideration in these meetings. The board continued drawing on each department's information until the members felt that they had the best information available, then its members prepared NSC briefing papers. These papers were drafts summarizing the question under consideration, facts the Planning Board had uncovered about the situation, general objectives to be obtained by following certain policies, operational suggestions, and estimates of the cost of the suggested policy. If the board had not reached unanimous agreement, Cutler provided two columns of information on the page starkly and completely outlining differences of opinion. If time permitted, the board circulated the papers to each member department ten days before the NSC meeting at which it was to be discussed to allow the departments time to digest the information and formulate their positions.

At NSC meetings, the special assistant initiated discussion by outlining each paper, including the differences of opinion, and identifying various alternatives by the agencies that advocated them. Eisenhower actively participated in the discussion and made the ultimate decision.

> When he became President, General Eisenhower transformed the Council into a forum for vigorous discussion against a background of painstakingly prepared

and carefully studied papers. He likes nothing better than the flashing interchange of views among his principal advisers. Out of the grinding of the minds comes a refinement of the raw material into valuable metal; out of the frank assertion of differing views, backed up by preparation that searches every nook and cranny, emerges a resolution that reasonable men can support. Differences of views which have developed at lower levels are not swept under the rug, but expressed.[29]

NSC meetings generated a Record of Action to which Eisenhower added clarification, if necessary. Following the NSC meeting, the Operations Coordinating Board, chaired by the under secretary of state, shaped steps to implement each decision as policy. In addition, Eisenhower occasionally summoned small groups of key policy makers into his office for informal discussions, during which he would make additional decisions regarding operations.[30]

Eisenhower shared with Truman a belief that the making of national security policy should remain a presidential prerogative. Though he created the office of the special assistant and used the NSC in ways unapproached during Truman's tenure, Eisenhower continued his predecessor's reliance on the secretary of state as the prime mover with regard to policy making. Secretary of State Dulles too felt that he had to work directly with the president on all important developments in world affairs and that no one should come between him and Eisenhower.

Cutler (and his fellow ANSAs) was therefore necessarily restricted to the important but subsidiary role of coordinator. Even though Cutler chaired the Planning Board and initiated discussion at NSC meetings, consequently exercising greater managerial responsibilities than Truman's executive secretary, his primary responsibility lay in amassing information from the various departments, ensuring that the Planning Board considered all points of view, and summarizing these findings at NSC meetings. He was not the primary—nor even a major—initiator of policy. Instead, he was the essential coordinator, defining options for NSC consideration and monitoring the implementation of these decisions. In the job of physically managing the daily flow of information and operational memoranda to and from the president, he was assisted by Eisenhower's staff secretary, General Andrew Goodpaster, who kept the president informed of pending and completed actions.[31]

Fred Greenstein and John P. Burke have further clarified the role of the Eisenhower ANSA, which, they argue, consisted of "maintaining the quality and character of advising as a process, not simply . . . expressing those views and positions he and his staff formed."[32] Their detailed analysis of the January 8, 1954, NSC meeting on Vietnam, for example, reveals that Cutler was concerned that current discussion be related to prior decisions, to guarantee an orderly policy-making process. He took care to ensure that NSC deliberations stayed on track while encouraging participants to voice their policy views, and sought to avoid letting any decision be made without consideration of the short- and long-term implications of each option.[33]

Cutler's authority ended with the NSC decision—the top of the "policy hill" that was his domain. The Operations Coordinating Board, chaired by the undersecretary of state, devised ways to implement NSC decisions. Even when the SANSA chaired the OCB, however, he posed no threat to the State Department's primacy in foreign affairs. The department had a voice in Planning Board sessions, a dominating personality on the NSC in the person of Dulles, and major responsibility for transforming national security decisions into governmental action. The "great partnership" between Eisenhower and Dulles also gave the State Department a direct line to the White House that was less common in subsequent administrations.

▐ The Policy Hill

Eisenhower's principal contribution to the development of the policy-making process with regard to national security lay, as we have noted, in the formalization of the advisory process. Under Eisenhower, an NSC system was established with the council at the apex of a highly formalized set of procedures for formulating policy and implementing decisions. The linchpin of the system was Robert Cutler, who had advised the newly elected Eisenhower on reorganizing the national security apparatus. Cutler, unlike his predecessors in the Truman administration, Sidney Souers and Robert Lay, was designated special assistant for national security affairs, rather than executive secretary to the NSC. In effect, Cutler's standing as a White House aide, rather than an NSC functionary, was an important landmark in the rise of the national security adviser to the upper ranks of decision makers.

As a member of the White House staff and not simply the director of the NSC's secretariat, Eisenhower's ANSA served two presidential objectives. While supervising the NSC staff, Cutler was to ensure that the policy-making process worked to the advantage of the president. However, as ANSA, Cutler was also expected to be the president's agent on the NSC and not an independent actor. Though a secretary of state may be permitted a certain independence, a national security adviser who sets up shop for himself would be moved out of the White House. In sum, the Office of the Special Assistant for National Security Affairs was created to send a clear message to the departments that a White House official, with presidential authority, was in charge of the advisory process. The end of the State Department's monopoly on advising the president on foreign affairs can be dated as beginning here.

The necessary complement to Cutler's heightened status was an NSC system, which "consisted of the Central Council supported by a grid of highly standardized procedures and staff relationships and a complex interdepartmental committee substructure."[34] We have used Cutler's term, the "policy hill," to describe the process of policy formulation and implementation in the Eisenhower administration. The National Security Council sat at the top of the hill with the Planning Board on one side and the Operations Coordinating Board on the other.

> Policy recommendations moved up one side of the hill, through the Planning Board to the Council, where they were thrashed out and submitted to the

President. Approved by the Chief Executive, the new policy traveled down the other side of the policy hill. . . . A short distance down this side of the hill was the OCB, to which the President referred the new policy for coordination and operational planning with the relevant departments and agencies.

The up side of the policy hill was the Planning Board, which was responsible for evaluating department recommendations, resolving interagency differences, and preparing policy papers for consideration at council meetings. Less formal than NSC meetings, Planning Board meetings, held every Tuesday and Friday afternoon, were what Alexander George called "'warm-up' sessions . . . that provided opportunities for genuine policy debate."[35] Members of the Planning Board were at the assistant secretary level and represented those agencies also represented on the NSC (for example, the Departments of State and Defense and the CIA). Nominated by their departments and approved by the president, "they were expected to have the personal confidence of their agency heads . . . [and] they inevitably tended toward institutional advocacy."[36] The chairman of the Planning Board was the ANSA, whose role as a nonvoting participant was primarily "to ensure that the board's papers were adequate and that they satisfactorily reflected the views of the members. When 'splits' could not be avoided, [he] was responsible for presenting them to the council as clearly and accurately as possible."[37] As noted earlier, these policy splits were sometimes outlined in parallel columns, identified by agency, and circulated to the NSC members in advance of each meeting.

The Planning Board also drew up the agenda for NSC meetings and prepared the papers that were the basis for deliberations. Although all participants had the documents well in advance of the NSC meetings and had discussed them with their representative on the Planning Board, the special assistant was responsible for initiating discussion by summarizing each paper. After Cutler would point out the splits and identify the agencies that had advocated the various positions, a free-flowing discussion would ensue, with each agency defending its side of the disagreement.[38]

Eisenhower, of course, made the final decision. The NSC's small permanent staff, which consisted largely of career civil servants, sought to guarantee continuity and uniformity in policy making. It reviewed policy papers for coherence and completeness and called attention to policy gaps and issues not receiving enough attention.[39] The NSC secretariat thus provided the ANSA, and in turn the NSC, with an independent source for analyses of departmental recommendations.

In September 1953, the OCB was formed. According to Cutler, its purpose was "to coordinate, 'ride herd on,' and report to the council on the performance by the departments and agencies charged with responsibility to carry out national security policies approved by the President."[40] Prior to September 1953, the State Department had been responsible for coordination. Probably for that reason, the OCB was initially chaired by the under secretary of state. Members included the deputy secretary of defense, the CIA director and the director of the United States Information Agency. Most members were at the under-secretary level to ensure that they had enough authority within their own agencies to see that policies were carried out.

After an NSC decision, the Operations Coordinating Board would consider steps for implementation. OCB working groups prepared plans for putting the NSC policy into action, biweekly progress reports, and weekly status summaries. Formal reports were prepared by the working groups, then reviewed first by the assistants and finally by board members before being presented to the NSC.[41] The circle was then completed: Policy Planning Board to National Security Council to Operations Coordinating Board to National Security Council again.

OCB meetings were held on Wednesdays and consisted of an informal lunch followed by a formal meeting. "Operation plans for implementing national security policy were discussed, revised and approved at these meetings. . . . Preparation . . . helped participating departments and agencies identify, clarify and resolve differences of policy interpretation or operating responsibility." Resolving differences over operational plans necessarily meant that the OCB would make new policy decisions. The SANSA in 1957 was made vice chairman of the Operations Coordinating Board in "recognition of the important interrelationship between policy formulation and policy implementation." In 1960 Eisenhower sought to further improve coordination by having the SANSA chair the OCB, replacing the under secretary of state. According to Gordon Gray, Ike thus "eliminated a situation in which a protagonist was also expected to be an 'impartial chairman.' "[42]

The structure established under Eisenhower for the making of national security policy is one of the best illustrations of what Richard Tanner Johnson calls the "formalistic" model of management. This model is characterized by well-defined procedures, hierarchical lines of communication, and a structured staff system.[43] The benefits of such a model are twofold: (1) An orderly decision-making process fosters more thorough analysis, and (2) the decision makers' time and attention is conserved for the big decisions.[44] In following a formalistic model Eisenhower sought to structure an optimal decision by making more efficient "the gathering and analysis of facts, and the arranging of the findings of experts in logical fashion."[45] The Eisenhower system has also been applauded as providing the most efficient means for coping with the NSC's heavy workload. "The aim was not just to get top officials to consider every issue of consequence; it was to have a set of written general policies approved by the President which would serve as guidance for the overall government."[46] Other cited merits of the Eisenhower system are "meticulous staff work, free and open discussion, . . . use of cabinet-level meetings to clarify official policy among those responsible for its execution, and . . . its function as a means of developing an effective crisis management team."[47]

President Eisenhower created the most institutionalized and formalized National Security Council thus far. Though the Eisenhower NSC was noted for its administrative regularity, several criticisms have been directed at its decision-making procedures.[48] First, a decision-making hierarchy that screens information may also distort it, and hierarchical systems have a tendency to respond slowly in crises.[49] Second, Ike's NSC was criticized for sacrificing quality for quantity. Third, some have argued that because policy was shaped in interdepartmental forums, the decision making suffered from such traditional committee problems as "agreement by exhaustion" (a term used by Dean Acheson) and compromise rather than optimal choice. Fourth, because policy questions were handled through set channels, many issues whose interdisciplinary nature did not fit squarely within one policy arena received little attention. All of these criticisms were finally to become the subject of intense scrutiny by Senator Henry Jackson's subcommittee on National Security Policy in 1961, as will be discussed in greater detail in the next section.

Eisenhower's national security advisers were Robert Cutler (1953–1955 and 1957–1958), Dillon Anderson (1955–1956), and Gordon Gray (1958–1961). Of these three, Cutler was by far the most important, partly because he helped create the Eisenhower NSC system and partly because he served the longest. Though the special assistant exercised significant authority, he was still an assistant to the president, not an independent actor. During Eisenhower's term, not once was there a major struggle between the special assistant and Secretary of State John Foster Dulles. Cutler and his successors realized that their job was to coordinate matters, as would a good manager, and that the principal actors—the secretary of state and the president—were the primary policy makers.

Cutler, Dillon, and Gray served Eisenhower in a very specific, well-defined role: They coordinated the development and implementation of policy within the framework of the National Security Council and in accordance with the president's desire to formalize the policy-making structure with regard to national security. As special assistants to the president, these national security advisers brought to the White House a great deal of control over what came to be a powerful policy-making structure. Although the Eisenhower SANSAs served as neutral coordinators within a process dominated by a powerful secretary of state, they brought attention to the potential power of both their office and the NSC staff for the presidential conduct of foreign affairs.

■ Eisenhower's Administrative Style

The Jackson Subcommittee on National Security Policy criticized the NSC system under Eisenhower as "bureaucratic, burdensome, inflexible, and inflated with unnecessary paperwork." Instead of an "intimate forum" for "searching discussion and debate," it said, the council had become the "apex of a comprehensive and highly institutionalized system." Implying that the Eisenhower NSC was too dependent on its staff, to the detriment of presidential leadership, the subcommittee argued that a new president should dismantle the policy hill. In effect, the Eisenhower NSC was portrayed as a vehicle for ensuring consensus and as promoting the least common denominator of a policy rather than diversity and innovative proposals.[50]

The Jackson subcommittee's critique of the Eisenhower NSC was enormously influential in its day and afterward. For the Kennedy administration, it suggested another approach to making national security policy and a new role for the national security adviser. The subcommittee's sweeping but often stereotypical indictment of the Eisenhower advisory process persisted at least until the recent revisionist view associated with Fred Greenstein's *The Hidden-Hand Presidency* and Stephen Ambrose's presidential biography. Certainly the NSC's procedures did not prohibit promising proposals, even if they did not guarantee dissent. The fairest appraisal of the Eisenhower NSC may have been offered almost twenty-five years ago: "By 1960, the NSC had developed into a highly complicated but nonetheless smoothly operating machine, with clear lines of authority and responsibility and elaborate yet systematized staff work."[51] After all, the policy hill worked for Eisenhower, who valued careful planning, detailed coordination, and a staff that was compatible, complementary, and carefully trained. Further, NSC conversations appear to have been a great deal more candid than supposed, and Eisenhower, to have "regarded the NSC process as only one of several components in the shaping of foreign policy."[52] Eisenhower was hardly a captive of his policy-making machinery; rather, he used it to complement his decision-making style.

Certainly, Cutler was no chief of staff for international relations. If that were anyone, it would have been Secretary of State Dulles, who enjoyed unchallenged preeminence as Eisenhower's chief deputy for foreign affairs (even though the State Department did not share the secretary's status). On the other hand, Cutler was no mere "clerk," as he was often labeled. Cutler (as well as his successors, Dillon Anderson and Gordon Gray) saw himself as the custodian of the NSC rather than as the director of national security policy. Future national security advisers would use this position as a mechanism for providing presidents with independent analyses of foreign policy. Those who held the position under Eisenhower, however, had the classical "passion for anonymity" that is supposed to characterize presidential staffers. Most important, they never overtly challenged the State Department's role in formulating and executing foreign policy.

Fred Greenstein has termed many aspects of Eisenhower's leadership and management style "hidden-hand" tactics. For example, Eisenhower was much more than the "simple soldier" he pretended to be; indeed, Stephen Ambrose believed that the simple-soldier manner was a public relations technique.[53] Stephen Hess gave another example of Eisenhower's hidden-hand tactics, arguing that Eisenhower deliberately delegated authority to construct an "elaborate maze of buffer zones that gave himself considerable freedom of action."[54] As "buffers" Eisenhower's staff often took the blame for policies that were, in reality, the president's. Press Secretary James Hagerty recalled a conversation with Eisenhower as follows: "President Eisenhower would say, 'Do it this way.' I would say, 'If I go to that press conference and say what you want me to say, I will get hell.' With that he would smile, get up and walk around the desk, pat me on the back and say, 'My boy, better you than me.' "[55] Eisenhower's relationships with his staff generated so much loyalty that they seemed to take the beatings willingly.[56] Similarly, Secretary of State Dulles's tough public manner nicely complemented Eisenhower's easy-going appearance and served to deflect criticism from the boss to the deputy.

Greenstein has also argued that Eisenhower believed that his hidden-hand strategy had been useful in bringing an end to the Korean conflict: "When Eisenhower entered the White House he was convinced that the Chinese forces were so well entrenched on the current truce line that a negotiated settlement was the best course of action."[57] As Eisenhower put it, "we dropped the word, discreetly, of our intention . . . to move decisively without inhibition in our use of weapons, and . . . no longer be responsible for confining hostilities to the Korean Peninsula. . . . We felt sure it would reach Soviet and Communist ears."[58] Eisenhower felt this hidden-hand strategy had been effective, since almost immediately after the word was dropped in February 1953, the Chinese became more open to negotiations.

The "hidden-hand" nature of Eisenhower's presidency can be seen very clearly in the dynamics of the Eisenhower–Dulles relationship. Dulles knew precisely who was the boss and acted accordingly. Sherman Adams has quoted Dulles as having observed to Eisenhower at the start of the administration that "with my understanding of the intricate relationships between the peoples of the world and your sensitiveness to the political considerations involved, we will make the most successful team in history."[59] Dulles may have been exaggerating here, but as partnerships go, Eisenhower and Dulles's was a great success in foreign affairs.

What enhanced Dulles's role as secretary of state was his ability to win the president's unlimited confidence. Dulles did this in three ways: (1) He had a prodigious mastery of the details of foreign affairs, which could not but impress any chief executive, even one as well versed in the subject as Eisenhower; (2) he used his time with Eisenhower as economically as possible, not "thinking out loud" but presenting all the possible courses of action. (Dulles would indicate his own preferred solution but not present a purely "parochial" State Department viewpoint, and would also assess the likely effects of a decision on other policies and departments);[60] and (3) he embodied the foreign policy views of many Republicans and conservative Democrats and nicely complemented the president's obvious internationalism.

"Dulles worked for Eisenhower and was dependent on him."[61] "Indeed, few Secretaries of State have ever been more conscious of dependence on the President, and none has been more careful of his White House credit."[62] These two observations by Richard Neustadt point out the subordinate relationship Secretary of State Dulles had to President Eisenhower. Despite the president's apparent passivity, Eisenhower maintained firm control over foreign policy making while using Dulles as a confidant and adviser. Eisenhower believed Dulles to have a grasp of foreign affairs that was without equal among his advisers; most important, the president trusted his secretary of state to faithfully execute his policy decisions. Eisenhower, however, set the general direction of policy. As he observed, "I don't like to make a speech on foreign policy that my Secretary of State disagrees with."[63] The clear implication is that once Eisenhower had decided on a course of action, he would tolerate no disagreement.

Dulles, for his part, was extremely jealous with regard to his prerogatives as the president's premier adviser on foreign affairs. As we have noted, various presidential staffers whose domains overlapped Dulles's witnessed the determination with which he would protect his fiefdom. Overall, relations between the State Department and the White House during Dulles's tenure in office were quite amicable. Certainly, the special assistant for national security affairs did not seek to challenge the secretary of state's paramount position. As already noted, this would be a later development in the administration of American foreign policy, the consequences of which would undermine the president's credibility and capacity to govern.

For all the criticism that Eisenhower has received from commentators regarding his management, the fact is that he initiated many administrative procedures with far-reaching significance. Examples are the creation of a cabinet secretariat and a White House chief of staff and formalized decision-making procedures within the presidential office. Indeed, the formalization of the decision-making process with regard to national security ranks as one of Eisenhower's greatest contributions to the office of the presidency. As we have noted, the NSC policy-making process was criticized as a cumbersome paper-mill. More recently, however, the system has been judged to have had a number of merits including meticulous staff work, free and open discussion of various policy proposals at the subcabinet level, and the systematic coordination of policy decisions among those responsible for its execution. The process may have been time-consuming, but its very formality imparted to the Eisenhower administration's foreign policy a coherence and accountability that, unfortunately, would be conspicuously absent from that of some later administrations.

NOTES

1. For dissenting opinions, see Samuel Lubell, *Revolt of the Moderates* (New York: Harper, 1956).

2. Fred I. Greenstein, "Eisenhower as an Activist President: A Look at New Evidence," *Political Science Quarterly* 94 (Winter 1979–1980): 577.

3. Fred I. Greenstein, *The Hidden-Hand Presidency: Eisenhower as Leader* (New York: Basic Books, 1982), pp. 102–105.

4. Greenstein, *The Hidden-Hand Presidency*, pp. 105–114; Sherman Adams, *Firsthand Report: The Story of the Eisenhower Administration* (New York: Harper & Brothers, 1961), pp. 52–53; Stephen Ambrose, *Eisenhower: The President* (New York: Simon & Schuster, 1984), pp. 37 and 103.

5. Adams, *Firsthand Report*, p. 87.

6. Ibid., p. 102.

7. Townsend Hoopes, *The Devil and John Foster Dulles* (Boston: Little, Brown, 1973), p. 277.

8. Ibid., p. 279.

9. Ibid., p. 277.

10. Ibid., p. 283.

11. Cecil V. Crabb, Jr., and Kevin V. Mulcahy, *Presidents and Foreign Policy Making: FDR to Reagan* (Baton Rouge: Louisiana State University Press, 1986), pp. 178–179.

12. Ibid., p. 181.

13. Ibid., p. 325.

14. Hoopes, *The Devil and Dulles*, p. 143.

15. Ibid., p. 141.

16. J. F. Dulles, Ann Whitman file, Dulles–Herter, Box 7, June 4, 1957, Eisenhower Library, Abilene, Kansas.

17. Adams, *Firsthand Report,* p. 275.

18. Dwight D. Eisenhower, *Waging Peace* (Garden City, N.Y.: Doubleday, 1965), p. 365.

19. Dwight D. Eisenhower, *The White House Years: Mandate for Change* (Garden City, N.Y.: Doubleday, 1963), p. 87.

20. Stanley L. Falk, "The National Security Council under Truman, Eisenhower, and Kennedy," *Political Science Quarterly* 79 (September 1964): 418.

21. U.S. Congress. Senate. Committee on Government Operations. Subcommittee on National Policy Machinery. *Organizing for National Security.* 86th Cong., 2d sess., 1961, vol. 2 (Washington, D.C.: Government Printing Office, 1961), pp. 439–468, hereafter referred to as *Jackson Subcommittee Report*; Greenstein, *The Hidden-Hand Presidency,* pp. 102–105 and 124–138; Eisenhower, *Mandate for Change;* p. 114; and Robert Cutler, *No Time for Rest* (Boston: Little, Brown, 1965); pp. 300 and 306–307.

22. R. Gordon Hoxe, "The National Security Council," *Presidential Studies Quarterly* 12 (Winter 1982): 109.

23. Falk, "The National Security Council," p. 431.

24. Sidney W. Souers, "Policy Formulation for National Security," *American Political Science Review* 43 (July 1949): 536.

25. Cutler, *No Time For Rest,* p. 300.

26. Ibid., pp. 306–307.

27. Greenstein, *The Hidden-Hand Presidency,* p. 126.

28. Michael P. McConackie, "The National Security Council: Patterns of Use of Presidents Truman and Eisenhower." Paper presented at the annual meeting of the Southwest Social Science Association, Houston, March 16–19, 1983, p. 20.

29. Paul Y. Hammond, "The National Security Council as a Device for Interdepartmental Coordination: An Interpretation and Appraisal," *American Political Science Review* 54 (December 1960): 904.

30. Greenstein, *The Hidden-Hand Presidency,* pp. 126–128; *The President and the Management of National Security,* ed. Keith C. Clark and Lawrence J. Legere (New York: Praeger, 1969), pp. 61–62.

31. Clark and Legere, *The President and the Management of National Security,* pp. 61–62; Stephen Hess, *Organizing the Presidency* (Washington,

D.C.: Brookings Institution, 1976), p. 74; Joseph G. Bork and Duncan L. Clarke, "The National Security Assistant and the White House Staff: National Security Policy Decisionmaking and Domestic Political Considerations, 1947–1984," *Presidential Studies Quarterly* 16 (Spring 1986): 260.

32. Fred Greenstein and John P. Burke, "Comparative Models of Presidential Decision-Making: Eisenhower and Johnson." Paper presented at the annual meeting of the American Political Science Association, Washington, D.C., August 28–31, 1985, pp. 13–14.

33. Ibid., pp. 14–15.

34. Harry B. Yoshpe and Stanley L. Falk, *Organization for National Security* (Washington, D.C.: Industrial College of the Armed Forces, 1963), p. 93.

35. Ibid., p. 97.

36. Alexander George, "Presidential Management Styles and Models," in *Presidential Decisionmaking in Foreign Policy: The Effective Use of Information and Advice* (Boulder, Colo.: Westview Press, 1980) p. 152.

37. Clark and Legere, *The President and the Management of National Security*, pp. 63–64.

38. Ibid., p. 64.

39. Greenstein, *The Hidden-Hand Presidency,* p. 129. See also Cutler, *No Time for Rest,* pp. 314–315.

40. Philip Henderson, "Advice and Decision: The Eisenhower National Security Council Reappraised," in *The Presidency and National Security Policy,* ed. R. Gordon Hoxe (New York: Center for the Study of the Presidency, 1984), p. 159.

41. Yoshpe and Falk, *Organization for National Security,* p. 95.

42. Anna Kasten Nelson, "National Security I: Inventing a Process" in *The Illusion of Presidential Government,* ed. Hugh Heclo and Lester M. Salamon (Boulder, Colo.: Westview, 1981), p. 248. See also *Jackson Subcommittee Report,* vol. 2, pp. 195–201.

43. Henderson, "Advice and Decision," pp. 173–176.

44. George, "Presidential Management Styles," p. 148.

45. Richard Tanner Johnson, *Managing the White House* (New York: Harper & Row, 1974), p. 238.

46. Henderson, "Advise and Decision," p. 156.

47. I. M. Destler, "National Security Advice to U.S. Presidents: Some Lessons from Thirty Years," in *U.S. National Security: A Framework for Analysis,* ed. Daniel J. Kaufman, Jeffrey S. McKitrick, and Thomas J. Leney (Lexington, Mass.: D. C. Heath, 1985), p. 184.

48. Crabb and Mulcahy, *Presidents and Foreign Policy Making,* p. 169.

49. See Johnson, *Managing the White House,* p. 238; and George, "Presidential Management Styles," p. 165.

50. Nelson, "National Security Council I," p. 254; Henry N. Jackson, ed., *The National Security Council: Jackson Subcommittee Papers on Policymaking at the Presidential Level* (New York: Praeger, 1965), p. 32.

51. Falk, "The National Security Council," p. 418.

52. Nelson, "National Security I," p. 249.

53. Ambrose, *Eisenhower: The President,* p. 18.

54. Hess, *Organizing Presidency,* p. 65.

55. Quoted in R. Gordon Hoxe, ed., *The White House: Organization and Operations* (New York: Center for the Study of the Presidency, 1971), p. 4.

56. Greenstein, *The Hidden-Hand Presidency,* p. 91.

57. Ibid., pp. 61–62.

58. Eisenhower, *Mandate for Change,* p. 181.

59. Adams, *Firsthand Report,* pp. 89–90.

60. Roscoe Drummond and Gaston Colelenty, *Duel at the Brink; John Foster Dulles's Command of American Power* (Garden City, N.Y.: Doubleday, 1960), pp. 32–33.

61. Richard E. Neustadt, *Alliance Politics* (New York: Columbia University Press, 1970), pp. 64–65.

62. Ibid., p. 103.

63. Quoted in Morton H. Halperin, *Bureaucratic Politics and Foreign Policy* (Washington, D.C.: Brookings Institution, 1974), p. 220.

CHAPTER 6

National Security Policy in the Johnson Administration: The Adviser as Counselor

In terms of its impact on American national security policy, the administration of President Lyndon B. Johnson was one of the most momentous in American history. This generalization applies both to the process of decision making in national security affairs and to substantive decisions, concepts, and principles deriving from the administration's experience, some of which continue to guide national security policy today.

Following the format of the other case studies, we begin by examining the context in which national security decision making occurred in the Johnson White House. After that, we shall look more closely at the roles of certain specific actors in the decision making process. Finally, the legacy of the Johnson administration for national security policy will be outlined and evaluated.

▮ The Kennedy Legacy and Foreign Affairs

A unique characteristic of the Johnson presidency, of course, was the tragic sequence of circumstances that brought the vice president and former senator from Texas Lyndon B. Johnson to the Oval Office. After an administration of "a thousand days," on November 22, 1963, President John F. Kennedy was struck down by an assassin's bullet in Dallas, Texas.[1] Within a few hours after Kennedy's death, Vice President Johnson was sworn in as the thirty-sixth president of the United States. (In retrospect, these events remind us that any system of national security policy making in the United States must allow for the possibility that an incumbent president may not serve out a normal term of office. As President Richard M. Nixon showed, the chief executive may relinquish office for one reason or another, voluntarily or involuntarily.)

Until he was reelected as chief executive in his own right in 1964, Lyndon Johnson was conscious that he was an "accidental president" who lacked a demonstrable public mandate. LBJ also believed that, in view of the circumstances that brought him into the White House, he was required to continue the policies of the late President Kennedy.[2] To understand LBJ's approach to national security issues, we must therefore briefly examine President John F. Kennedy's diplomatic legacy.

In the most globally pervasive and momentous aspect of external policy—relations with the Soviet Union—the Kennedy heritage was clearly mixed. On the one hand, in company with every post–World War II chief executive before and after him, President Kennedy accepted and continued the containment policy as the foundation of American policy toward Moscow. As illustrated by Kennedy's widely quoted statement at the Berlin Wall—"*Ich bin ein Berliner*" ("I am a Berliner")—JFK was determined to resist any new communist encroachments in Europe or elsewhere against the free world.

At the same time, Kennedy was equally mindful of the growing threat of global nuclear war and of the necessity for the two superpowers to somehow reduce that danger. He believed that the United States and the Soviet Union must conduct themselves with restraint and seek new opportunities for resolving their differences peacefully.[3] Accordingly, JFK encouraged such steps as a renewal of Soviet–American arms control negotiations and installation of the "hot line," permitting instantaneous communications between Washington and Moscow. The hot line was to contribute significantly toward preventing "war by accident" between the two superpowers.[4]

Toward the European allies, President Kennedy reiterated America's commitment to Western defense and undertook to strengthen the North Atlantic Treaty Organization. One specific step involved promulgating a new defense strategy for NATO based on two related strategic principles known as "forward strategy" and "flexible response." "Forward strategy" means that the NATO allies will defend Europe as far to the east as possible. In other words, in contrast to what happened in World War II, NATO seeks to actively defend noncommunist Europe, not merely "liberate" it after the region has been overrun by an enemy. "Flexible response" means that NATO will attempt to repel any threat initially by conventional (nonnuclear) weapons but, if this defense is unsuccessful, might then, if necessary, use nuclear weapons—that is, resort to "massive retaliation." In contrast to the earlier strategic doctrine of "massive retaliation" identified with the Eisenhower–Dulles era, this new strategy was designed to give the president and his advisers a wider range of options in responding to diverse threats to Western security. Even under the new strategy, it must be emphasized, it was possible that the NATO allies might ultimately have to resort to nuclear weapons in responding to a full-scale Soviet military invasion of Western Europe. Under the revised NATO strategy, however, other and much more limited responses were now available to Western policymakers; they would not, for example, automatically engage in massive nuclear retaliation against an enemy but would do so only as a last resort to defend the NATO area.[5]

Another development affecting NATO was the phenomenon known as "Gaullism," named for the president of the Fifth Republic of France, General Charles de Gaulle. Neither President Kennedy nor his successors in the Oval Office could convince de Gaulle and his followers that the United States would actually use its strategic arsenal to defend the European continent, thereby risking a nuclear attack upon American soil. Because of these doubts, France decided to construct its own nuclear arsenal (the *Force de Frappe*.)[6]

In dealing with Latin America, the diplomatic record of the Kennedy White House was also decidedly mixed. Early in 1961, President Kennedy had authorized the ill-fated Bay of Pigs invasion of Cuba, a CIA-sponsored expedition designed to overthrow Fidel Castro's government and install a new regime headed by Cuban exiles in the United States. The operation failed and was the most graphic diplomatic reversal in the experience of the Kennedy White House.[7]

By contrast, in October 1962, during the Cuban missile crisis, President Kennedy achieved his most conspicuous diplomatic triumph, carrying out one of the most dramatically successful undertakings in American diplomatic tradition. Confronted with irrefutable evidence that the Soviet Union was seeking to install intermediate-range missiles in Cuba—less than a hundred miles from the United States—President Kennedy and his advisers undertook a thorough and secret analysis of the challenge, carefully considered the available alternatives, and in the end decided on a naval "quarantine" (or blockade) of Cuba as the best method for gaining the removal of the Soviet missiles. After a brief period of extreme global tension—the closest that the United States and the Soviet Union have actually come to hostilities since World War II—the Kremlin agreed to remove its missiles from Cuba and to refrain from sending more. Under these conditions, the United States lifted its naval quarantine of Cuba, and the most ominous Soviet–American confrontation in recent memory passed into history. Nonetheless, the Cuban missile crisis had several lasting consequences for contemporary international relations. For example, after 1962, successive presidents declared that the United States could not tolerate "another Cuba" in the Western hemisphere.[8]

The Kennedy administration was also responsible for launching the Alliance for Progress, a kind of Western hemispheric Marshall Plan for promoting Latin American modernization and development. Initially entailing a U.S. commitment of some $10 billion, this program was designed in response to the Latin America complaint that Washington had too long neglected the needs of its neighbors.[9]

In the Middle East, the Kennedy White House predictably continued America's close ties with Israel. After the Suez crisis of 1956, the United States had to repair the resulting breach in the Western alliance. In addition, officials of the Kennedy Administration attempted (with no noteworthy success) to resolve the long-standing Arab–Israeli conflict.[10]

Under President Kennedy, an abortive attempt was also made to heal the breach between the United States and Communist China that had existed since the communist victory on the Chinese mainland in 1949. A "trial balloon" sent up by officials of the Kennedy foreign policy team indicating a desire to reestablish normal Sino–American relations generated no public or congressional support for the idea.[11]

Throughout the Third World, President John F. Kennedy was in some respects the most popular chief executive since Franklin D. Roosevelt. While serving in the Senate, Kennedy had identified himself with anticolonial causes in African and other Third World countries. Under his administration, American policy makers came to terms with the dominant diplomatic strategy of the Third World: nonalignment with the superpowers. Kennedy recognized that a stance of nonalignment was in effect a powerful affirmation of national independence by the nations of the Third World. Moreover, JFK believed that contemporary nonalignment was remarkably similar to the position that a weak and vulnerable American Republic had itself assumed during its early history as a new nation.[12]

Yet, among all the dimensions of American foreign policy under Johnson, the diplomatic legacy of the Kennedy White House in Southeast Asia had perhaps the most crucial impact. Like Presidents Truman and Eisenhower before him, JFK was clearly disturbed about communist advances in Southeast Asia, because he believed that behind the expansionism of Communist North Vietnam lay the reality of Soviet and Communist Chinese power. Though Kennedy opposed Western colonialism in Asia and elsewhere, he was no less apprehensive about efforts by North Vietnam, China, and the Soviet Union to bring Indochina and nations adjacent to it within the communist orbit. (In the early 1960s, Kennedy and his advisers were particularly concerned about the growing communist threat to Laos.) The evidence leaves little doubt that President Kennedy regarded the containment of communism in Southeast Asia as an urgent diplomatic goal of the United States.[13] Rightly or wrongly, President Kennedy viewed the defense of Southeast Asia against communism as a vital U.S. security interest, although why was never very clearly articulated by spokesmen for the New Frontier.[14] At the same time, JFK also recognized that in the final analysis, the successful containment of communism in Southeast Asia would depend on the attitudes and actions of the people and the political leaders of the region.[15]

▌ Challenges to National Security under LBJ

As our discussion has emphasized, when he entered the Oval Office, President Lyndon B. Johnson believed he had a strong obligation to maintain the continuity of American external policy, as established by President Kennedy and earlier chief executives. Toward Western Europe, for example, LBJ preserved the American commitment to NATO, reiterating several times Washington's determination to defend the European continent from aggression and calling for greater consultation among the Western allies in dealing with common problems. As indicated, however, President Johnson was no more successful than his predecessors in convincing Gaullists that the commitment of the United States to European defense was firm and dependable;

thus, LBJ and his advisers were not able to prevent France from developing its own nuclear arsenal.[16] Problems in the Western Hemisphere continued to present the Johnson White House with some of its most difficult challenges. During LBJ's presidency, for example, officials in Washington were disturbed about the degree to which Cuba and the Soviet Union were honoring the agreement ending the Cuban missile crisis of 1962. (As late as the Carter administration in 1979, American intelligence units discovered a large Soviet troop presence in Cuba. Incredibly, this force had apparently been "left over" from the missile crisis in 1962 and had gone undetected by the United States for some 17 years! In turn, this intelligence failure was one reason that opinion in the Senate became highly negative toward the proposed SALT II strategic arms control agreement between the United States and the Soviet Union, because adherence to its terms largely depended on each side's ability to monitor compliance by the other. SALT II has, therefore, remained an un-ratified arms control agreement.)[17]

Also during the Johnson administration, Panamanian nationalist senti-ment, directed primarily against exclusive control of the Panama Canal by the United States, continued to grow. Though no change was made in the status of the Panama Canal (that was not done until new treaties were ratified under the Carter Administration), in the Johnson period groundwork was laid for future negotiations that would produce new agreements regulating the use and defense of the Panama Canal by the United States.[18]

Yet, in relations with Latin America, the dominant problem confronting the Johnson administration was the crisis in the Dominican Republic that erupted in April 1965.[19] Officials of the Johnson administration believed that communist elements were seeking to exploit conditions of economic, social, and political instability for the purpose of imposing a Marxist regime on the Dominican people. As political turbulence in the country increased—and as the lives of Americans and other foreigners were eventually placed in jeopar-dy—President Johnson finally ordered U.S. Marines to land in the Dominican Republic to restore order and prepare the country for new national elections. The Dominican intervention revived memories of earlier intervention in Latin America during the era of "Big Stick" diplomacy. Critics also charged that reliance on armed force by the United States did little to correct the underlying conditions engendering political turbulence in the Dominican Republic.

Yet President Johnson's Dominican intervention did avert an immediate communist threat in the Dominican Republic. The ensuing Dominican elec-tions (supervised by foreign observers) were the freest in the nation's history, and under the new government, the Dominican Republic at least was given an opportunity to solve its acute domestic problems and to evolve in a democratic direction.[20]

In the sphere of Soviet–American relations, developments under the Johnson administration paralleled the approach of the Kennedy White House. Like other post–World War II chief executives, LBJ left no doubt about his determination to oppose communist expansionism abroad. In the Johnson White House, containment remained the cornerstone of American national security policy.

Yet, like his predecessor, President Johnson also believed that a nuclear cloud hung over humanity, endangering the future of civilization. LBJ was convinced that, since the death of Stalin in 1953, Soviet leaders had moderated their behavior at home and abroad and had become increasingly concerned with domestic problems. Furthermore, by the early 1960s, American officials believed that, in some spheres at least, the Kremlin was prepared to collaborate with the United States to reduce global tensions. Like Kennedy, LBJ believed that the two superpowers must exercise restraint in pursuing their global objectives. President Johnson therefore instructed his subordinates to respond positively to Soviet overtures for more-cooperative superpower relations, and he urged members of his official family to deescalate Cold War rhetoric.[21]

Even more significantly, the Johnson White House usually exhibited restraint in situations (such as the Vietnam War and the Middle East conflict of 1967) that might lead to overt conflict between the superpowers. For example, in July 1968, when Soviet and other Warsaw Pact forces invaded Czecho-slovakia to suppress the nation's movement toward democratization, the U.S. government did little more than protest.

President Johnson also advocated a policy of "building bridges" between the United States and the Soviet satellites in Eastern Europe. He was convinced that expanding political, economic, cultural, and other ties between the United States and the communist states of Eastern Europe would lead in time to a loosening of the Soviet Union's grip on the satellite countries. This is an approach that has been continued by his successors in the Oval Office.[22]

The high point of Soviet–American collaboration during the 1960s was perhaps the summit conference between Soviet Premier Aleksey Kosygin and President Johnson in Glassboro, New Jersey, in June 1967. There, the two leaders reiterated their interest in preserving peace and avoiding the calamity of nuclear war; they discussed outstanding Cold War issues, such as ongoing conflicts in the Middle East and Southeast Asia; they emphasized the urgency of reducing the level of strategic armaments; and they agreed that both nations should endeavor to limit the proliferation of nuclear weapons throughout the world. Otherwise, like most spirits, "the spirit of Glassboro" proved ephemeral and difficult to translate into concrete actions. The principal result of the conference was the signing (almost exactly a year later) of the nuclear nonproliferation treaty by the Soviet Union, the United States, and fifty-nine other nations. (This treaty's utility was limited, however, because several states, such as Communist China, France, and India, refused to sign the agreement.)[23]

❚ The Johnson Administration and the Vietnam War

Transcending all other foreign policy issues during the Johnson administration, was the Vietnam War—in some respects, the most divisive external challenge in American history. Over time, the conflict in Southeast Asia eclipsed most other national security problems. In the end, as every student of recent American history is aware, the war undermined the credibility of the Johnson administration, destroyed LBJ politically, drained his physical and psychological health, and frustrated his goal of building the Great Society in the United States.

It is neither necessary for our purposes nor possible to deal with the Vietnam War in great detail here.[24] It must suffice to emphasize a few points important for a better understanding of American national security policy.

As we have seen, America's commitment to defend Southeast Asia from communism antedated Johnson's presidency. In fact, some commentators trace its origins as far back as the Truman administration. Certainly, the Eisenhower White House regarded the preservation of Southeast Asian security as a major foreign policy objective of the United States. Yet President Eisenhower also recognized the overriding importance of getting other countries to join with the United States in containing communism in Asia.[25] The Eisenhower White House took the lead in creating the SEATO defense system for that purpose. (Created on September 8, 1954, the Southeast Asia Treaty Organization—SEATO—included Britain, France, Australia, New Zealand, the Philippines, Pakistan, Thailand, and the United States. SEATO became inactive after the Vietnam War ended.)

As we have already emphasized, on several occasions President Kennedy reiterated America's determination to preserve the security of Southeast Asia. By the end of 1963, a few weeks after Kennedy's death, the United States had some 15,000 troops in South Vietnam, and American financial aid to the country was approximately $500 million annually.[26]

As the months passed after LBJ entered the Oval Office, the American military commitment in Southeast Asia climbed steadily, reaching its peak in 1969, when 543,000 troops were stationed in South Vietnam. This escalation came about as the result of a familiar scenario. Officials in Southeast Asia and Washington presented to President Johnson an alarming picture of communist ambitions within the region. They warned him of the dire consequences to regional and global security that could be expected from new communist gains. They convinced him that progress was being made in containing communism within the region—and that even more progress would be achieved if the American military and financial commitment to regional security were increased.[27]

Relying heavily on computer-generated analyses of the comparative strengths of both sides, Secretary of Defense Robert McMamara and what were called his "Whiz Kids" in the Pentagon were extremely persuasive in pursuing this line of argument with President Johnson. Since LBJ possessed little or no firsthand knowledge of military strategy or of foreign affairs generally, he was heavily dependent on his advisers' assessments. Moreover, in wartime situations chief executives customarily give great weight to the judgments of high-ranking military commanders and civilian military experts.

Other high-ranking presidential advisers, such as Secretary of State Dean Rusk and National Security Adviser McGeorge Bundy, seldom dissented from the Pentagon's optimistic assessments.[28] For a period of several years, a high degree of unanimity—critics of LBJ's diplomacy have labeled it "groupthink"—

existed among the president's principal aides concerning the nation's proper course of action in Southeast Asia. In hindsight, most of these decisions were based upon highly dubious policy assumptions, faulty information, poor policy analysis, or were otherwise erroneous.[29]

By early 1968, some of President Johnson's most influential advisers were beginning to tell him that the United States could not win the war in Southeast Asia—at least, not at a cost the American people were willing to pay. As the weeks passed, this point of view gradually prevailed among the president's aides and was finally accepted by officials such as Secretary of State Dean Rusk and, eventually, if most reluctantly, by President Johnson himself. This realization led to LBJ's widely publicized announcement that he would not seek reelection to the White House—a de facto admission that his administration had lost its political credibility with the American people.[30] Richard M. Nixon, pledging to end the Vietnam War, was elected to the presidency in 1968. After a prolonged period of continued fighting in Southeast Asia—and of difficult diplomatic negotiations among the parties to the conflict—the war was formally ended on January 27, 1973.

▌ The National Security Council under LBJ

As our treatment thus far suggests, President Johnson continued to use the formal National Security Council mechanism established in 1947. Yet, as we shall see, the actual contribution of the NSC to the decision-making process changed considerably vis-à-vis that during the Eisenhower era.

Once again, we need to recall that the National Security Council includes three basic elements: the council itself, the highest-level executive committee for advising the president on national security issues; the president's assistant for national security affairs (ANSA); and the NSC staff (whose role became highly influential and prominent under the Reagan administration).

Under President Johnson, the National Security Council continued to meet and function (theoretically at least) as the highest-level executive committee in the national security field, though the frequency of its meetings declined. Moreover, several former Johnson aides have testified that NSC sessions became increasingly symbolic and only indirectly related to the council's original purpose. President Johnson seldom relied on the NSC to formulate national policy on crucial issues such as the Vietnam War. (America's basic commitment to the defense of South Vietnam, we must remember, had been established before LBJ took office.) Johnson viewed the NSC as too large and unwieldy a forum for policy formulation; and in time, the council also acquired a reputation as a major source of leaks to the news media, further limiting its usefulness in LBJ's eyes. In most instances, Johnson either had made his decision before the National Security Council met or depended on other (usually smaller and more informal) advisory forums for assistance in arriving at decisions.[31]

What purpose then did the National Security Council play in the Johnson White House? As one commentator has expressed it, LBJ used the council as a means of informing his subordinates about the direction in which presidential thinking was moving.[32] He also used it as a means of "signing doubters" on to the Johnson foreign policy team (such as UN Ambassador Adlai E. Stevenson).[33] (This particular use of the NSC appears to have been unsuccessful, since a number of Stevenson supporters in time became outspokenly critical of LBJ's diplomacy.) According to George W. Ball, President Johnson had nearly always decided on his course of action prior to meetings of the National Security Council. As Ball viewed it, NSC meetings actually served two purposes: They were occasions for informing his advisers of the president's impending decision; and they gave many members of LBJ's inner circle "the illusion of participation" in the decision-making process.[34]

In addition to the council itself, there is the presidential assistant for national security affairs (ANSA), who directs the NSC staff and assumes such other duties in the national security field as may be assigned by the President. In the Johnson administration, this position was held by McGeorge Bundy and (after Bundy's resignation in late 1965) by the economist W. W. Rostow. McGeorge Bundy had been a member of the Kennedy team and continued in the position under LBJ. Bundy came from a prominent New England family and was a Yale graduate, a former dean of Harvard University, and a relative of former Secretary of State (under Hoover) and former Secretary of War (under FDR) Henry L. Stimson. With these credentials, Bundy personified both the Eastern intellectual and the foreign policy establishment, whose members' viewpoints have often been decisive in shaping the course of American foreign policy since World War II. Bundy had been offered several other positions by President Kennedy before he finally accepted the appointment as White House aide for national security affairs. (Some commentators believe that Bundy aspired to become secretary of state, a goal that proved unattainable after he emerged as a vocal supporter of the Johnson administration's diplomacy in Southeast Asia, the Dominican Republic, and other settings.)[35]

As much as any other single individual in President Kennedy's retinue, Bundy exemplified "the best and the brightest." He had a reputation for possessing a sharp and highly developed intellect, and he was widely viewed as a symbol or "repository of national intelligence."[36] Bundy personified JFK's New Frontier—especially the supreme confidence of its devotees that, with intellectual prowess and sufficient energy, difficult problems confronting the American society at home and abroad could be solved. (Bundy's successor as ANSA, W. W. Rostow, was perhaps even more convinced that the combination of new and creative ideas with their forceful implementation was the key to attaining American goals abroad.) Yet, in reality, Bundy's firsthand knowledge of foreign affairs was extremely limited.[37] Indeed, among LBJ's closest advisers—Secretary of State Dean Rusk, Secretary of Defense Robert McNamara, and McGeorge Bundy—Rusk alone had prior experience in foreign affairs.

According to one official who served under both Kennedy and Johnson, it was McGeorge Bundy's responsibility as ANSA to supervise the "area where political and military considerations [of national policy] overlap" and to achieve a unified approach to national security issues. A cool, dispassionate, and skillful problem solver, Bundy exemplified the kind of pragmatic approach to national issues that became a hallmark of John F. Kennedy's New Frontier. As another analysis concluded, Bundy was a kind of "super administrator" and a "supreme mover of papers." Indeed, a critic once said that Bundy tended to view himself as a "clerk of the world."

Among presidential advisers during the 1960s, Bundy could usually be counted on to take a middle-of-the-road position. Toward Vietnam, for example, he favored neither a sharp escalation of the American military effort in Southeast Asia, nor (while he was in the government) a substantial reduction in the American commitment to the security of Southeast Asia. Along with the two presidents he served, Bundy accepted without serious question the "domino theory," which held that a communist victory in South Vietnam would ultimately lead to the communization of most of Asia.[38]

According to one account, as one of President Kennedy's White House aides, McGeorge Bundy quickly assumed "the management of day-to-day presidential foreign policy business"—a growing responsibility, as JFK increasingly transferred the conduct of foreign relations to the White House. Relying on his proximity to the Oval Office and his ready access to the president, Bundy increased significantly the ANSA's role in the decision-making process. President Kennedy's skepticism about the State Department—and his disillusionment with his advisers generally after the Bay of Pigs disaster—provided a favorable milieu for this development.[39] Under President Johnson, McGeorge Bundy served (with Secretaries Rusk and McNamara) as one of LBJ's most influential advisers in the sphere of national security policy. As ANSA, Bundy was largely responsible for the formulation of a well-informed, carefully thought-out "presidential" perspective on national security questions, including the objective presentation of available policy options from which the president could choose the most desirable course of action.

In the evolution of the White House national security staff, therefore, McGeorge Bundy played a pivotal role. As one study concluded, under Bundy the position of ANSA was transformed "from a neutral custodian of the machinery to what eventually amounted to a one-man NSC" (as it was to become a few years later, in the Nixon–Kissinger era).[40] Yet in certain other respects, as we shall see in chapter 6, McGeorge Bundy was not "another Kissinger" or the latter's equal. For example, Bundy seldom operated on the basis of a carefully thought-out diplomatic strategy, and from the evidence of the Johnson administration, there is no indication that he proposed original or novel ideas regarding national security.) Nor did Bundy have notably good relations with Congress or the news media.[41] In marked contrast to Kissinger later, Bundy did not emerge as the Johnson administration's leading foreign policy spokesman and negotiator.

After Bundy, however, it became customary for the ANSA to serve as one of the president's most influential foreign policy advisers, on a level of de facto equality with cabinet officers. In effect, McGeorge Bundy acquired cabinet rank in the Johnson White House. (It remained for Zbigniew Brzezinski, ANSA in the Carter White House several years later, to assert that President Carter had formally conferred cabinet rank on him. Yet neither Brzezinski nor any other ANSA was confirmed in the position by the Senate, as is required for cabinet appointments.) Primarily as a result of Bundy's conception of the role and his performance, the ANSA emerged as a true presidential counselor, whose viewpoints and activities sometimes had a crucial impact on external policy.

What did McGeorge Bundy actually do in his position as ANSA under Presidents Kennedy and Johnson? As we have noted, Bundy directed the activities of the National Security Council staff. Under his supervision, the staff became a kind of "intellectual center" in the White House, actively seeking out problems and questions confronting the United States abroad and undertaking detailed analyses of these problems. In a number of instances, Bundy and members of his staff prepared National Security Action Memoranda that (after being approved by the president) defined American policy toward particular issues. The NSC staff also analyzed and condensed memoranda and proposals from the State Department and other executive agencies for the president and identified possible courses of action the president could take in responding to them. Bundy usually insisted that the president also be presented with a full range of policy options (as during the Cuban missile crisis of 1962). During the Vietnam War, Bundy insisted that policy recommendations allow the president maximum flexibility in charting the nation's course abroad.

In his role as ANSA, Bundy was responsible for another innovation that made the president more independent of the executive bureaucracy: the establishment of a "situation room," or communications center, in the White House. For the first time, the White House received directly important communications from intelligence agencies, U.S. embassies abroad, and other sources. This development meant that the president was no longer totally dependent on the executive bureaucracy to supply the information needed to make national security decisions. Such changes made possible "a broad, government-wide presidential view encompassing diplomatic, military, and increasingly, economic elements in foreign policy." In other words, for the first time since the passage of the National Security Act of 1947, the White House staff had both the inclination and the resources to develop and present to the president an independent viewpoint that did not merely reflect the ideas, biases, and bureaucratic vested interests of the established executive departments. (As the Iran–Contra affair that impaired the credibility of the Reagan administration during the 1980s clearly illustrated, members of the White House or NSC staff can, of course, exhibit preconceptions, biases, and personal ambitions of their own that directly affect their judgment and performance.)[42]

In addition, Bundy and the members of the NSC staff coordinated the flow of information and papers to the president. Bundy communicated the wishes and decisions of the president to departments, supervised the coordination of executive efforts in external policy, served as a liaison between the White House and cabinet officers, undertook analyses of problems requiring a presidential decision, acted as a policy "facilitator" throughout the government, and monitored the implementation of presidential decisions.[43]

In addition (foreshadowing the extremely active role that Henry Kissinger played in the Nixon administration), McGeorge Bundy sometimes undertook fact-finding and other diplomatic missions for President Johnson. After or during some of these trips abroad, Bundy submitted reports and made policy recommendations, as in his belief that the United States must increase its military commitment to the security of South Vietnam. In a mission to the Dominican Republic in 1965, Bundy attempted (without success) to establish a coalition government for that politically turbulent nation. Bundy also suggested that President Johnson travel to Hawaii in early 1966 to meet with Asian leaders for the purpose of underscoring the firmness of America's commitment to South Vietnamese independence. (Another objective of the trip was to shift the spotlight of public attention from Capitol Hill, where the Senate was investigating the Vietnam War, to the White House.) In addition, as the president's chief assistant for national security affairs, Bundy also served as a link between the White House and American ambassadors (such as Ambassador Maxwell Taylor in South Vietnam.)

Under both Presidents Kennedy and Johnson, Bundy headed interagency task forces established to study and make recommendations on selected national security problems. As President Kennedy viewed it, the role of these task forces was to enable the White House to "stay ahead of events," instead of merely reacting to them on an ad hoc basis. (Yet, ironically, the Kennedy–Johnson era is widely cited as a period in which "incremental," or ad hoc, decision making was in fact the rule!)[44]

Implicit in the concept of ANSA as counselor is the idea that McGeorge Bundy sometimes had a crucial impact on the substantive policies adopted by the Kennedy and Johnson White House. Predictably, as a Republican and a kinsman of Henry L. Stimson, Bundy was firmly opposed to communism, which he believed threatened the security of the United States and other nations. Moreover, he was convinced that the United States must use its great power to contain communist expansionism abroad. Bundy both shared and articulated the "anticommunist consensus" that served as the foundation of the nation's foreign policy from the end of World War II until the early 1970s. With other prominent members of the Eastern foreign policy establishment, Bundy's thinking about international issues had been profoundly influenced by the "lessons of Munich" and by recent experience (as in the early postwar era) in dealing with Moscow.

Predictably, therefore, Bundy could nearly always be counted on to approve the growing American commitment to preserving the independence of South Vietnam—a commitment he believed could be traced back at least to the Eisenhower administration. For Bundy and other presidential advisers, America's willingness to honor this commitment was a kind of litmus test of its diplomatic credibility generally. For several years, therefore, Bundy opposed the views of those (such as Under Secretary of State George Ball) who urged LBJ to reduce, and ultimately to liquidate, the nation's commitment to the security of South Vietnam. Yet, as a pragmatist, even Bundy was compelled as time passed to acknowledge that the United States was in the process of losing the Vietnam War. In light of that fact, Bundy ultimately reversed his position and urged President Johnson to reduce the American presence in Southeast Asia.[45]

Some changes occurred in the role of ANSA when W. W. Rostow replaced McGeorge Bundy late in 1965. Rostow was an economist who had previously served on the State Department's policy planning staff and had also been one of McGeorge Bundy's assistants on the NSC staff. Rostow was especially interested in the Third World and the process of national development. Among LBJ's advisers, Rostow was known as a vocal and imaginative "ideas man." Along with Bundy, he served as one of President Johnson's links with the academic community, although in time (because of their hawkish views on the Vietnam War) both Bundy and Rostow largely lost their rapport with academia. Indeed, Rostow's attitude toward the Vietnam War earned him the label "super-hawk" from President Johnson. Rostow advocated the intensive bombing of North Vietnamese industries as a step he was convinced would lead to the defeat of communism in Southeast Asia. (As events proved, this and other strategies tried by the U.S.—such as "counter-insurgency"—failed to achieve American goals in Southeast Asia.) Other officials (such as Secretary of State Dean Rusk) came to regard most of Rostow's ideas as excessively theoretical and impractical—a viewpoint ultimately shared by President Johnson.[46]

▌ Other Advisory Channels and Mechanisms

As our discussion thus far has suggested, President Lyndon Johnson, perhaps more than most chief executives, was disinclined to rely heavily on formal and complex advisory mechanisms. He preferred to seek advice from individuals, singly or in small groups, in whom he had confidence. With the passage of time, these informal ad hoc advisory channels became increasingly influential in the national security decision-making process in the Johnson White House.

For example, LBJ reposed considerable confidence in two of his cabinet officers: Secretary of State Dean Rusk and Secretary of Defense Robert Mc-Namara. Throughout most of the Johnson presidency, these individuals played a highly influential role in shaping the administration's policies on the Vietnam War and other important global issues.

A protégé of Secretaries of State George Marshall and Dean Acheson during the Truman period, Dean Rusk had been appointed by President Kennedy to head the State Department, and he continued in that office under President Johnson. Serving from 1961 until early 1969, Rusk served longer than any other secretary of state except Cordell Hull under Franklin Roosevelt. Before joining the State Department, Rusk had served in the U.S. Army in Asia, where he rose to the rank of colonel. (In the State Department, Rusk was always sympathetic to the military viewpoint and inclined to defer to what he viewed as the "expert opinion" of officials in the Pentagon.) In his prior State Department service, Rusk had been in charge of the Far Eastern bureau and also served as assistant secretary of state for United Nations affairs. Rusk left the department in 1952 to become president of the Rockefeller Foundation, where he became involved with the problems of the Third World. Dean Rusk had been recommended for appointment as secretary of state by his mentor, former Secretary of State Dean Acheson, and by others whom President Kennedy consulted.[47]

In contrast to McGeorge Bundy, W. W. Rostow, and other New Frontier—men, Dean Rusk was not noted for his intellectual brilliance, forceful personality, or supreme confidence in the ability of the United States to solve intractable global problems. In fact, as a rule Rusk was highly skeptical of the ability of New Frontier programs to decisively and quickly resolve such problems. (Many of JFK's other advisers scarcely concealed their disdain for Rusk, whom they looked upon as passive, unimaginative, and seemingly uninterested in protecting his bureaucratic turf against interlopers.)

Rusk was known as a State Department traditionalist: He exemplified the department's preference for established procedures and routines, for "quiet diplomacy," and for a conviction that only limited results would likely be achieved by American moves abroad. Having entered the State Department in the early postwar era, Rusk shared the anticommunist consensus that was the basis of American foreign policy until the end of the Vietnam War. As a matter of deep conviction, Rusk advocated the containment policy—earlier, he had urged President Truman to resist the communist threat to South Korea—and supported the growing effort to protect Southeast Asia from communist hegemony.[48]

In his position as the head of the State Department, Rusk followed certain principles and practices he had learned from his mentors, such as Secretaries Marshall and Acheson. One was to withhold his own counsel until he could convey it privately to the president. This practice gave Rusk the reputation of being unimaginative and passive (the term frequently applied to him was *Buddha-like*) vis-à-vis other presidential advisers. Another precept Rusk followed (which Acheson had taught him) was to be the last person to communicate advice to the president before the latter arrived at a decision. In other words, Rusk always tried to get the "last shot" in before the decision became final. Again following in Acheson's footsteps, Dean Rusk almost never publicly disagreed with or questioned the president's diplomatic decisions. Like Acheson, Rusk understood clearly that the ultimate power of decision making resided in the Oval Office. Nor did Rusk appear resentful that President Johnson routinely consulted a wide range of advisers before making a decision in foreign affairs. Throughout his term in the White House, President Johnson relied heavily on Secretary Rusk for advice. According to some accounts, LBJ "trusted" the quiet and methodical Rusk more than he did any of his other counselors. Johnson repeatedly expressed confidence in Rusk and conferred the Medal of Freedom on him for his long and dedicated service to the nation.[49]

The other cabinet officer on whom both Presidents Kennedy and Johnson leaned heavily for advice—especially during the Vietnam War—was Secretary of Defense Robert McNamara. McNamara's background and personality were totally different from Dean Rusk's. The former had a background as a highly successful, aggressive executive of the Ford Motor Company. In the words of one study, McNamara had "blown into Washington in 1961 like a brisk and exhilarating wind." As the civilian head of the Pentagon, he had exhibited "a swift and powerful mind," a firm grasp of the principles of modern management, and a determination to do whatever was necessary to impose order on the "warring tribes" of the Defense Department.[50] In brief, McNamara was expected to do what no one else had been able to do since 1947: really manage the Pentagon, making it efficient and responsive to the presidential will. To achieve this goal, McNamara surrounded himself with a coterie of extremely bright and energetic assistants (called his "Whiz Kids") and proceeded to vigorously carry out his assigned mission. Among McNamara's numerous reforms were the introduction of new management techniques and computer-based studies of national security problems.

In marked contrast to Secretary of State Rusk's customary diffidence, Secretary McNamara tended to dominate meetings of President Johnson's advisers. He was extremely forceful, outspoken, and authoritative—if not in some respects overbearing.[51] Nearly always, McNamara's proposals were impressively "documented" with computer-generated analyses. Regarding the Vietnam War, time and again McNamara's studies supported two crucial conclusions: that the United States was winning the contest with communism in Southeast Asia and that a decisive victory over communism could be expected in the near future, provided that even more American resources and personnel were committed to achieve the goal. Such optimistic projections were almost never effectively refuted by Secretary of State Rusk or other members of LBJ's foreign policy team.[52] It must be remembered, of course, that (although it had not been officially declared) the United States was in fact at war in Southeast Asia. During wartime, as in World War II, the military viewpoint normally overrides all others.

Both Presidents Kennedy and Johnson regarded Secretary McNamara as perhaps their ablest adviser. As for McNamara, the military has seldom had a more capable or persuasive spokesman for its point of view. Yet, by October 1966, Robert McNamara had begun to lose his enthusiasm for American participation in the Vietnam War, and he began to express his doubts to President Johnson. For several months, McNamara tried to persuade the president to seek a political solution to the conflict. Then in late 1967 McNamara resigned his position with the Defense Department to become president of the World Bank. McNamara was succeeded at the Pentagon by the "old Washington hand" and eminent lawyer, Clark Clifford, who had served successive presidents going back to the Truman administration. Supported by other advisers, Clifford was finally able to convince President Johnson that the Vietnam cause was lost.[53]

President Johnson consulted Secretaries Rusk and McNamara both individually and collectively, as exemplified by the "Tuesday lunch group," which in some respects may have been the most influential advisory body in the Johnson White House. Originally, the core of this group consisted of Secretary Rusk, Secretary McNamara, presidential assistant McGeorge Bundy, and President Johnson. In time, other officials—such as LBJ's press secretary, the director of the CIA, the chairman of the Joint Chiefs of Staff, and other White House aides—attended the meetings. Although its membership gradually changed, this group continued to serve as an influential advisory mechanism until the end of the Johnson presidency.

In contrast to the National Security Council, the Tuesday lunch group was an informal body lacking statutory authority. It was established, and largely controlled, by President Johnson. The group had no announced agenda. (Not knowing what would be discussed, departmental representatives were therefore hard-pressed to prepare for the meetings.) No formal record of the meetings was kept or circulated. As a result, it was difficult for participants to know what precisely had been "decided" at the meetings or what the exact responsibility of different departments and agencies was for implementing decisions reached. Not infrequently, subsequent meetings of the National Security Council were held to "ratify" decisions the president had arrived at as a result of advice received in the Tuesday lunch group.[54]

Perhaps primarily because of his prior service in Congress, President Johnson had a wide circle of friends, cronies, and contacts on whom he leaned for advice in dealing with a variety of national issues. For example, UN Ambassador Adlai Stevenson and (his successor in the position) former Supreme Court Justice Arthur Goldberg conveyed their views to LBJ on issues such as the Vietnam War. Supreme Court Justice Abe Fortas was also one of LBJ's old friends and advisers. Among experienced military leaders, World War II General Omar Bradley, along with Korean War commander General Maxwell Taylor, were called on to communicate their views to the Johnson White House. Among experienced diplomatic figures, none was courted more intensively for his counsel than former Secretary of State Dean Acheson. Acheson was another leading member of the Eastern foreign policy establishment, which tended both to intimidate President Johnson and to play an influential role in the decision-making process of the Johnson White House.[55]

In 1965, President Johnson constituted what came to be called the "Senior Advisory Group on Vietnam," otherwise known as "the Wise Men." As noted earlier, the Wise Men consisted of a group of experienced and distinguished former public servants who devoted countless hours to considering America's increasingly frustrating involvement in the Vietnam conflict. Initially, the group supported the Johnson administration's policies in Southeast Asia (several members of the Wise Men had, after all, played an influential role in the promulgation and implementation of the containment policy).[56]

With time, however, led by Dean Acheson, George Ball, and Clark Clifford, the Wise Men concluded that the United States could not achieve its objectives in Southeast Asia at a price the American people were prepared to pay. In a word, the policies of the Johnson White House in Southeast Asia were a failure. Needless to say, this was not a conclusion that President Johnson and several of his closest advisers accepted easily. But, reluctantly, the president did accept this outcome, which in turn led to his decision not to seek reelection and to agree to a negotiated settlement of the Vietnam War.

■ National Security Policy under LBJ: An Assessment

From the perspective of the evolution of American national security policy, the Kennedy–Johnson era was an important period. Both presidents contributed significantly to this evolution, primarily in terms of the use to which they put established advisory mechanisms. Before his death, President Kennedy was quite clearly moving in the direction of greater control over foreign relations directly by the president himself. As had been true of President Franklin D. Roosevelt during World War II, Kennedy was approaching the model of the chief executive's acting as "his own secretary of state." His successor did not carry the process as far as Kennedy, but in decision making concerning the Vietnam War, Johnson also made many key decisions himself, and he left no doubt where the ultimate authority in diplomatic decision making resided.[57]

Both chief executives moved outside the formal advisory structure in making crucial decisions in the field of external policy, a fact that clearly cautions against the notion that Congress can specify in detail how or where a president is to seek advice. Congress may create elaborate advisory structures like the NSC, but it cannot determine by law precisely how an incumbent President will rely on them in responding to external challenges.

As our treatment has emphasized, under President Johnson the principal value of the National Security Council and its associated organizational structure (the council itself, the NSC staff, and the ANSA) lay perhaps in facilitating the emergence of an independent "presidential" viewpoint on national security issues, in contrast to the narrower perspective of the State, Defense, and other executive departments. On balance, this was a positive development, allowing the White House to counter bureaucratic provincialism and vested interests and to approach global issues more objectively from the perspective of a national interest, as exemplified by the office of the president.

In his position as ANSA, McGeorge Bundy played a key role in this transition. More than anyone serving in the position since 1947, Bundy was a capable advocate of an independent presidential viewpoint on national security problems. His elevation of the position of ANSA to the level of a counselor or de facto equality with the department heads indicated that Presidents Kennedy and Johnson approved of this development.

Obvious as it might seem, it is essential to bear in mind that the major purpose of the National Security Council and other formal advisory mechanisms is to produce the best policy possible in the national security field. By this admittedly ideal standard, the national security advising process—including both its formal and informal components—must, on balance, be judged a failure during the Johnson era. Though there were unquestionably positive accomplishments during Johnson's presidency (for example, some mitigation of Cold War animosities), primarily because of the Vietnam War, his administration's record shows more losses than gains. The war greatly strained interallied relations, creating internal stresses within NATO. Its outcome left doubts, unsolved problems and fundamental questions that posed obstacles to the solution of national security questions for many years after the Vietnam conflict ended.[58]

With regard to two other continuing problems affecting national security policy—executive–legislative relations, and intraexecutive relations in the foreign policy sphere—the Johnson administration's record was clearly mixed, with setbacks outweighing accomplishments. By the late 1960s, as we have seen, relations between the White House and Congress had deteriorated badly, reaching perhaps the lowest point since the McCarthy era of the late 1940s and early 1950s. For a prolonged period after the Vietnam War (and the War Powers Resolution of 1973 was a conspicuous example), Congress continued to react against what its members viewed as the Johnson administration's disregard of legislative viewpoints, and the kind of manipulation of Congress that had become a hallmark of the Johnson presidency. In more general terms, such behavior was widely viewed as characteristic of the "imperial presidency," or executive-branch domination of the foreign policy process. During the 1970s and 1980s, much of congressional activism in the foreign policy field could be interpreted as a continued reaction against this conception of the president's role.[59]

With regard to the problem of intraexecutive relations under Johnson, five observations can be made briefly. First, there did not occur the kind of open conflict (Secretary of State George Shultz called it "guerrilla warfare") among the president's advisers that characterized the Reagan administration during its second term. In contrast to the Reagan era, during the 1960s the ANSA and members of the NSC staff refrained from advocating, and in some cases actually implementing, national security policies of their own. In the vast majority of instances, McGeorge Bundy's views coincided with those of President Johnson, Robert McNamara, Dean Rusk, and other high-level presidential advisers.

Second, although we have described McGeorge Bundy's role in the Johnson White House as that of "counselor," the limitations on that role must be understood clearly. Bundy's impact on the evolution of the office of ANSA was unquestionably great: During the 1960s, it was without question more influential than it had been during the Truman or Eisenhower periods. Furthermore, we must assume that this transition occurred with the full support of the chief executives whom Bundy served. (As our discussion indicated, the ANSA's influence declined after W. W. Rostow succeeded Bundy in the office.) At the same time, it must also be emphasized that, though Bundy achieved de facto cabinet rank as ANSA, he did not, in contrast to Henry Kissinger under Nixon, directly challenge the position of the secretary of state, attempt to eclipse it, and endeavor to serve as the president's recognized principal deputy and spokesman on foreign policy. For the most part, relations between the State Department and the staff of the National Security Council during the Johnson period were reasonably good.

Third, throughout the 1960s, the "anticommunist consensus" that had served as the foundation of American foreign policy since the end of World War II remained durable and was not widely questioned.[60] This was a crucial fact that went far toward explaining the relative lack of intra-executive conflict on foreign policy issues during the Kennedy–Johnson period. Underlying this consensus were at least three basic beliefs: (1) that communism—identified specifically with the Soviet Union—was antithetical to democracy and the American way of life; (2) that, as evidenced during and after World War II, communism was inherently expansive, especially with regard to regions in which a "power vacuum" existed; and (3) that the United States could and must effectively resist communist expansion by applying the containment policy. Not until near the end of the Johnson administration, after it became evident that the United States could not win the contest in Southeast Asia, did the American people and Congress question one or more elements of this consensus.[61]

Fourth, the Johnson presidency is often widely cited as a leading example of the phenomenon known as "groupthink"—or unanimity among the president's advisers achieved by coercion, the elimination of dissent, and other steps designed to maintain a preconceived viewpoint consonant with the president's known inclinations. On the basis of the evidence, many of the arguments made by critics of groupthink seem undeniable.[62] For example, in the Johnson White House early dissenters such as Under Secretary of State George Ball were discouraged from stating their views and encountered the idea that they were somehow "disloyal" to the president when they challenged prevailing policies. Yet President Johnson always contended that the advice he received was full and balanced.

It must also be remembered that a high degree of intraexecutive unity was characteristic of the Truman Administration as well, during the heyday of "bipartisan" cooperation on foreign policy in the postwar period.[63] Yet the term "groupthink" has never consistently been applied to that era. It is certainly conceivable, therefore, that the problem was not so much unity among President Johnson's advisers. The later experience of the Reagan administration indicated convincingly that a lack of unity among the president's aides can be a no less serious problem for national security policy. During the 1960s, the serious defect in national security policy was unanimity in behalf of unsound policies. This was why, based on the results it produced, the national security policy advisory system during the Johnson presidency must be judged at least a partial failure.

Fifth, the Johnson administration's national security efforts must also be viewed as less than successful for another reason. Ever since the concept of national security policy gained currency in the early post–World War II era, a fundamental question has confronted the President, Congress, and the

American people. This is the question of defining the circumstances under which the nation's armed forces are to be used for foreign policy ends. By the late 1960s, the American people had made clear their view that the defense of Southeast Asia from communism was not a vital interest of the United States. (By contrast, and despite General MacArthur's widely quoted dictum against becoming involved in "a land war on the Asian continent," the defense of South Korea has remained a vital American interest since the beginning of the Korean War in June 1950.)

Seriously lacking in the Johnson period was a redefinition of the nation's vital diplomatic interests, in light of the outcome of the Vietnam conflict. Insofar as the evidence indicates, the National Security Council was never used for that purpose. The Nixon administration later attempted such a basic redefinition of national policy, in the form of the "Nixon Doctrine," which became perhaps fatally tarnished by the Watergate affair that destroyed President Nixon's credibility.[64] In that sense, twenty years or so after the National Security Act of 1947, the president and his chief advisers had still failed to formulate a clear and comprehensive national security policy. It was a lack that was to impede the effectiveness of the nation's external policies— toward Central America, toward the Persian Gulf area, toward East Asia—for many years to come.

NOTES

1. Detailed discussions of the Kennedy administration's diplomacy are included in Theodore C. Sorensen, *Kennedy* (New York: Harper & Row, 1965); Arthur M. Schlesinger, Jr., *A Thousand Days: John F. Kennedy in the White House* (Boston: Houghton Mifflin, 1965); and Roger Hilsman, *To Move a Nation: The Politics of Foreign Policy in the Administration of John F. Kennedy* (Garden City, N.Y.: Doubleday, 1967).

2. See Lyndon B. Johnson, *The Vantage Point: Perspectives of the Presidency, 1963–1969* (New York: Holt, Rinehart & Winston, 1971), pp. 197–198; and Eric F. Goldman, *The Tragedy of Lyndon B. Johnson* (New York: Knopf, 1969), p. 175.

3. Soviet–American relations during the 1960s are discussed in Joseph L. Nogee and Robert H. Donaldson, *Soviet Foreign Policy since World War II*, 2nd ed. (New York: Pergamon Press, 1984), pp. 101–146; and Adam B. Ulam, *The Rivals: America and Russia since World War II* (New York: Viking Press, 1971), pp. 299–397.

4. Schlesinger, *A Thousand Days,* pp. 889–923.

5. See Edwin H. Fedder, *NATO: The Dynamics of Alliance in the Postwar World* (New York: Dodd, Mead, 1973); and Alfred Grosser, *The Western Alliance: European–American Relations since 1945* (New York: Continuum, 1980).

6. Schlesinger, *A Thousand Days,* pp. 842–889. For more comprehensive analyses of General de Gaulle's views, see Alexander Werth, *De Gaulle:*

A Political Biography (New York: Simon & Schuster, 1966); and Roy C. Macridis, ed., *De Gaulle: Implacable Ally* (New York: Harper & Row, 1966).

7. Sorensen, *Kennedy,* pp. 291–310; Schlesinger, *A Thousand Days,* pp. 233–267.

8. Sorensen, *Kennedy,* pp. 667–719; Schlesinger, *A Thousand Days,* pp. 794–819; and Robert F. Kennedy, *Thirteen Days: A Memoir of the Cuban Missile Crisis* (New York: New American Library, 1969).

9. See Sorensen, *Kennedy,* pp. 533–540. More-detailed treatment is available in J. Walter Nystrom and Nathan A. Haverstock, *The Alliance for Progress* (Princeton, N.J.: Van Nostrand, 1966).

10. The Middle East was a relatively low priority region with the Kennedy White House. See Schlesinger, *A Thousand Days,* pp. 508 and 564–567. On the challenge of repairing U.S. relations with Arab states after the Suez crisis of 1956, see William R. Polk, *The United States and the Arab World* (Cambridge: Harvard University Press, 1965), pp. 261–284.

11. The Kennedy administration's overture to Communist China is discussed more fully in Hilsman, *To Move a Nation,* pp. 275–361.

12. See, for example, JFK's views on French colonialism, in Schlesinger, *A Thousand Days,* pp. 320–323; on the "neutralization" of Southeast Asia, pp. 329–334; and on America's relations with black Africa, pp. 551–585.

13. Regarding Kennedy's strong opposition to communist inroads in Southeast Asia, see Wesley R. Fishel, ed., *Vietnam: Anatomy of a Conflict* (Itasca, Ill.: F. E. Peacock, 1968), pp. 142–148; Schlesinger, *A Thousand Days,* pp. 320–343; and Hilsman, *To Move a Nation,* pp. 91–159. According to one "revisionist" study of the Kennedy administration, JFK's diplomacy was motivated by a militant opposition to communism and radical political change. See Richard J. Walton, *Cold War and Counter-Revolution: The Foreign Policy of John F. Kennedy* (Baltimore: Penguin, 1973).

14. When John F. Kennedy entered the White House, there were some 600 U.S. military advisers in Vietnam. In late April 1961, JFK approved an increase in this number, by an additional 100 advisers—called the first step in the rapid escalation of American forces in Southeast Asia. A few weeks later, Kennedy agreed to send an additional 400 Special Forces troops to conduct covert warfare against communism in Southeast Asia. See Walton, *Cold War and Counter-Revolution,* p. 169. See also the discussion of JFK's views toward Southeast Asia in Chester Bowles, *Promises to Keep: My Years in Public Life, 1941–1969* (New York: Harper & Row, 1971), pp. 407–410. Bowles believes it was President Kennedy who "upset the balance," giving the military a disproportionate voice in shaping U.S. policy toward Vietnam.

15. See JFK's views, as quoted in Sorensen, *Kennedy,* pp. 654–655.

16. The Johnson administration's diplomacy toward Western Europe is examined in greater detail in Johnson, *The Vantage Point,* pp. 305–322; John Pinder and Roy Pryce, *Europe after de Gaulle* (Baltimore: Penguin, 1969); and Robert Aron, *De Gaulle* (New York: Harper & Row, 1966), pp. 133–201.

17. See Jimmy Carter, *Keeping Faith: Memoirs of a President* (New York: Bantam Books, 1982), pp. 262–265.

18. Johnson, *The Vantage Point*, pp. 180–183.

19. A brief treatment of the 1965 Dominican intervention may be found in Cecil V. Crabb, Jr., *The Doctrines of American Foreign Policy: Their Meaning, Role, and Future* (Baton Rouge: Louisiana State University Press, 1982), pp. 215–277. More-detailed accounts are Abraham F. Lowenthal, *The Dominican Intervention* (Cambridge: Harvard University Press, 1972); Theodore Draper, *The Dominican Revolt: A Case Study in American Policy* (New York: Commentary Reports, 1968); and John B. Martin, *Overtaken by Events* (Garden City, N.Y.: Doubleday, 1966).

20. See the evaluation of LBJ's Dominican diplomacy in Crabb, *The Doctrines of American Foreign Policy*, pp. 262–277.

21. See LBJ's ideas on "thawing" the Cold War, in Johnson, *The Vantage Point*, pp. 462–492. For more extended discussion, see Nogee and Donaldson, *Soviet Foreign Policy since World War II*, pp. 101–137 and 248–300; and Ulam, *The Rivals*, pp. 299–405.

22. Johnson, *The Vantage Point*, pp. 470–474. An extended discussion can be found in Robert F. Byrnes, ed., *The United States and Eastern Europe* (Englewood Cliffs, N.J.: Prentice-Hall, 1967).

23. Johnson, *The Vantage Point*, pp. 481–485 and 587–590.

24. The Vietnam War has engendered a long and ever-growing list of commentaries. The following is merely a sampling of available studies: George C. Herring, *America's Longest War: The United States and Vietnam, 1950–1975* (New York: Wiley, 1979); Larry Berman, *Planning a Tragedy: The Americanization of the War in Vietnam* (New York: Norton, 1982); Paul Kattenberg, *The Vietnam Trauma in American Foreign Policy, 1945–1975* (New Brunswick, N.J.: Transaction Books, 1980); Stanley Karnow, *Vietnam: A History* (New York: Viking Press, 1983); Herbert Y. Schandler, *The Unmaking of a President: Lyndon Johnson and Vietnam* (Princeton, N.J.: Princeton University Press, 1977); James P. Harrison, *The Endless War: Fifty Years of Struggle in Vietnam* (New York: Free Press, 1982); W. Scott Thompson and Donaldson D. Frizzell, eds., *The Lessons of Vietnam* (New York: Crane Russak, 1977); James E. Veninga and Harry A. Wallace, eds., *Vietnam in Remission* (College Station: Texas A&M University Press, 1985); and Robert L. Galluci, *Neither Peace nor Honor: The Politics of American Military Policy in Vietnam* (Baltimore, Md.: Johns Hopkins University Press, 1975).

25. See Harry S Truman's memoirs, *Years of Trial and Hope* (Garden City, N.Y.: Doubleday, 1956), pp. 421–422; and George M. Kahin and John W. Lewis, *The United States in Vietnam* (New York: Dell, 1969), pp. 21–31 and 325–327.

26. One of President Kennedy's advisers believed that the commitment to protect the security of South Vietnam had initially been undertaken by President Eisenhower in 1954. See Sorensen, *Kennedy*, p. 650; and Kahin and Lewis, *The United States in Vietnam*, pp. 43–126.

27. Our scenario summarizes the decision-making process in the Johnson White House. See, for example, I. M. Destler, *President, Bureaucrats, and Foreign Policy: The Politics of Organizational Reform* (Princeton, N.J.: Prin-

ceton University Press, 1972), pp. 95–154; Johnson, *The Vantage Point,* pp. 112–154, 232–270, and 365–425. Another commentator believes that Secretary McNamara and the Pentagon had a decisive influence on decisions concerning the Vietnam War, in large part because they successfully insisted that questions related to the war were mainly "strategic" (rather than political) in nature. See Charles W. Yost, *The Conduct and Misconduct of Foreign Affairs* (New York: Random House, 1972), p. 156. Yet Goldman believes it is a mistake to view President Johnson as a "captive" of the military; basically, LBJ accepted the Pentagon's viewpoint because he usually agreed with it. See Goldman, *The Tragedy of Lyndon B. Johnson,* pp. 472–473.

28. See the provocative analysis by Irving L. Janis, *Groupthink,* 2nd ed. (Boston: Houghton Mifflin, 1982). Compare with Kearns' view that if LBJ had wanted a different, more heterogenous set of advisers who would have made different recommendations on global issues, he would have changed the membership of his inner circle. See Doris Kearns, *Lyndon B. Johnson and the American Dream* (New York: Harper & Row, 1976), p. 275. George W. Ball's assessment is that President's Johnson's advisers—specifically, Secretaries Rusk and McNamara—deliberately endeavored to present him with a common viewpoint, thereby sparing LBJ the necessity of making difficult choices among divergent opinions. Yet in his view, the same adversary process that exists in the legal profession ought to be used in advising the president. George W. Ball, *The Past Has Another Pattern* (New York: Norton, 1982), p. 332.

29. See Johnson, *The Vantage Point,* pp. 365–462.

30. President Johnson indicated that he decided in March 1968 to initiate peace overtures in the Vietnam War and, concurrently, not to seek reelection to the White House. He announced his decision on March 31, 1968. See Johnson, *The Vantage Point,* pp. 423–424.

31. For President Johnson's view of the role and contribution of the National Security Council, see Chester L. Cooper, *The Lost Crusade: America in Vietnam* (New York: Dodd, Mead, 1970), pp. 222–223; and Merle Miller, *Lyndon: An Oral Biography* (New York: Ballantine, 1980), pp. 492–494.

32. See Cooper, *The Lost Crusade,* p. 223.

33. See, for example, Chester Cooper's recollection of NSC meetings and their purpose, as recounted in Kearns, *Johnson and the American Dream,* pp. 338–339; and David Halberstam, *The Best and the Brightest* (New York: Penguin Books, 1972), pp. 631–632.

34. See George Ball's assessment of the National Security Council in his *Diplomacy for a Crowded World: An American Foreign Policy* (Boston: Little, Brown, 1976), pp. 198–199. See also Townsend Hoopes, *The Limits of Intervention: An Inside Account of How the Johnson Policy of Escalation in Vietnam Was Reversed,* (New York: David McKay, 1969), pp. 5–6. The view of Clark and Legere was that with the passage of time LBJ looked to the NSC and its staff less and less for original ideas and policy initiatives. NSC's function became mainly "educational . . . or ceremonial." *The President and the Management of National Security,* ed. Keith C. Clark and Laurence J. Legere (New York: Praeger, 1969), p. 83–88.

35. See Thomas Parker, *America's Foreign Policy—1945–1976: Its Creators and Critics* (New York: Facts on File, 1980), pp. 13–14; the *New York Times* edition of *The Pentagon Papers* (New York: Bantam Books, 1971), p. 630; and Philip Geyelin, *Lyndon B. Johnson and the World* (New York: Praeger, 1966), p. 130.

36. See Miller, *Lyndon*, pp. 539–541; Paul Joseph, *Cracks in the Empire: State Politics in the Vietnam War* (Boston: South End Press, 1981), pp. 271–273; and Hugh Sidey, *A Very Personal Presidency: Lyndon B. Johnson in the White House* (New York: Atheneum, 1968), p. 253.

37. See Roger Hilsman, *The Politics of Policy Making in Defense and Foreign Affairs* (New York: Harper & Row, 1977), pp. 167–168; Halberstam, *The Best and the Brightest*, p. 56; and Parker, *America's Foreign Policy*, p. 13.

38. McGeorge Bundy's pragmatic orientation to problem solving is conveyed by his observation that "gray is the color of truth." Bundy's views are quoted in Henry Brandon, *Anatomy of Error: The Inside Story of Asian War on the Potomac, 1954–1969* (Boston: Gambit, 1969), p. 112. See also Parker, *America's Foreign Policy*, p. 114.

39. Henry F. Graff, *The Tuesday Cabinet: Deliberation and Decision on Peace and War under Lyndon Johnson* (Englewood Cliffs, N.J.: Prentice-Hall, 1970), pp. 20–21. Another of Kennedy's advisers, Arthur M. Schlesinger, Jr., believes that McGeorge Bundy came very close to realizing JFK's expressed hope of establishing a semisecret State Department in the White House, where foreign affairs were actually conducted. See Parker, *America's Foreign Policy*, p. 14; and Schlesinger, *A Thousand Days*, pp. 406–407.

40. Lincoln P. Bloomfield, *The Foreign Policy Process: A Modern Primer* (Englewood Cliffs, N.J.: Prentice-Hall, 1982), p. 49. See also Graff, *The Tuesday Cabinet*, pp. 47–48.

41. See Geyelin, *Lyndon B. Johnson and the World*, p. 150. For a somewhat contrary view, emphasizing Bundy's understanding of the role of Congress, see Graff, *The Tuesday Cabinet*, p. 48.

42. Bundy, for example, equated the defense of South Vietnam with earlier American firmness in resisting communist pressures in the cases of Berlin, South Korea, and more recently, during the Cuban missile crisis. See Brandon, *Anatomy of Error*, p. 16. For a vigorous defense in McGeorge Bundy's own words of President Johnson's policies in opposition to communism, see Bundy's "The Presidency and the Peace," *Foreign Affairs* 42 (April 1964): pp. 353–366. See also *The Pentagon Papers*, pp. 254–255; and the discussion of McGeorge Bundy's views on American policy in Vietnam in Walter Isaacson and Evan Thomas, *The Wise Men: Six Friends and the World They Made* (New York: Simon & Schuster, 1986), pp. 679–680.

43. More-detailed discussion of McGeorge Bundy's actual duties and responsibilities as ANSA may be found in Miller, *Lyndon*, pp. 485–724; *The Pentagon Papers*, pp. 126–127, 389–390, 400–401, 405, 442–443, and 506–527; Joseph, *Cracks in the Empire*, pp. 156 and 231; Graff, *The Tuesday Cabinet*, pp. 48–49 and 94–95; and Johnson, *The Vantage Point*, pp. 122–123, 128–129, 181–203, 234–235, 240–243, 299–302, and 373.

44. See Arthur Cyr, "How Important Is National Security Structure to National Security Policy?" in James M. McCormick, ed., *A Reader in American Foreign Policy* (Itasca, Ill.: F. E. Peacock, 1986), pp. 268–269.

45. See Johnson, *The Vantage Point,* pp. 516–518; and Hoopes, *The Limits of Intervention,* pp. 159–168.

46. See Schlesinger, *A Thousand Days,* pp. 420–421. See also Richard Brown, "Toward Coherence in Foreign Policy: Greater Presidential Control of the Foreign Policy Machinery," in R. Gordon Hoxie, ed., *The President and National Security Policy* (New York: Center for the Presidency, 1984), pp. 334–335. W. W. Rostow's ideas on economic and political issues—especially his theories about development in the Third World—are conveyed in his *The Stages of Economic Growth* (Cambridge: Harvard University Press, 1960); his *Politics and the Stages of Growth* (New York: Cambridge University Press, 1971); and his memoirs while serving in the Kennedy and Johnson administrations, *The Diffusion of Power: An Essay in Recent History* (New York: Macmillan, 1972). President John F. Kennedy said of Rostow that he had "ten ideas every day," only one of which was worthwhile. Quoted in Brandon, *Anatomy of an Error,* pp. 28–29. Miller classifies Rostow as among those who seriously misadvised President Johnson during the Vietnam War. See Miller, *Lyndon,* pp. 539–540.

47. For a more detailed discussion of the process by which President Kennedy decided to appoint Dean Rusk secretary of state, see Sorensen, *Kennedy,* pp. 256–278. See also Dean Acheson, *Present at the Creation: My Years in the State Department* (New York: Norton, 1969), pp. 255, 402, 423, and 432.

48. See the characterizations of Dean Rusk by Sorensen, *Kennedy,* pp. 252–270, 287–289, 391, 590–599, and 726; by Schlesinger, *A Thousand Days,* pp. 407–413, 433–438, 612–613, 986–993, and 1017; and by one of the earliest State Department dissenters on the Vietnam War, Paul Kattenberg, in *The Vietnam Trauma,* pp. 126–127. W. Averell Harriman believed that on many aspects of Vietnam policy, Rusk was guilty of "ceding policy making to the Pentagon." See Isaacson and Thomas, *The Wise Men,* pp. 636–637. During the Korean War, after a series of American defeats at Chinese hands, Dean Rusk had felt compelled to "buck up" the military when it was in a defeatist mood. Ibid., pp. 678–679.

49. See Acheson, *Present at the Creation,* pp. 402 and 423; David S. McLellan, *Dean Acheson: The State Department Years* (New York: Dodd, Mead, 1976), p. 320; Dean Rusk, "The President and the Secretary of State," in *Virginia Papers on the Presidency,* ed. Kenneth Thompson (Lanham, Md.: University Press of America, 1980), p. 9; Hoopes, *The Limits of Intervention* p. 172; and the portrait of Dean Rusk in Isaacson and Thomas, *The Wise Men,* pp. 703–705.

50. Hoopes, *The Limits of Intervention,* p. 17.

51. More-detailed evaluations of Robert McNamara's performance as secretary of defense under Presidents Kennedy and Johnson are William W. Kaufmann, *The McNamara Strategy* (New York: Harper & Row, 1964); and

C. W. Borklund, *Men of the Pentagon: From Forrestal to McNamara* (New York: Praeger, 1966). A highly critical account is John C. Donovan, *The Cold Warriors: A Policy-Making Elite* (Lexington, Mass.: D. C. Heath, 1974), pp. 150–175.

52. Numerous concrete examples of Secretary McNamara's views on the Vietnam War are contained in the *New York Times* edition of *The Pentagon Papers.*

53. The process by which Clark Clifford gradually changed from a defender to a critic of the Johnson administration's policies toward Southeast Asia is described in his own account, "A Viet Nam Reappraisal," *Foreign Affairs* 47 (July 1969): 601–623. See also Hoopes, *The Limits of Intervention,* pp. 159–225.

54. An informative treatment of the "Tuesday lunch group" as an advisory forum is Graff, *The Tuesday Cabinet.*

55. One study emphasizes that, in the advisory processes of the Johnson White House, individuals were always more important to LBJ than were formal mechanisms and institutions. See Clark and Legere, *The President and the Management of National Security,* p. 83. Another study calls attention to the degree to which President Johnson delighted in bypassing the established procedures of the State and Defense departments by relying heavily on unofficial advisers outside the government. See Goldman, *The Tragedy of Lyndon Johnson,* pp. 453–454.

56. See the recent study of several influential members of what was sometimes called "the elders," by Isaacson and Thomas, *The Wise Men.* See also Parker, *America's Foreign Policy;* Brandon, *Anatomy of Error,* pp. 118–140; Hoopes, *The Limits of Intervention, pp. 139–202;* and Johnson, *The Vantage Point,* pp. 365–437 and 493–532.

57. After the disastrous Bay of Pigs invasion of Cuba in 1961, President John F. Kennedy was motivated to take the conduct of foreign relations more directly into his own hands. One account holds that in responding to the Dominican crisis of 1965, President Johnson directly "assumed the direction of day-to-day policy" and served in effect as "the Dominican desk officer" in the State Department! See Ball, *The Past Has Another Pattern,* p. 329. For a detailed analysis of the pattern by an earlier president who served as "his own secretary of state"—Franklin D. Roosevelt—see Cecil V. Crabb, Jr., and Kevin V. Mulcahy, *Presidents and Foreign Policy Making: From FDR to Reagan* (Baton Rouge: Louisiana State University Press, 1986), pp. 82–122.

58. The problem of disunity and disarray within NATO during the Vietnam War and the period that followed are dealt with more fully in Johnson, *The Vantage Point,* pp. 305–322; Henry A. Kissinger, *The Troubled Partnership* (New York: McGraw-Hill, 1965); Thomas J. Kennedy, Jr., *NATO Politico-Military Consultation* (Washington, D.C.: National Defense University Press, 1984); and John Palmer, *The Crisis in Atlantic Relations* (New York: Oxford University Press, 1988).

59. For a comprehensive evaluation of the concept, see Arthur Schlesinger, Jr., *The Imperial Presidency* (Boston: Houghton Mifflin, 1973).

The Johnson presidency is examined on pp. 177–208. Congressional activism in foreign affairs since the Vietnam War is the principal theme of Cecil V. Crabb, Jr., and Pat Holt, *Invitation to Struggle: Congress, the President and Foreign Policy,* 2nd ed. (Washington, D.C.: Congressional Quarterly Press, 1984). See also Thomas Franck and Edward Weisband, *Foreign Policy by Congress* (New York: Oxford University Press, 1979).

60. In President Johnson's view, he had been chosen by the American people to decide the nation's foreign policy. See Miller, *Lyndon,* pp. 530–531; and Sidey, *A Very Personal Presidency,* p. 253.

61. See George H. Quester, *American Foreign Policy: The Lost Consensus* (New York: Praeger, 1982); Albert Cantrill, *The American People, Vietnam, and the Presidency* (Princeton, N. J.: Princeton University Press, 1976); and Ralph B. Levering, *The Public and American Foreign Policy, 1918–1978* (New York: Morrow, 1978).

62. See again the basic contention of Janis in *Groupthink.* Yet Clark Clifford's position was that President Johnson's senior adviser supported his effort to contain communism in Southeast Asia as a matter of basic conviction, not of coercion. See Clifford's views, as reported in Miller, *Lyndon,* p. 531. Another commentator's view is that in reality, LBJ "listened eagerly to any alternatives [to existing policy] that anyone could think up." But he demanded "loyalty" from his subordinates once a choice had been made among these alternatives. See Sidey, *A Very Personal Presidency,* p. 254.

63. The concept of bipartisanship in early post–World War II American foreign policy is examined in detail in Cecil V. Crabb, Jr., *Bipartisan Foreign Policy: Myth or Reality?* (New York: Harper & Row, 1957). See also H. Bradford Westerfield, *Foreign Policy and Party Politics* (New Haven, Conn.: Yale University Press, 1955). A more recent analysis of the phenomenon is Paula Stern, *Domestic Politics and the Making of American Foreign Policy* (Westport, Conn.: Greenwood Press, 1979).

64. The Nixon Doctrine is examined more fully in Crabb, *The Doctrines of American Foreign Policy,* pp. 278–325.

CHAPTER 7

The Nixon Administration:
The National Security Adviser
as Agent

The Nixon administration witnessed a dramatic turnaround in both the substance of American foreign policy and its administration. President Richard Nixon, with the collaboration of his National Security Adviser Henry Kissinger, introduced far-reaching revisions in the conduct of American foreign affairs. The Nixon Doctrine introduced the concept of detente with the Soviet Union and the normalization of relations with the communist government of mainland China. Kissinger, with the NSC staff, served as an indispensable instrument in one of the most dramatic redefinitions of American security interests ever. Kissinger not only emerged as the president's chief aide in this process but also developed and supervised an NSC system that effectively displaced the State Department as the locus of foreign policy making. Whatever criticisms there may be of Nixon and Kissinger personally, and of detente and their NSC system, there is no question that the policies Nixon and Kissinger inaugurated in the early 1970s reoriented the principles on which the United States would conduct its international relations.

▌ Detente as Deterrence

Given America's experience with the war in Vietnam, which seemed both endless and victoryless, the need for a reassessment of the nation's international priorities to reflect military capabilities was painfully evident.

In particular, the restoration of American power in world politics would entail the following prerequisites: first, a liquidation of the Vietnam conflict in a way that would avert a dangerous polarization of American society and still preserve the reputation of the United States as a country that sustained its commitments; second, a realistic reordering of the nation's priority interests so as to avoid squandering its resources in the service of idealistic goals peripheral to the central balance of military and geopolitical power; third, the development of a concept of international order—that while consistent with the priority interests of the United States—would provide a standard of legitimacy to which most nations could attach themselves, and, finally, purposeful and dramatic action on global issues so that this country's leaders, once again, would be looked to as the main pace-setters in the international arena.[1]

A key element in this so-called Nixon Doctrine was the need for the U.S. to retrench its foreign commitments so it could more effectively and efficiently use its power. As President Nixon said, "I began with the proposition that we would keep all our existing treaty commitments, but that we would not make any more commitments unless they were required by our own vital interests."[2]

When Nixon thus asserted that national interests must shape security commitments, rather than the other way around, he was echoing a doctrine of international relations that has been termed *realpolitik.* As a guide for national security, realpolitik assumes the primacy of a "balance of power" and the national interest.[3] According to this doctrine, as nations seek to further their interests in world politics, a central goal of American foreign policy must be to construct an international environment that is supportive of American security and well-being. Implicit in such a conception of a stable international order is a recognition of the interests that other nations pursue in world politics. For example, Anatol Rapaport has argued that successful detente between the United States and the Soviet Union must be predicated on a de facto acceptance of the stake that each has in maintaining its respective international interests and influence.[4]

Under the Nixon Doctrine the realization of detente—that is, an easing of tension between the U.S. and the USSR—was seen as a necessary precondition for a "structure of peace." The general goal of detente required negotiation of specific arms control agreements and an overall reduction in competitive tensions. This, in turn, required that both the United States and the Soviet Union recognize a basic parity in strategic weaponry and accept each other's security interests. What Nixon and Kissinger proposed, in effect, was a new world order in which the United States would no longer seek to act as the "policeman of the free world." Rather, different spheres of influence would be recognized in which allied nations would bear the responsibility for maintaining regional security interests. As Henry Kissinger put it, "We can continue to contribute to defense and positive programs, but we must seek to encourage and not stifle a sense of local responsibility. Our contribution should not be the whole or principal effort, but it should make the difference between success and failure."[5] In effect, the essential precondition for American support of an endangered ally would be the willingness of the country in question to demonstrate an ability to provide for its own security.

The "realism" involved in such a policy has not been without critics from different parts of the American political spectrum. For many, the Nixon–Kissinger approach eschewed more far-reaching goals such as military superiority or a just world order. As an alternative model of strategic thinking, the Nixon Doctrine represented an effort to reassess America's role in the international order in light of the limits on power that had become evident in America's

Vietnam experience. It may be understood as seeking "to enable the United States to do essentially as much in the world as before, but with an economy of means, a fairer distribution of burdens, and a more rational allocation of tasks among allies."[6]

The most immediate foreign policy problem that faced the Nixon administration was to achieve an "honorable" resolution to the war in Vietnam. Disengaging from the war, however, proved to be a long and politically volatile process that was not finally completed until January 27, 1973—four years after Nixon became president. Nixon and Kissinger pursued a two-pronged approach toward ending this "endless war." First was the phased withdrawal of American troops from the ground war while continuing air support. The second phase consisted of following the "de-Americanization" of the war with its "Vietnamization." This involved modernizing the South Vietnamese army to enable it to assume full responsibility for the fighting. The United States would "train, equip, and inspire the South Vietnamese to fill the gap" created by the withdrawal of American ground forces.[7] Of course, the success of this Vietnamization policy depended on the willingness of the Hanoi government to give its adversaries in Saigon the breathing space they needed to rearm as the American presence was phased out. Significantly, the North Vietnamese government agreed to recognize the political sovereignty of the American-backed regime, allowing the Nixon administration to disengage from hostilities with the appearance of honor. However, what Hanoi conceded in January 1973 it regained in the spring of 1975, when the Saigon government collapsed precipitously in the face of a North Vietnamese military offensive.

The so-called loss in Vietnam was proof to some that the United States lacked not only the power but the determination to fulfill its commitments to allied nations. Others argued that Nixon's Vietnamization policy had protracted a conflict that was militarily hopeless, morally indefensible, or both. Regardless, this loss freed the United States to refocus its attention on the crucial and neglected matter of strategic balance between itself and the Soviet Union. In effect, the Nixon administration cut its losses in a protracted land war in Asia to recoup broader American security interests. If Vietnam was lost, this was necessary to the success of detente.

As John Spanier has noted, "at the center of detente with the Soviet Union stood the Strategic Arms Limitation Talks (SALT)."[8] While the United States was engaged in Vietnam, the Soviet Union had moved from a position of strategic inferiority to one of parity with the United States, and possibly of superiority in at least some categories of nuclear weaponry. Significant figures within the foreign policy community argued that qualitative and quantitative increases in the Soviet nuclear arsenal had undermined the "balance of terror" on which the system of mutual deterrence was based.

In particular, the Nixon administration concluded that the Soviet Union had developed a first-strike capacity that would allow it to destroy American land-based missiles without fear of retaliatory annihilation. If the two superpowers could come to a mutually acceptable arms agreement, this would constitute recognition of the strategic parity and diplomatic equality between the two nations that was the basis of detente. "SALT, in brief, became a symbol of detente. With it, detente seemed to be blossoming; without it detente seemed to be fading. A SALT agreement or failure to arrive at an agreement became the barometer of detente."[9]

Negotiations directed at achieving a Soviet–American arms control agreement began in late 1969 and culminated on May 21, 1972, when Richard Nixon and Leonid Brezhnev signed the SALT I accords. These efforts were directed at securing agreement on a quantitative limitation on nuclear arms—one that limited the number of delivery vehicles (such as missiles and bombers) each country possessed. (In contrast to the SALT II agreement that followed in the late 1970s but that was never ratified, SALT I did not restrict the overall nuclear firepower allowed each superpower.) In essence, SALT I sought to preserve the prevailing nuclear symmetry by freezing the number of missile launchers that each country was allowed to possess. SALT I also prohibited both nations from converting short-range missiles into long-range ones and taking other steps that would alter the military equilibrium that had been established.

When SALT I was signed in 1972, the United States had 1,054 land-based intercontinental ballistic missiles compared to the Soviet Union's 1,618. Note that the SALT agreements dealt only with the quantity of nuclear weapons each country had and did not address other characteristics of other existing weapons systems.[10] For example, SALT I did not apply to mobile ICBMs such as the much-debated MX missile system. The SALT I accords also did not apply to intermediate range, or so-called theater, nuclear weapons. These would be the subject of the Intermediate Nuclear Force (INF) Treaty negotiated in 1988 and the yet to be concluded START, or Strategic Arms Reduction Talks. What is important to remember, however, is that SALT I represented the first time that the two superpowers had agreed to limit the number of strategic weapons each could possess. If nothing else, SALT I thus established an invaluable precedent for superpower cooperation in limiting their nuclear arsenals.

To speak of detente as if it were only a Soviet–American matter would be a mistake. Along with SALT I and Vietnamization, the normalization of relations with the People's Republic of China (PRC) was a necessary third element of the Nixon Doctrine's defensive reassessment. Indeed, it can be argued "that detente with China was a prerequisite for detente with the Soviet Union."[11] From a realpolitik perspective, normalizing relations with the PRC represented an opportunity for the United States to take advantage of a falling out between its two principal adversaries. Kissinger argued "that the Soviets were more likely to be conciliatory if they feared we would otherwise seek a rapprochement with Peking."[12] The Sino–American alliance created a new balance of power within the international system, one in which China would serve to check the Soviet Union's superiority in conventional military forces as the United States checked its nuclear power.

It could be judged "a major event in American foreign policy when a president declared that we have a strategic interest in the survival of a communist country, long an enemy, and with which we had no contact."[13] As we have indicated, the "China card" that the United States played in normalizing relations with the PRC was meant to trump the Soviet Union's long suit in conventional military forces. All trumps, however, must be played selectively. As the United States was careful to remind the Soviet Union, the Sino–American friendship was not a defensive alliance between the two countries, nor was the United States, as the architect of detente, interested in intensifying conflict between the Soviet Union and other nations. Nonetheless, American (and Soviet) officials were aware of the strategic advantages of a close relationship with China. These advantages were influential in changing the course of Soviet–American, as well as Sino–American, relations. In this, and in the other ways we have discussed, detente represented a historic diplomatic volte-face—that is, an almost unprecedented turnaround in the relations between the two superpowers.

▌ The Nixon–Kissinger NSC System

With Richard Nixon's assumption of the presidency in 1969 came a dramatic overhaul of the national security advisory process. Where Truman and Eisenhower had regarded the secretary of state as the principal architect of foreign policy, and even Kennedy conceded him pride of place, Nixon actively opposed granting his secretary of state a major role in policy formulation. Kissinger, acting as Nixon's solitary surrogate for foreign affairs virtually replaced Secretary of State William P. Rogers, and the NSC functioned as a "rival State Department." As assistant for national security affairs (ANSA), Henry Kissinger was, in effect, the president's foreign secretary. Later in the Nixon administration, Kissinger would achieve de jure what he had de facto: that is, he would serve concurrently as secretary of state and national security adviser.

Whatever personality traits may have disposed Nixon toward an insular style of governance, his deep hostility to the State Department seemed to derive from his perception of the department as the epitome of the Eastern establishment. Nixon seemed to harbor resentment over what he had perceived as snubs by Foreign Service officers when he was vice president; in reaction, as president, he was determined to circumvent the State Department's traditional role in foreign policy making and to conduct foreign policy from the White House.[14] As Nixon observed in his memoirs, "Therefore I regarded my choice of a National Security Adviser as crucial."[15] Nixon's diminution of the State Department's standing in the day-to-day policy-making process and his concurrent enhancement of the NSC staff's role allowed for the creation of a new system dominated by Kissinger as national security adviser. In his role as ANSA Kissinger combined the duties of Eisenhower's special assistants (coordinating policy planning) with those of Bundy and Rostow (serving as personal presidential counselors) to achieve an unparalleled preeminence.[16]

Kissinger recommended that Nixon institute more-formal operations for the NSC than Johnson had used. President Johnson's decision-making process, according to Kissinger, comprised too many informal meetings without adequate staff work, records of decisions, and follow-up procedures. Too often, departments could interpret the outcomes of such informal meetings as they saw fit. On the other hand, Kissinger thought that Nixon should avoid Eisenhower's highly formalized system, under which "the policymaking process resembled the formulation of treaties among sovereign departments."[17] As noted, Nixon's elimination of the State Department from serious participation in the day-to-day policy-making process and his enhancement of the role of the NSC staff created a new system dominated by Kissinger in his personal capacity as a White House aide. Where previous administrations had seen incremental shifts in decision-making responsibility from the departments to the White House, the Nixon–Kissinger organizational scheme was a radical alteration in the locus and process of national security policy making.

First, presidents before Nixon recognized, at least in principle, the primacy of the State Department and its secretary in the conduct of international relations. William Rogers, however, was largely a cipher in an NSC system that was essentially a dyad comprising the president and his assistant for national security affairs.

Second, despite early pronouncements about the importance of "cabinet government," it was obvious from the early days of the Nixon administration that the Kissinger-directed NSC would concentrate power in the White House to the exclusion of the departments and agencies that had traditionally handled national security matters. Even as Nixon insisted that William Rogers was "the chief foreign policy adviser and chief foreign policy spokesman of the Administration," he also asserted with regard to foreign policy and national security policy that Kissinger was responsible for "the coordination of these policies."[18]

Third, the NSC staff reported to the Office of the Assistant to the President for National Security Affairs, while Kissinger reported to Nixon alone. In place of the issue-specific study groups of the Kennedy administration, Kissinger organized the NSC staff into regional and functional units that competed with the bureaus of the line agencies. Kissinger, not a State Department official, chaired the important interdepartmental committees such as the Washington Special Action Group (set up to deal with international crises) and the Senior Policy Group (a top-level deliberative body for reviewing the studies prepared by working groups).[19]

Overall, the purpose of Kissinger's NSC system was to strengthen the intellectual and bureaucratic resources of the White House to ensure direct presidential control over national security policy making.[20] Kissinger succeeded admirably in realizing Nixon's intention. Administratively, the State Department was displaced to the periphery of policy formulation; politically, the White House situation room replaced the State Department's seventh floor as the forum for decision making.

Kissinger's power as ANSA reflected Nixon's management style as president. "It suits Nixon to deal with the foreign affairs government principally through one man, and his trust in Kissinger grew very strong very early."[21] In particular, Nixon had a strong desire for solitary, personal decision making. Circumventing departmental officials and entrusting representation of the presidential will to a White House aide fulfilled the first criterion. Developing an avenue of communications with foreign leaders that supplemented the usual diplomatic cables and intelligence sources fulfilled the second. Nixon and Kissinger used the White House situation room as a communications center for negotiating major diplomatic initiatives, such as the normalization of relations with China and the preliminary protocols to SALT I. As Kissinger suggests below, these breakthroughs were personal covenants, privately arrived at.

> As time went by, the President, or I on his behalf . . . came to deal increasingly with key foreign leaders through channels that directly linked the White House Situation Room to the field without going through the State Department—the so-called backchannels. This process started on the day after Inauguration.[22]

After his tenure at the State Department, Kissinger declared his conviction, while admitting that he had not held it while working at the White House, that the secretary of state should be every administration's chief foreign policy spokesman. The national security adviser, in contrast, should play only a coordinating role in ensuring that all points of view on a proposed policy are heard, he said. "If the security adviser becomes active in the development and articulation of policy, he must inevitably diminish the Secretary of State and reduce his effectiveness."[23] This, of course, was exactly Secretary Rogers's experience.

In *Years of Upheaval,* Kissinger expanded further on the proper role of the ANSA, emphasizing that the security adviser's contact with media and foreign diplomats should be minimal. The secretary of state, Kissinger argued, should be responsible for the articulation and conduct of foreign policy in conjunction with the president. The national security adviser, on the other hand, should be responsible for running the interdepartmental machinery that prepares policy options. The preferred characteristics of the ANSA are "fairness, conceptual grasp, bureaucratic savvy and a willingness to labor anonymously."[24] General Brent Scowcroft, in his first tenure as ANSA under President Ford, has been cited as an outstanding example of the qualities necessary for the successful occupant of this position.

Of course, Kissinger's record as national security adviser evinced the exact opposite of this ideal role behavior. As ANSA, Kissinger dominated the processes involved in formulating national security policy—making many decisions himself, advocating others, and acting as the primary presidential representative for foreign affairs. This virtually eliminated any distinction between the duties of the assistant and those of the secretary of state: "The staff man became the key line operator in every important respect."[25]

Before the end of Nixon's first term, Kissinger was unquestionably the prime presidential adviser on foreign affairs. "If Bundy had intruded on the role of the Secretary of State, Kissinger obliterated it. In so doing, he became Nixon's agent."[26] As the president's agent, Kissinger not only briefed Nixon daily on the nation's security but increasingly spoke on behalf of the president and finally served as the principal negotiator in matters relating to Vietnam, China, and SALT. Since (a) these were the main items on the Nixon foreign policy agenda, (b) Kissinger was the focal point for both their conceptual and operational realization, and (c) the NSC system was the means by which foreign policy could be conducted from the White House, Kissinger was firmly installed atop the bureaucratic structure, with decisive control over both the formulation and the conduct of policy. The de facto powers this position gave him were greater than those granted by the Constitution to the secretaries of state and defense. Exploited and extended to become a vehicle for Kissinger's extraordinary talents, that position of power created a new pattern of government in Washington for foreign relations.

The Nixon administration represents the high point of what has been termed "the rise of the Assistant." Kissinger demonstrated the kind of role that the ANSA could create for himself by fully exploiting the office's potential. To be a Kissinger is to be a national security adviser who exercises virtually unchallenged plenipotentiary powers as the president's agent. The likelihood of another ANSA acting like Kissinger would be improbable if not impossible. It would require a special combination of extraordinary personal skills, relatively weak bureaucratic competitors, and a well-organized and well-staffed NSC system. Above all else, Kissinger flourished because Nixon chose to administer foreign policy directly from the White House and put his confidence in Kissinger as his agent in executing his plans.

Upon assuming the presidency in 1969, Richard Nixon pledged to revitalize the National Security Council and restore to it the position and authority that it had held during the Eisenhower administration. This is not surprising, for, having served as Eisenhower's vice president, Nixon was well versed in the process of formulating and implementing a complex system of national security policy. On the surface, Nixon spoke of returning the NSC to the role it had played during the 1950s, but clearly the new president had something else in mind. By instituting new policy channels and reorganizing the flow of policy to the top, Nixon made his NSC system "a kind of command and control center for his foreign policy."[27]

The NSC system that Kissinger devised and maintained rivaled the Eisenhower system in its structural complexity. A fundamental difference between the two systems, however, lay in the role of the national security adviser and the purpose of the interdepartmental committee structure. Where Robert Cutler, as Eisenhower's assistant, operated essentially as a neutral custodian of the advisory machinery, Kissinger ran the system as its undisputable leader. In the Eisenhower system, departmental differences were carefully noted for NSC resolution, and implementation was left as a departmental responsibility under the review of the Operations Coordinating Board; in contrast, the Nixon administration, through the NSC system, sought to concentrate power in the White House, to the exclusion of the departments and agencies that had traditionally handled national security matters. Cutler had served to coordinate policy made largely by Eisenhower himself in a system dominated by the State

Department and its secretary, John Foster Dulles. Kissinger, on the other hand, was a powerful substantive actor and quickly dominated national security matters to the exclusion of the State Department.

Some note needs to be made of the principal NSC components that assisted Kissinger in advising President Nixon. The basic building blocks of the Kissinger system were interdepartmental groups (IGs). These were made up of representatives at the assistant secretary level from the Departments of State and Defense, the CIA, the Joint Chiefs of Staff, and the NSC staff. Organized into working groups by either region or function, IGs worked up options—but did not make recommendations—for later action. Although chaired by a State Department official, IGs reported to Kissinger as assistant for national security affairs. The policy papers prepared by the IGs were in turn reviewed by the Senior Review Group (SRG) before being forwarded to the NSC or the president. Composed of the deputy secretaries of state and defense, the CIA director, and the chairman of the JCS, and chaired by Kissinger as ANSA, the Senior Review Group made specific policy recommendations in the form of national security study memoranda (NSSM), providing directives for specific courses of action to be undertaken by the particular departments that were to be responsible for implementing specific policy decisions and specifying the goal to be achieved, who was responsible for achieving it, and when it was to be achieved.

Through his chairmanship of the Defense Program Review Committee (responsible for military budgets), the NSC Intelligence Committee (responsible for reviewing and evaluating intelligence reports), and the Verification Panel (responsible for making recommendations on arms control subjects), Kissinger exercised broad supervision over politico-military decision making. In addition, he chaired the Washington Special Action Group, which served as an operations center for the management of sudden crises and emergencies.

Overall, Kissinger involved himself in every major policy issue. All policy issues had to pass him before reaching the president. Kissinger was assisted by a staff of more than 130 (of whom about 50 were policy professionals) in operating this "little State Department" at the White House. With Kissinger's help, Nixon could effectively manage the formulation and elaboration of national security policy from within the precincts of the west wing. Eventually, the frequency of National Security Council meetings would diminish dramatically as Nixon, with Kissinger's advice and the support services of the NSC staff, centralized foreign policy making in the White House.

The Nixon administration marked a clear turning point in what has been described more fully as the "rise of the Assistant." As the author of a 1977 study on national security affairs stated, "under President Nixon the NSC was restored to a central, if not dominating, role in the policy process, acting as the major vehicle and conduit for the formation of national security policy."[28] To the extent that this statement is true, Nixon was very successful in implementing a national security system that worked for him. He trusted few people, and this distrust brought about a predominance of activity in the White House, with extraordinary power vested in his assistant for national security affairs.

▮ Kissinger as National Security Adviser

It may be that the virulence of university politics (a characterization attributed to a former political science professor, Woodrow Wilson) provides good training for the bureaucratic battlefield of the White House. Kissinger was hardly the first college professor to hold high public office: FDR, JFK, and LBJ had all made extensive use of professorial talent. Kissinger's immediate predecessors as national security adviser, McGeorge Bundy and W. W. Rostow, were professors, as was Zbigniew Brzezinski in the Carter administration. Nonetheless, no one has assumed this position with such a well-developed theory of international relations as Kissinger, and no one since World War II has commanded the foreign policy making process so effectively for so long.

In his Harvard doctoral dissertation, Kissinger developed a full-scale interpretation of international relations through a study of European diplomatic history in the generation after Napoleon's fall. Published in 1957, *The World Restored: Castlereagh, Metternich, and the Restoration of Peace, 1812–1822* was an unusual combination of *tour d'horizon* and personal reflection. Even as a doctoral student, Kissinger had formulated certain basic notions, such as the distinction between "legitimate" and "revolutionary" states, that were to inform not only his later writings but also his policies as ANSA and secretary of state.[29] One commentator has argued for the continuity in Kissinger's thinking as follows: "His diplomacy as Secretary of State is deeply rooted in the insights of the young doctoral student at Harvard. . . . It is, in fact, a virtual transplant from the world of thought into the world of power."[30]

It is beyond the scope of this study to discuss fully Kissinger's theories about the conduct of international relations.[31] However, three elements of his thinking warrant discussion here, particularly because of their relationship to the Nixon Doctrine. These may be summarized as follows:

1. A stable world order is a necessary precondition for a peaceful world.
2. Stability rests on a shared belief among nations in the legitimacy of the world order.
3. The ever-changing political goals of nations must be accommodated through periodic reformulations of the balance of power.

Metternich's fundamental insight was that Napoleon represented a revolutionary force that the state system then existing could not accommodate. Following Napoleon's defeat, Austria, Prussia, Russia, and a rehabilitated France formed the Concert of Europe, which guaranteed stability for a century. Kissinger's fundamental insight was that the USSR and the PRC had ceased being revolutionary powers and had come to accept the post–World War II balance of power. Soviet–American nuclear parity, in particular, gave every nation a stake in the survival of this world order—however flawed and in need of revision. The great challenge was to accommodate competing and conflicting interests without resort to a general war, especially when this carried the possibility of an all-out thermonuclear exchange.

For Kissinger, the possibility of a nuclear calamity made maintenance of the balance of power necessary, not as a static system but as a dynamic process that could respond and adapt to developments within the status quo. This power balance required an ongoing equilibrium to be maintained among the various nations, and especially between the superpowers, that would allow international political adjustments without a breakdown in the system itself. In essence, this necessary equilibrium depended on the commitment of the superpowers to a system of mutual acceptance that, while often precarious, provided an alternative to nuclear anarchy.

Kissinger's selection as Nixon's national security adviser was considered unusual because he had no prior friendship with the reclusive president-elect. Moreover, Kissinger had been a campaign adviser to Nixon's rival for the 1968 nomination, Nelson Rockefeller, and had not thought favorably of Nixon.[32] By dint of unflagging personal loyalty, however, Kissinger established a close bond between himself and President Nixon. Kissinger was the only post-election acquaintance of Nixon to achieve such a personal intimacy with the president.[33] Most important, the closeness Kissinger cultivated with Nixon allowed him to become the most successful of the "foreign policy intellectuals" who had come to serve in the government during the past fifty years.

This new class of actors in the foreign policy making process was a loose category of individuals associated with major university research centers (such as the Johns Hopkins University School of Advanced International Studies), think tanks specializing in the study of national security issues (such as the Rand Corporation), and private foundations (such as the Carnegie Endowment for International Peace and the Council on Foreign Relations). Kissinger was a prominent member of this intellectual class before entering the White House: as a Harvard professor; the author of *Nuclear Weapons and Foreign Policy;* a frequent contributor to *Foreign Affairs*, published by the Council on Foreign Relations; and a consultant to the State Department on various arms control panels. If there was a foreign policy establishment, Kissinger was a member in good standing.

What principally distinguishes Kissinger from others with a similar background—such as McGeorge Bundy, W. W. Rostow, and Zbigniew Brzezinski—was the unparalleled power that he exercised as the assistant for national security affairs. Indeed, Kissinger was one of the most influential presidential assistants to have emerged in the fifty-year history of the Executive Office of the President. Kissinger's influence was restricted to foreign affairs, but no White House aide has ever enjoyed greater command of such a key policy area of American government. Perhaps only Harry Hopkins (when he ran the Lend–Lease program for FDR), Sherman Adams (when he served as the assistant to the president under Eisenhower), and H. R. Haldeman (Nixon's chief of staff before Watergate) have rivaled Kissinger in their political importance as White House aides. Even so omnipotent a chief of staff as Haldeman did not encroach on Kissinger's foreign policy turf.[34] A contemporary account of the Nixon administration certified Kissinger's importance and added, "What no one saw at first, though, was that he would quickly become the President's closest confidant, his principal negotiator, his troubleshooter, his First Minister, overshadowing members of the Cabinet—would become . . . no less than the second most powerful man in the world."[35]

Though this evaluation contains a heavy dose of journalistic license, Kissinger's preeminence in foreign affairs was certainly unequalled. On the other hand, it would be a major error to jump to any conclusions about the presidential assistant superseding the president. Even more than cabinet secretaries (who may enjoy independent political standing or the protection of a powerful interest group), White House aides must faithfully mirror the interests of their sole protector—the president. For all of his stature, Kissinger was no exception to this rule. He himself commented on how dependent a White House aide was on the president's favor and how any aide needed to cater to the president's whims, because an assistant's power derives almost exclusively from the confidence of the president.[36] This presidential confidence is, as we have seen and will continue to see, the necessary adhesive for any successful policy-making relationship, regardless of the particular policy or president involved.

To make use of the historical comparisons that are so often attached to Kissinger, the assistant for national security affairs was no Richelieu or Bismarck conducting foreign affairs virtually independently of the head of state. U.S. foreign policy under Nixon was always more Nixon's than it was Nixon and Kissinger's. We need to emphasize again that Kissinger's influence was as great as it was because his views were in accord with President Nixon's. They saw eye-to-eye on the objectives of American foreign policy and the best means for achieving them. When Nixon said that "the only time in the history of the world that we have had extended periods of peace is when there is a balance of power," he was not quoting Kissinger.[37] Rather, both men echoed Metternich's formulation of a stable world order. Nixon and Kissinger also both subscribed to the realpolitik approach of pursuing national security with alliances rooted more in geopolitical realities than in ideology or principle.

If Nixon was the princely patron, Kissinger was the court architect. Kissinger supplied the machinery that translated presidential conceptions into policies. For example, Kissinger had secret meetings with Chinese leaders to block out the specific details of a bilateral agreement that in turn allowed President Nixon and Chairman Mao to negotiate the broad principles of mutual understanding. Since Nixon was uncomfortable in unstructured conversations and disliked appearing ill-prepared at meetings, Kissinger prepared detailed briefing papers, which Nixon would memorize.[38] Kissinger also briefed the press (with whom Nixon felt uneasy) and often served as the administration's foreign policy spokesman. However, Kissinger disabused anyone who might mistake his role as agent with that of principal.

> Presidents, of course, are responsible for shaping the overall strategy. They must make the key decisions; for this they are accountable and for it they deserve full credit no matter how much help they receive along the way. When they attempt

the tactical implementation of their own strategy they court disaster. Nixon never made that mistake.[39]

The compatibility of Kissinger's personality with Nixon's and the similarity of their objectives were essential to Kissinger's success as Nixon's agent. What enabled Kissinger to consolidate and expand his favor with the President was the institutional support the staff of the National Security Council provided. Kissinger used his position as director of the NSC staff to develop an administrative apparatus that could supply the technical support necessary for the successful execution of foreign policy. Where presidents before Nixon may have sought to challenge the State Department's authority, Kissinger created an NSC staff that displaced the department as a policy-making body.

From the earliest days of the Nixon administration, Kissinger established "a near monopoly on the time, attention, and respect of the President of the United States on all matters of foreign policy."[40] As noted earlier, the NSC system that was created advanced Kissinger's power by placing him at the head of an expanded foreign policy-making apparatus within the White House, giving him effective control over the formulations and conduct of national security policy. When combined with his formidable personal skills, Kissinger's White House position represented a new pattern of government for foreign relations. In effect, Kissinger as Nixon's ANSA had "de facto powers greater than the de jure constitutional authority of the Secretaries of State and Defense."[41] As Kissinger observed, such an extraordinary accumulation of decision-making authority resulted from Nixon's long-standing determination "to conduct foreign policy from the White House, his distrust of the existing bureaucracy, coupled with the congruence of his philosophy and mine and the relative inexperience of the new Secretary of State."[42]

▋ The Nixon–Kissinger Era Evaluated

Richard Nixon's departure from the White House in the aftermath of the Watergate scandal in 1973 eclipsed his reputation as an architect of foreign affairs. Over the next decade few references were made to the Nixon Doctrine as a touchstone of American foreign policy. Nonetheless, the principles of the Nixon–Kissinger approach to international relations continued and continue to exercise considerable influence in debates about the proper role of the United States in world affairs. Ironically, the most sustained opposition to these principles came from conservative critics who argued that detente was based on a fundamental misconception: that the Soviet Union would become a responsible international actor if its security were enhanced by strategic parity with the United States. On the other hand, liberal critics have never been comfortable with the primacy that Nixon and Kissinger attached to realpolitik criteria, rather than promoting north–south economic justice or human rights.

Indeed, much of the importance of the Nixon administration's foreign policy lay in its assertion that a nation's foreign policy must approximate its capabilities, rather than its fantasies—military or moral. For Nixon and Kissinger, American national security was founded on the realization that the United States could no longer police the world and that the United States had to adapt to the Soviet Union's achievement of equality in nuclear weaponry.

The Nixon Doctrine was a needed corrective to the almost limitless diplomatic ambitions of the United States from the end of World War II until the end of the Vietnam War. In effect, the Soviet Union was being recognized as a coequal superpower, on the assumption that this would result in a lessening of global tensions and would lead to Soviet restraint in exploiting any power vacuums that might affect American interests.

> U.S.–Soviet arms control efforts, particularly the Strategic Arms Limitation Talks (SALT), were linked by Nixon and Kissinger to this grand strategy. SALT became the most visible and dramatic symbol—and test—of the Soviets' willingness to moderate their power competition with the United States and be bound by mutually acceptable rules.[43]

In effect, Nixon and Kissinger were asking the Soviet Union to join the United States in forming a world concert to guarantee international stability. This new concert was similar to the post-Napoleonic Concert of Europe in being an international arrangement that would facilitate a rational and controlled management of power relations.[44] Successful management of such a concert requires certain preconditions of its members. These include a shared sense of values, mutual recognition of moral and political equality, an agreed-upon means for readjusting power relations, and a long-term commitment to the system. Above all, concert members must have a sufficient stake in the system to make the adjustments necessary to ensure its survival.[45] It is a testimony to the strength of the Nixon–Kissinger concert that, whatever the state of U.S.–Soviet relations in the 1970s and 1980s, the system of joint superpower responsibility for maintaining world peace has endured.

The practical effect of the Nixon doctrine of detente was to replace the Cold War emphasis on verbal confrontation and military containment with a more conciliatory approach that accepted the legitimacy of communist political systems. Nixon's visit to China and the acceptance of strategic parity with the Soviet Union formalized by the SALT I agreements were clear signs that the Cold War was diminishing and a concert was emerging.[46] On the other hand, Soviet cooperation was not simply to be assumed or taken on verbal assurances alone; rather, continued detente was "linked" to continued evidence of Soviet (and Chinese) restraint in international affairs.

In effect, linkage was a new name for an older principle invoked by Truman and Acheson in dealing with the Soviet Union: The United States would look at Soviet actions and not rely simply on words. The linkage principle, for example, specified that detente could not be maintained in the face of Soviet-sponsored "wars of national liberation" in the Third World. The Soviet invasion of Afghanistan in the late 1970s was a blow to detente and further arms control agreements, whereas the Soviet withdrawal ten years later signaled a warming of superpower relations and improved prospects for the treaty on intermediate nuclear forces in Europe. Whether it achieved a full-blown concert or not, the Nixon Doctrine represented a pragmatic attempt to create an international system based on mutual awareness by the U.S. and the USSR that, in this nuclear age, some semblance of order is preferable to disorder.

Apart from its reformulation of superpower relations, the Nixon-Kissinger era will have continuing import because of the changes it introduced in the process of making foreign policy. For the first time, the secretary of state was effectively excluded from diplomatic decision making by the national security adviser. From the beginning, Kissinger recognized the potential of his position in the White House, and he acted decisively to expand his power. Besides having the advantage of a strong background in foreign affairs, he also realized that his position on the White House staff gave him the incomparable additional advantage of propinquity to the president.

Most important, Kissinger realized that national security is a peculiarly presidential responsibility and that presidents are often likely to prefer the advice of a White House aide over that of a cabinet secretary. Statutory provisions now prevent another Kissinger from serving as both assistant for national security affairs and secretary of state. Nevertheless, the success of Kissinger's "rival State Department" serves as a possible model to be emulated by presidents and national security advisers who would dominate foreign policy making from the White House.

For all the international success of the Nixon administration, the president ran up against some fundamental rules governing the making of American public policy. In particular, the official wrongdoing associated with the Watergate scandal led to a general repudiation of President Nixon and his policies.[47] Watergate (as would the Iran–Contra affair) triggered a new aggressiveness on the part of Congress to reassert its constitutional prerogatives in formulating foreign policy. Congressional frustration over the "imperial presidency" came to a head with the Nixon administration's attempt to exercise nearly absolute power. The War Powers Act of 1973 was the most dramatic assertion of the rights of Congress against the president's pretensions in foreign policy making. As events indicated, the importance of the War Powers Act may be more symbolic than real—President Nixon vetoed the legislation, though his veto was overridden, and subsequent presidents have declared themselves opposed to the resolution's provisions. Regardless, the War Powers Act served notice on presidents that Congress would demand to be included in the foreign policy process as a constitutionally mandated partner.

Similarly, Congress protested against the lack of accountability that resulted when foreign policy initiatives were formulated and executed by White House assistants who invoked the doctrine of "executive privilege" to insulate themselves from legislative oversight. In particular, the NSC staff was criticized for engaging in "secret diplomacy" that left the State Department and Congress ignorant of even the basic objectives being negotiated. Critics demanded that there be "no more Kissingers" at the White House beyond the reach of congressional oversight.

On the other hand, a strong national security presidency has been one of the enduring expectations of the public and Congress itself. The strange career of Richard Nixon may have somewhat chastened future presidents with regard to imperialist claims to supremacy in foreign policy making. However, both Presidents Reagan and Bush have taken expansive views of their powers in the conduct of American foreign affairs. Indeed, the exigencies of world affairs reaffirm continually the need for a president who is firmly in control of national security policy making.

NOTES

1. Seyom Brown, *The Crisis of Power: An Interpretation of United States Foreign Policy during the Kissinger Years* (New York: Columbia University Press, 1979), pp. 2–3.

2. Richard Nixon, *The Memoirs of Richard Nixon* (New York: Grosset & Dunlap, 1978), p. 395.

3. For a full discussion of realpolitik, see Cecil V. Crabb, Jr., *Policy-Makers and Critics: Conflicting Theories of American Foreign Policy* (New York: Praeger, 1976), pp. 165–214.

4. Anatol Rapaport, *The Big Two: Soviet-American Perceptions of Foreign Policy* (New York: Bobbs-Merrill, 1971), p. 86.

5. Henry A. Kissinger, "Central Issues in American Foreign Policy" in *Agenda for the Nation,* ed. Kermit Gordon (Washington, D.C.: Brookings Institution, 1968), p. 612.

6. Earl C. Ravenal, "Nixon's Challenge to Carter," *Foreign Policy* 29 (Winter 1977): 37.

7. Nixon, *Memoirs,* p. 392.

8. John Spanier, *American Foreign Policy since World War II,* 9th ed. (New York: Holt, Rinehart, & Winston, 1983), p. 191. For a detailed discussion of detente, see Coral Bell, *The Diplomacy of Detente* (New York: St. Martin, 1977).

9. Spanier, *American Foreign Policy,* p. 193.

10. See Richard Burt, "The Scope and Limit of SALT," *Foreign Affairs* 56 (Summer 1978): 751–771; Aaron L. Freidberg, "What SALT Can and Cannot Do," *Foreign Policy* 33 (Winter 1978–1979): 92–101.

11. Spanier, *American Foreign Policy,* pp. 187–188.

12. Henry Kissinger, *The White House Years* (Boston: Little, Brown, 1979), p. 182.

13. Ibid., p. 182.

14. Ibid., pp. 11–12.

15. Nixon, *Memoirs,* p. 340.

16. For a summary description of the Nixon "palace guard pattern," see Cecil V. Crabb, Jr., and Kevin V. Mulcahy, *Presidents and Foreign Policy Making: FDR to Reagan* (Baton Rouge: Louisiana State University Press, 1986), p. 327.

17. Kissinger, *White House Years,* p. 29–30.

18. I. M. Destler, *Presidents, Bureaucrats, and Foreign Policy* (Princeton, N.J.: Princeton University Press, 1972), p. 131.

19. Mark M. Lowenthal, *The National Security Council: Organizational History* (Washington, D.C.: Congressional Research Service, 1978), pp. 76–77.

20. Alexander George, *Presidential Decisionmaking in Foreign Policy* (Boulder, Colo.: Westview Press, 1980) p. 177.

21. Destler, *Presidents, Bureaucrats, and Foreign Policy,* p. 125.

22. Kissinger, *White House Years,* p. 29.

23. Ibid., p. 30.

24. Henry Kissinger, *Years of Upheaval* (Boston: Little, Brown, 1982), p. 437.

25. I. M. Destler, "National Security II: The Rise of the Assistant," in *The Illusion of Presidential Government,* ed. Hugh Heclo and Lester M. Salamon (Boulder, Colo. Westview Press, 1981) p. 271.

26. I. M. Destler, Leslie H. Gelb, and Anthony Lake, *Our Own Worst Enemy: The Unmaking of American Foreign Policy* (New York: Simon & Schuster, 1984), pp. 208–209.

27. John P. Leacacos, "Kissinger's Apparat," *Foreign Policy* 5 (Winter 1971–1972): 3.

28. U.S. Senate, Committee on Foreign Relations, *The National Security Adviser, Role and Accountability.* 96th Cong., 2nd sess. (Washington, D.C.: Government Printing Office, 1980), p. 25.

29. Harvey Starr, "The Kissinger Years," *International Studies Quarterly* 24 (December 1980): 488.

30. John Stoessinger, *Henry Kissinger: Anguish of Power* (New York: Norton, 1976), p. 7.

31. For a summary of Kissinger's thinking about international relations, see Stephen R. Graubard, *Kissinger: Portrait of a Mind* (New York: Norton, 1974), pp. 13–53. For a critical view, see George Liska, *Beyond Kissinger: Ways of Conservative Statecraft* (Baltimore: Johns Hopkins University Press, 1975).

32. Kissinger, *White House Years,* p. 12.

33. Martin Kalb and Bernard Kalb, *Kissinger* (Boston: Little, Brown), p. 168.

34. For Kissinger's relations with Haldeman, see Kissinger's *Years of Upheaval,* pp. 95–97.

35. Henry Brandon, *The Retreat of American Power* (New York: Doubleday, 1973), p. 24.

36. Kissinger, *White House Years,* pp. 30–31.

37. *Time,* January 3, 1972.

38. For some of Kissinger's observations about Nixon's personality, see *White House Years,* pp. 45, 78, 480–482, 917, and 1475–1476, and *Years of Upheaval,* pp. 103 and 1181–1184.

39. Kissinger, *White House Years,* p. 142.

40. Roger Morris, *Uncertain Greatness: Henry Kissinger and American Foreign Policy* (New York: Harper & Row, 1977), p. 145.

41. Ibid., p. 47.

42. Kissinger, *White House Years,* p. 47.

43. Brown, *Crisis of Power,* p. 143.

44. Stephen A. Garrett, "Nixonian Foreign Policy: A New Balance of Power or a Revived Concert?" *Polity* 8 (Spring 1976): 408.

45. James A. Nathan, "Commitments in Search of a Roost: The Foreign Policy of the Nixon Administration," *Virginia Quarterly* 50 (Summer 1974): 338–339.

46. Garrett, "Nixonian Foreign Policy," p. 398.

47. See Kissinger, *Years of Upheaval,* pp. 122–127, 300–301, and 414–416; Chalmers McRoberts, "Foreign Policy under a Paralyzed Presidency," *Foreign Affairs* 52 (July 1971): 75–89; and McGeorge Bundy, "Vietnam, Watergate and Presidential Powers," *Foreign Affairs* 58 (Winter 1979–1980): 397–407.

CHAPTER 8

Disunity and Disarray in National Security Policy Making: The Carter and Reagan Administrations

Foreign policy making proved to be the political and administrative Achilles' heel of the Carter and Reagan administrations. American policies were widely judged to have been poorly conceived (the Carter administration's actions in Iran and the Reagan administration's in Central America), disastrously managed (the attempted rescue of the American hostages in Iran and the deployment of Marines in Lebanon), or unnecessarily provocative (the development of the MX missile and the deployment of Euromissiles). Of equal importance has been continuing criticism of the foreign policy-making process itself. Both Carter and Reagan were faulted for policies that lacked conceptual coherence and suffered from administrative fragmentation. Underlying such fragmentation has been the long-standing and still unresolved conflict between the secretary of state and the assistant for national security affairs over who would function as the president's chief spokesman for foreign affairs.

Beginning with McGeorge Bundy in the Kennedy administration (see chapter 6), and culminating in Henry Kissinger under Nixon and Ford (see chapter 7), the assistant to the president for national security affairs has often been the equal, and, in some cases, the superior, of the secretary of state in the foreign policy process. Moreover, the National Security Council staff, which the presidential assistant directs, has become institutionalized as a policy-making body. The NSC staff has achieved such decision-making importance that it can now initiate policies of its own, in addition to evaluating and coordinating those of cabinet departments—including the Department of State.

By the 1980s, a national security assistant could claim that he alone comprehended the full scope of American international relations and the policy options involved, whereas cabinet members represented various specialized bureaucratic interests. Finally, the White House staff was directly and actively involved in the foreign policy-making process. Previously, the political and domestic assistants to the president had largely eschewed involvement in diplomacy; this had remained the preserve of a separate foreign policy advisory system (including, of course, the assistant for national security affairs). As discussed in this chapter, however, the ill-fated careers of both Cyrus Vance and Alexander Haig suggest that in any struggle between the State Department and the White House for control of foreign policy, the secretary of state will lose unless he has established a good working relationship with the senior White House aide. Today, the secretary of state cannot maintain power by simply asserting institutional preeminence in foreign policy making.

In this chapter we discuss the ultimately unsuccessful efforts of the secretary of state to establish himself as *the* presidential adviser on foreign policy, focusing primarily on Alexander Haig. To comprehend properly Haig's claims to being the "vicar" of foreign policy, however, it is necessary to understand the earlier relationship between Secretary of State Cyrus Vance and National Security Adviser Zbigniew Brzezinski in the Carter administration. Though not claiming the title of vicar, Vance nevertheless believed himself to be the rightful spokesman for American foreign policy; Vance's efforts to control foreign policy, however, proved as unsuccessful as Haig's were to be. Vance ran afoul of an ambitious presidential assistant in the person of Brzezinski; Haig's conception of his office no longer corresponded to the realities of national security policy making. Both Vance and Haig should have realized from their persistent problems that their claims were impossible. Competition between the president's chief diplomatic adviser and the assistant to the president for national security affairs had become endemic to the foreign policy process.

Whether or not such fragmentation of the policy-making process will continue to characterize American foreign relations is still unclear. The Iran–Contra episode, which will be discussed at length in the next chapter, dramatized the consequences of disunity and disarray in national security policy making. The international political risks associated with continuation of this state of affairs do not need to be reemphasized, but the serious domestic political problems that have also resulted do. The internecine warfare between Vance and Brzezinski caused not only a great deal of skepticism about the reliability of President Carter's foreign policy, but also questioning of Carter's competence with regard to presidential management.

Ronald Reagan also found foreign policy to be a major domestic political liability. This was true not only with regard to the commitment of American troops in foreign operations (such as in Lebanon and Central America) but also with regard to the administrative disarray that resulted from the conflict between the State Department and the NSC under both Alexander Haig and George Shultz. Indeed, as the bureaucratic conflict broadened and persisted, the question of whether or not anyone was in command of American foreign policy making arose. On several occasions, Ronald Reagan had to go to some lengths to persuade the public that he was neither a "part-time president," nor the captain of a chartless and rudderless ship of state. Both Carter and Reagan came to recognize the importance of President Truman's truism about where the buck stopped. Providing direction for the nation's foreign policy is a peculiarly presidential responsibility, and every president needs to adopt a decision-making model appropriate to his or her style of governance and then accept responsibility for the outcomes of the policies that result.

■ The Secretary of State Versus the ANSA

Jimmy Carter entered the White House in 1977 promising to be a "managerial president." This was a pledge in which Carter took great pride and one that he felt eminently qualified to fulfill. In his view, presidential management required order and systemization in government, and though he lacked experience in national affairs, Carter believed that his engineering education at Annapolis and early background as an officer in the nuclear-submarine service provided him with an affinity for exact procedure.[1] It can be argued, however, that Carter's strong concern with the minutiae of administrative procedure, though a commendable personal predilection, left him personally overwhelmed and the government devoid of policy leadership. Paradoxically, it was precisely a lack of systemization in foreign policy management that proved to be one of the great weaknesses of the Carter administration.

Carter's main concern in foreign policy making was to establish an administrative process that would avoid the Nixon administration's extreme centralization of power. As already noted, when Henry Kissinger was the assistant for national security affairs, he virtually displaced the secretary of state and ultimately held both positions simultaneously.[2] Carter wanted Secretary of State Cyrus Vance to be his principal adviser for foreign policy and the State Department to provide the necessary staff work. The ANSA, Zbigniew Brzezinski, and the NSC staff were to play a less active and assertive role in the foreign policy–making process. In particular, policy was to be coordinated among the principal actors—the secretaries of state and defense, the presidential assistant, the CIA director, and the vice-president—through collegiality rather than by means of a national security adviser serving as chief of staff for foreign policy.[3] However, as happened in many earlier administrations that began with a commitment to cabinet government and collegial decisionmaking, the politics of foreign policy making resulted in administrative arrangements other than those originally intended.

Carter's nomination of Cyrus Vance as secretary of state differed from the practice of other presidents in that it preceded the appointment of lesser-ranking State Department officials and the national security adviser. Yet Vance's appointment was widely applauded as a politically and administratively astute decision. As a former secretary of the Army under President Kennedy and deputy secretary of defense under President Johnson, Vance was knowledgeable about a broad range of international politico-military problems. As a Wall Street lawyer, Vance had close connections with the so-called foreign policy–making establishment centered in New York, and as an early supporter of

Sargent Shriver's presidential candidacy in 1976, he had strong credentials with the liberal wing of the Democratic party. President Carter described him as "cool under pressure" and a "natural selection" for secretary of state who had received the virtually unanimous recommendation of his advisers.[4] In the judgment of I. M. Destler, "Cyrus Vance was an experienced foreign policy professional with overwhelming establishment support."[5]

Despite a very limited background in foreign affairs—not unusual, of course, among presidents—Carter saw himself "as a policy initiator and manager who would make his own decisions from the range of views provided by his senior advisers."[6] The president's desire to have the option of acting "as his own secretary of state" would in itself limit any secretary of state's freedom to act as a presidential surrogate for foreign policy. Moreover, Zbigniew Brzezinski in the White House proved aggressive in gaining the president's confidence and access to him. With the career of Henry Kissinger as precedent, any assistant for national security affairs would have reason to entertain visions of administrative grandeur, and Brzezinski was no ordinary presidential assistant. As a professor of political science at Columbia University and a member (along with both Carter and Vance) of the Trilateral Commission during the 1970s,[7] he had strong views about American foreign policy that he was accustomed to arguing with great force. To have expected Brzezinski to take a backseat in foreign policy making, especially when sitting next to the driver in the White House, would have meant expecting him to become a different person.

As an early supporter of Carter's presidential candidacy, Brzezinski had gained experience in advising Carter on foreign policy during the campaign and had become acquainted with Carter's Georgia staff, who later held key White House positions. Brzezinski claimed early on that he did not see his job as involving policy making but simply as heading the president's operational staff for coordinating foreign policy.[8] Yet, even if Brzezinski had not had strong views on foreign policy (which he did—particularly concerning detente and SALT II), he would have been drawn into the foreign policy–making process at the president's behest. President Carter, in his memoirs, disclosed that he chose Brzezinski for his national security adviser despite some warnings that he might prove too aggressive, too inclined to speak too forcefully on controversial issues, and too competitive with the secretary of state.

> Knowing Zbig, I realized that some of these assessments were accurate, but they were in accord with what I wanted: the final decisions on basic foreign policy would be made by me in the Oval Office, and not in the State Department. I listened carefully to all the comments about him, considered the factors involved, and decided that I wanted him with me in the White House.[9]

In retrospect, Carter seems to have ignored some prescient advice in making this choice. On the other hand, Carter's appointment of Brzezinski points up a facet of presidential decision making that needs emphasizing: The president is constitutionally responsible for foreign policy and will choose the decision-making style most compatible with his or her personal preferences, political goals, and conception of the executive office. Because Cyrus Vance's cautious, lawyerlike style and avoidance of the limelight were at odds with President Carter's desire to have an outspoken advocate of the administration's foreign policy, one who was able to take the heat under the inevitable criticism, this task fell to Brzezinski.[10]

Moreover, the president liked the company of his ANSA and valued his advice.

> To me, Zbigniew Brzezinski was interesting. He would probe constantly for new ways to accomplish a goal, sometimes wanting to pursue a path that might be ill-advised—but always thinking. We had many arguments about history, politics, international events and foreign policy—often disagreeing strongly and fundamentally— but we still got along well. Next to members of my family, Zbig would be my favorite seatmate on a long-distance trip; we might argue, but I would never be bored.[11]

Physical propinquity may not account for preeminence in policy making, but when coupled with presidential approval and administrative adroitness, it can give one considerable power in the conduct of American foreign affairs.

The very qualities that made Brzezinski valuable to Carter ultimately became the source of antagonism between the secretary of state and the national security adviser. The more Brzezinski came to define and defend the administration's foreign policy objectives, the more Vance objected to these intrusions on the prerogatives of the State Department and its secretary. As time passed, Brzezinski acted more and more as Carter's foreign policy spokesman and, on occasion, became directly involved in diplomatic operations (for example, in negotiations on the normalization of relations with China). By the middle of 1978, Brzezinski had transformed his role as private presidential adviser to one of vigorous public advocate for important foreign decisions (especially those concerning the Soviet Union and, later, Iran).[12] Moreover, by 1978 a serious Brzezinski–Vance split was publicly manifest.[13]

President Carter, apparently at the secretary of state's request, instructed his national security adviser not to speak out on foreign policy issues in ways that pointed up differences between the White House and State Department.[14] Such restrictions however, did not last long; indeed, they could not be expected to be effective given the circumstances. The reality was that Brzezinski spoke out as forcefully as he did because the president encouraged his activities. As Carter observed, "The underlying State Department objection was that Brzezinski had spoken at all."[15] In any administration, few officials other than the president or the secretary of state have the stature to command attention as definitive formulators of foreign policy. The White House assistant for national security affairs can play that role if the president so wishes, and Carter did.[16] Brzezinski was not only an eager and indefatigable defender of the president's policies, but, in contrast to Secretary Vance, he willingly served as a lightning rod for criticism that would otherwise have been directed at Carter. An assistant like this can prove an invaluable asset to any president. Unfortunately for the Carter administration's credibility, however, the policy differences between Vance and Brzezinski became identified as a conflict between the State Department and the White House bureaucracies for control of American foreign policy making.

Vance and Brzezinski always denied that any organizational rivalry existed and went to great lengths to emphasize the high personal regard that they had for each other.[17] In actuality, it is difficult to see how the Brzezinski–Vance rivalry could have been avoided. With a president who was determined to make foreign policy decisions personally but who had little background on international issues, whoever emerged as Carter's top adviser would enjoy considerable control over foreign policy. The competition between Vance and Brzezinski continued unabated and unresolved until April 1980, when the secretary of state resigned because of his disagreement with Carter and Brzezinski over the military operation undertaken to rescue the American hostages in Iran.[18] By that time, however, the Carter administration's foreign policy had become characterized as badly fragmented, poorly designed, and improperly managed.[19] Just before Vance's resignation, the following exchange took place between him and Senator Edward Zorinsky (D–Neb.):

Senator Zorinsky: As you know, Mr. Secretary, I have sponsored legislation to require Senate confirmation of the President's Assistant for National Security Affairs. Next month, this committee is planning to hold hearings on this matter.

   With all due respect, isn't it true that we really have at least two Secretaries of State, you and Dr. Brzezinski? Why should one be subject to Senate confirmation and not the other when, in fact, both play a significant role in the foreign policy of this country?

Secretary Vance: The answer is no, there is only one Secretary of State. I am the Secretary of State. The Security Adviser has a very important role to play as an adviser to the President of the United States. This has long been the case, not only with the President but with other presidents, and it is appropriate that this should be the case.

   The only persons who speak for the United States, and the President has made this clear, in terms of foreign policy are the President of the United States and the Secretary of State.[20]

As we have seen, however, the Carter administration did essentially have more than one secretary of state at a time. Nor did the problem disappear after Vance's departure. Within months after his appointment, the new secretary of state, former Chairman of the Senate Foreign Relations Committee Edmund S. Muskie, complained that he had learned about Carter's decision to revise the nation's strategy with regard to nuclear war only after reading news reports about it.[21]

In a commentary about the continuing struggle between Muskie and Brzezinski for control of American foreign policy, Leslie Gelb, a former State Department official, argued that behind the competition for personal power was a more fundamental organizational competition. Seen in this light, the

Vance–Brzezinski rivalry derived from the differing perspectives of two institutions: the White House, in the person of the national security adviser and the NSC staff, and the Department of State, in the person of the secretary. This is really a modern replay of the historical conflict between the palace guard and the king's ministers, or between the personal staff and the line officers in any organizational structure.[22] From this perspective, Brzezinski's assertiveness was indicative of a process that had begun with McGeorge Bundy in the 1960s and was most dramatically exemplified by Henry Kissinger: the emergence of the White House assistant "as a major, visible foreign policy figure in his own right."[23]

Brzezinski made clear in his memoirs that he regarded himself an equal member, with the secretaries of state and defense, of a policy-making triad for foreign affairs. If he was not to become a Kissinger (dominating the policy-making process in the White House), neither was Vance to be a John Foster Dulles (monopolizing the president's attention for the State Department). Brzezinski also realized that as the president's assistant, the national security adviser was the guardian of the "presidential perspective" in decision making. This required transcending the interests of the various bureaucracies involved in foreign-policy—those representing the diplomatic corps, the military, the intelligence community, international economics, and other interests. Accordingly, Brzezinski used the NSC staff to sift through policy proposals to find those that would further Carter's avowed goals. According to Brzezinski, "coordination is predominance—and the key to asserting effective coordination was the right of direct access to the President, in writing, by telephone, or simply by walking into his office."[24]

What Vance forgot, and Brzezinski did not, is that there is no "perfect" process for foreign policy making—only one that serves the needs and interests of a particular president. Moreover, as Henry Kissinger had observed, and Brzezinski was aware, "every president since Kennedy seems to have trusted his White House aides more than his Cabinet."[25] Presidents may choose to work through a strong secretary of state (as Eisenhower did with Dulles), or they may rely exclusively on the assistant for national security affairs (as Nixon did with Kissinger). Carter preferred a middle course in which the secretary of state and the national security adviser competed for control of foreign policy making.

There is nothing necessarily wrong with such a model for policy making: A certain amount of rivalry among institutional actors is largely inevitable and may be constructively channeled to yield more-effective policies. In adopting such a model, however, a president needs to prevent the kind of institutionalized conflict between the State Department and the NSC staff that produces fragmented policy proposals and leaves the decision-making process in disarray. When President Carter could not, or would not, settle the differences between Vance and Brzezinski, this was precisely the result.[26] By relying on his national security adviser to retain control over foreign policy issues, Carter fatally undermined Vance's authority as secretary of state. The irony is that although Carter entered office pledged to oppose the Kissinger model of foreign policy making, the actual result was the concentration of nearly as much power in the White House as had been the case in the Nixon administration.

▌ The Secretary of State Versus the White House

Few secretaries of state have come to the office as well versed in White House politics as Alexander Haig, the first incumbent in that office under President Ronald Reagan. As a former deputy assistant to the president for national security affairs under Henry Kissinger, Haig served in the White House when it was the locus of American foreign policy making. While on the NSC staff, Haig rose from colonel to major general in the United States Army. After the resignation of H. R. Haldeman as Nixon's White House chief of staff, Haig served in this position through the Watergate crisis. His role in the final days of the Nixon administration may be one of the most remarkable ever played by a presidential assistant. Haig essentially orchestrated President Nixon's resignation while seeing that the basic functions of government operated despite a constitutional crisis.[27] Gerald Ford then appointed the four-star general Haig to be supreme commander of NATO, where, despite reservations by some allied governments because of his association with the discredited Nixon presidency, he enjoyed great success with the European military and diplomatic community.

Haig's almost-meteoric rise was not without criticism: He was said to be a "political general" who had had no actual combat experience and who had achieved his position because he was Henry Kissinger's protégé. (Haig jumped over thousands of other officers in his rapid promotions and was the only four-star general never to have been a divisional commander.) Critics also argued that Haig owed his political preeminence to an unseemly facility for bureaucratic intrigue and uncritical service to Henry Kissinger.[28] Still others were sharply critical of Haig for his role in the "Saturday Night Massacre," in which Haig told the acting attorney general to fire the Watergate special prosecutor, warning him, "Your Commander-in-Chief is giving you an order."[29] There were allegations that Haig was involved in illegal wiretapping of government officials, including his own colleagues on the NSC staff when he served as Kissinger's deputy. One commander put the strongest anti-Haig case as follows: "General Haig is the exemplar of the careerist: a man who will do anything for his master—anything likely, that is, to advance his own career. He evidently has no feeling for American constitutionalism, for restraint in the exercise of power."[30]

Despite the questions raised about Haig's connections with the Nixon administration generally, and Watergate specifically, his designation as secretary of state was considered a major commitment by the Reagan administration to a strong presence in foreign policy making. In particular, Haig was judged to have received a mandate to take command of the State Department to prevent a repetition of the vacillation and uncertainty that had characterized American foreign policy under Carter because of the feud between Secretary of State Vance and National Security Adviser Brzezinski.[31] What surprised most observers, including the Reagan White House staff, was how quickly, insistently, and dramatically Haig asserted his prerogatives—not only as secretary of state but also as principal policy maker and premier cabinet secretary. According to one senior official, "he acts more like an assistant President than a coequal Cabinet member."[32]

For all the problems of "turf and temperament" that later developed between the State Department and the White House, Alexander Haig and Ronald Reagan shared the same worldview, especially regarding the need to counter the growing power of the Soviet Union. Haig and Reagan were sharply critical of the Carter administration for what they deemed an overly conciliatory policy toward Moscow. Despite his own participation in formulating the Nixon–Kissinger foreign policy, Haig declared in 1980 that the "twin pillars" of that policy, detente and deterrence, had failed.[33] At the core of Haig's foreign policy was a commitment to resisting Soviet expansionism beyond Eastern Europe. According to what has been called the "Haig Doctrine," increased security assistance was to be provided to Third World countries to increase their internal stability and their ability to resist externally sponsored aggression.[34]

Yet, despite such hard-line positions, in reality Haig was probably a moderating influence on the Reagan administration's foreign policy. Haig was strongly opposed, for example, to ideas identified with right-wing Reagan supporters such as Senators Jesse Helms (R–N.C.) and John Tower (R–Texas). He was particularly upset by the suggestions of Richard Pipes, a Harvard professor and Eastern European analyst for the NSC, that seemed to countenance the possibility of a preemptive nuclear strike by the United States, and he rejected as well the comments of Richard Allen, the assistant for national security affairs, concerning the allegedly pacifist sentiments of many Europeans involved in the campaign against the deployment of Euromissiles.[35]

In general, Europeans regarded Haig highly for his firmness of manner and knowledge of international issues. At home, however, Haig became increasingly embroiled in ideological quarrels, especially over the background of State Department appointees. Many of these officials, such as the undersecretary for political affairs (Laurence Eagleburger) and certain regional assistant secretaries (for example, Richard Burt for European affairs and John Holdridge for Eastern affairs), had been members of Kissinger's NSC staff. Conservative Republican senators opposed their confirmation on the grounds that such appointments were a betrayal of Ronald Reagan's foreign policy principles.

How a policy maker's personality may affect his standing is uncertain. Regardless, White House aides were reported to have concluded that tensions between themselves and the secretary had been exacerbated by Haig's "volatile" and "unusual" temperament.[36] The most dramatic incidence of this occurred on March 30, 1981, when President Reagan was wounded in an assassination attempt. In the resulting confusion and the absence of Vice-President George Bush, Haig arrived in the White House to announce before the assembled press corps, "I'm in charge here." That such an announcement was obviously wrong (the constitutional order of succession was through the vice-president to the speaker of the House of Representatives and the president pro tempore of the Senate) was bad enough;[37] what was worse was Haig's televised appearance: shaken, exhausted, anything but in control.

It may be that Haig's reputation never recovered from that event. Though his intention must have been to assure the nation and the world that the machinery of government was operating without interruption, he appeared to be pushy and presumptuous. For the White House staff this incident was indicative of Haig's obsession with all matters relating to his secretarial prerogatives. Haig's bureaucratic skills and background in foreign affairs had led both political insiders and the general public to expect him to be the most powerful figure in the Reagan administration, "but in barely two months he is reported angry, brooding, near resignation over a series of poisonous bureaucratic struggles with the White House, whose power in such matters he knows so well, or should."[38]

Haig's difficulties with the White House reached major proportions in the dispute over who was to head the crisis management team established by President Reagan—the secretary of state or Vice-President George Bush. Both Henry Kissinger and Zbigniew Brzezinski had used their positions as crisis managers to make the situation room of the White House the focal point for directing international operations. Brzezinski, for example, used crisis management to formulate Persian Gulf policy independently of the Departments of State and Defense. Haig was determined to prevent the growth of a competing foreign policy center in the White House, such as had hampered his immediate predecessors; he wanted a return to the Eisenhower–Dulles model, in which the secretary of state acted as crisis manager. The struggle over precedence was also one over who would eventually control policy making. Haig stressed that he had the president's mandate to be the "chief formulator and spokesman for foreign policy." To delegate crisis management responsibilities to another official would diminish his authority.[39] After a highly publicized series of rumors about Haig's threatened resignation and his arguments with the chief of staff, James A. Baker, Jr., and White House Counselor Edwin Meese III, the White House announced that the vice-president would chair the crisis management team.[40]

Haig did not resign, although he publicly blamed the senior White House staff for mishandling the matter. For his part, President Reagan reaffirmed Haig's position as his "primary adviser on foreign affairs," while blaming reporters for the controversy over the secretary's remarks.[41] Haig was reported to be a "wounded lion" in the aftermath of the crisis management incident; as indicated earlier, he was particularly resentful of the role of the White House staff.[42] The secretary had reason to believe that he had been "had" by the White House, but he behaved in a way that demonstrated a fatal misunderstanding of decision-making power in the Reagan administration.

First, by publicly criticizing Baker and Meese, Haig transformed the existing rivalry into a public feud and formalized a breach between the White House and the State Department over foreign policy making.

Second, Haig's actions confirmed the early perception of the Reagan staff that the secretary was not a "team player" in an administration that strongly emphasized such behavior.

Third, and more important, the White House became convinced that Haig was preempting the president's role as the nation's chief diplomat. One presidential assistant was quoted as saying, "Haig thinks he's President."[43] As a past party to this kind of palace intrigue under the Nixon administration, Haig should not have underestimated the influence of the senior White House staff, whatever may have been President Reagan's expressed commitment to cabinet government.

Fourth, Haig made a serious strategic error by overreacting to the designation of Vice President Bush as chair of the crisis management team. As a former CIA director and ambassador to China, Bush had a background in foreign affairs second only to Haig's in the Reagan administration. Moreover, as vice-president, Bush could assert authority in the president's name and articulate a position independent of the perspective of a specific department. Haig was undoubtedly correct in his assessment that the White House staff was determined to "clip his wings" by denying him complete authority over foreign policy, but he might also have noted that it was the vice-president in the chair, not the assistant for national security affairs, as had been the case with Kissinger and Brzezinski.

Fifth, Haig was too quick to point to John Foster Dulles as a model for the conduct of foreign affairs. Haig seemed not to understand that Dulles's preeminence was principally the result of his close relationship with President Eisenhower, rather than of his official position as secretary of state. Haig forgot the fundamental tenet of successful secretarial–presidential relations in foreign policy making: It is the president who makes policy, and he is free to consult anyone he wishes and to establish whatever structural processes he deems necessary.

Sixth, Haig should have realized that though White House aides such as Baker and Meese had no particular expertise or interest in foreign affairs, they did have an inordinate interest in guarding the president's political well-being. With no interest in the personal management of foreign affairs, Reagan was strongly committed to Haig as a necessary alternative to the divisiveness of the Vance–Brzezinski years. The White House staff, however, did not wish to allow Haig to preempt complete responsibility for national security to the exclusion of Secretary of Defense Caspar Weinberger or CIA Director William Casey. Haig should have realized that in propounding his Dulles analogy he was overlooking the momentous changes that had broadened the scope of international relations beyond the State Department's traditional emphasis on diplomacy and that made White House officials reluctant to delegate this new domain to diplomats alone.[44]

Without a strong national security adviser, the White House staff was understandably fearful that a president who lacked a background in diplomatic and defense issues (unlike Eisenhower, who was knowledgeable about both) would become a pawn of departmental interests. As the keepers of Reagan's political future, Baker and Meese would inevitably have had to counter Haig's demands to dominate the process of foreign policy making or seem to have surrendered control to the general. Sherman Adams, as Eisenhower's chief of staff, could rely on the president to supervise foreign affairs while he concentrated on domestic policies, where Eisenhower was less knowledgeable. In contrast, with Alexander Haig as vicar, Ronald Reagan might seem only titular bishop of the diocese of foreign affairs.

Haig might still have achieved a de facto primacy in foreign affairs. But on Inauguration Day, he insisted, in a twenty-page memorandum, on a de jure grant of presidential authority that was more sweeping than had been accorded to his predecessors.[45] Though Haig did not get all that he proposed in his original memorandum, he was granted a broad authority over foreign policy making. For example, the secretary of state was designated chairman of a variety of interdepartmental working groups, although not those involving defense or international economic policies. Since these committees had in the most recent past been chaired by the assistant for national security affairs, this agreement was a major victory for Haig even if it was not the complete triumph that he had envisioned in his Inauguration Day memorandum. There was a Pyrrhic quality to Haig's organizational victory, however, because it put the White House staff and cabinet secretaries on alert that Haig was attempting a power play at their expense. A White House aide was quoted as observing that for Haig "everything beyond the water's edge was foreign policy."[46]

The inevitable result was battles over turf, as the secretary of defense asserted his primacy in areas such as the development of the neutron bomb and the MX missile system, and as the secretaries of treasury and commerce claimed leadership in questions involving foreign trade and international economic policy. The month-long delay before action was taken on Haig's original memorandum (see note 45) suggests that Meese deliberately stalled its implementation to allow a groundswell of opposition from within the administration to develop.[47] This should have been a signal to Haig that his plans for consolidation of the foreign policy–making process would not be unopposed.

While Haig was seeking to aggrandize his personal and institutional power, the assistant for national security affairs was doing a disappearing act in accordance with the president's publicized intention to make the secretary of state his principal foreign policy adviser. Like Brzezinski earlier, Richard Allen came to the office of ANSA from an advisory position in the Reagan campaign, where he had enjoyed considerable public exposure. Unlike Brzezinski or Kissinger, however, he did not have a background in the foreign policy establishment or a reputation as a scholar on foreign affairs. Allen consistently endorsed a conception of his job as presidential assistant as being that of a low-profile facilitator,[48] and he asserted that he had no intention of making policy, seeking "only to help coordinate the work of the various agencies in foreign policy."[49]

In a sharp break with a twenty-year tradition, the role of the national security adviser and his staff was deliberately scaled down, and the NSC was placed under the direct control of White House Counselor Edwin Meese. One would have to return to the Eisenhower national security system to find Richard Allen's administrative counterpart. Indeed, Allen likened himself to Eisenhower's aide, Gordon Gray, who, as the NSC staff secretary, was one of those presidential assistants with a "passion for anonymity."[50] Whereas previous national security advisers had had direct access to the president, Allen operated through Meese, although he continued to brief the president daily on the world situation and to prepare "talking points" for the president's conversations with foreign leaders.

The NSC staff was downgraded from a policy-making group to a conduit for departmental policy proposals. More significantly, Allen and his staff did not involve themselves either in the day-to-day operations of foreign policy or in independently formulating policy initiatives. As Allen put it, "the policy formulation function of the national security adviser should be offloaded to the Secretary of State." Theoretically, the national security adviser in the Reagan administration would concentrate exclusively on interagency coordination and "long-range thinking."[51] Appointees to the NSC staff positions were largely strongly conservative and, with certain exceptions (such as the controversial Harvard professors Samuel Huntington and Richard Pipes), lacked the professional visibility and experience that had typified earlier NSC staff members. In the administrative hierarchy, Allen ranked as a deputy secretary, compared to the cabinet-level status of his ANSA predecessors and his superior, Edwin Meese.[52]

Despite the absence of an identifiable challenger to Haig's preeminence, the secretary was engaged in open warfare less than three months into the administration. The incident over the crisis management team came after a mounting series of complaints from Haig that the White House was out to undermine his authority, accusations by both sides of inadequate or tardy briefing papers, claims and counterclaims of improper policy statements, and leaks by State Department and White House subordinates meant to settle their superiors' scores with the other side. At one point, Haig charged that someone in the White House, not identifiable (but not Richard Allen), was waging a "guerilla campaign" against him. It was widely rumored that Haig suspected Chief of Staff Baker. Clearly, White House senior staff, recognizing Allen's reduced powers and limited capabilities and wary of Haig's monopolistic goals, had moved into the foreign policy area themselves.[53]

Richard Allen was eased out as national security adviser in January 1982, ostensibly for his involvement with an unreported $1,000 honorarium from a Japanese magazine but really for his poor management of the NSC staff.[54] His successor was Deputy Secretary of State William P. Clark, who chose the veteran NSC staffer Robert McFarlane as his deputy. Clark was an old political friend of Ronald Reagan's from his gubernatorial days whom Reagan had appointed to the California Supreme Court. Judge Clark had no experience or background in foreign affairs and repeatedly stumbled over the names of foreign leaders (and the geographic location of their countries) during his confirmation hearings. This raised embarrassing questions about his qualifications for the department's second position. Clark, however, received high marks for his on-the-job learning, and he proved an invaluable emissary between Haig and the increasingly hostile senior presidential staff. In his move to the White House, Clark upgraded the status of the position of national security adviser, since he reported directly to the president rather than through Counselor Meese, and as a longtime friend of Reagan's he enjoyed an ease of access denied Allen (and Haig).

Clark and Haig had enjoyed a good working relationship at the State Department, but any hopes for improved relations between the secretary of state and the White House were quickly dashed. For one thing, Clark was closer to Reagan in ideology than was Haig. There were also recurring tensions over protocol and privileges, with Haig reported to have "bruised feelings" about slights to him in official ceremonies. By June 1982, he and Clark were reported to have confronted each other in what aides described as "shouting matches" over several issues.[55] When Haig finally resigned on June 26, 1982—citing unhappiness with the direction of foreign policy and his role as its director—his act was greeted as a foregone conclusion. For the White House staff, the move was long overdue. Though Reagan had come to respect Haig's intellect, he had also come to find his temperament intolerable.[56] Clark was the turning point: He had come to the White House as an admirer of Haig but quickly became disillusioned by the general's unwillingness to realize that foreign policy making was a presidential, not a secretarial, prerogative.

▌ No Vicar General

The new secretary of state, George P. Shultz, a former treasury secretary under Nixon, was a sharp contrast to Alexander Haig. Where the general had been mercurial, aggressive, and a political loner, the sometime economics professor was even-handed, conciliatory, and a team player. Whereas Haig (at least publicly) had been confrontational in diplomatic matters, Shultz deliberately opted for quieter, behind-the-scenes diplomacy to make his points. Most important, at least from the White House staff's perspective, Shultz was said to hold the view that as secretary of state he had no foreign policy of his own—only that of the president: "Shultz goes to extraordinary lengths to emphasize that Reagan is responsible for making foreign policy."[57] Shultz's preference for conciliation and compromise did cause speculation that he would lack the determination necessary for strong policy making. On the other hand, the incessant bureaucratic feuding of Haig's tenure had "projected a picture of a chaotic U.S. foreign policy and in the end sapped Haig's influence with the President."[58]

Noticeably absent with Shultz at the State Department was the incessant warfare between the secretary and the national security adviser. There was no

Clark–Shultz feud.[59] Both Shultz and Clark were personally loyal to Reagan and shared a nearly identical feeling about the role of the United States in world affairs. Clark, moreover, bore no similarity to national security advisers such as Kissinger and Brzezinski, who had liked to conceptualize about foreign policy formulations. Clark had the president's ear, though, and even with his scanty knowledge of foreign affairs, he was able to interest Reagan in the issues.[60]

Despite Clark's personal and political proximity to the president, however, Shultz continued to retain Reagan's confidence in his judgment. Although no personal confidant, Shultz was regarded as able and loyal and arguably the administration's most competent cabinet official. Differences did occur between the State Department and the White House (for example, over American military activities in Central America); in general, Shultz counseled a more moderate foreign policy, while Clark favored a harder line. Their conflicts never became conflagrations, however, as had been the case with Haig and the White House. When Clark left to become secretary of the interior, it was because he preferred to work on natural resource issues, with which he was more familiar, rather than on foreign policy, where he was, by self-admission, out of his depth.

Shultz's personal characteristics were widely agreed on ("conservative, methodical and calm"), as were his administrative qualities ("an incrementalist, a problem solver and a mediator"), although these qualities sometimes earned Shultz criticism: His calmness was seen as passivity, his team playing as timidity. Though the new secretary's views were virtually identical to Haig's, Shultz did not have the same broad experience in foreign affairs. On the other hand, "unlike Mr. Haig, he does not push those positions that are contrary to what he thinks are presidential inclinations. Unlike Mr. Haig, he subordinates himself at every opportunity to Mr. Reagan." Of course, this was one of Shultz's major goals: to end the rancor that had existed when Haig was secretary of state. Shultz was fond of saying, "It is Mr. Reagan's policy." Many critics, though, maintained that the president was not inclined to develop policy himself and, that as a result of Shultz's attitude, American foreign policy remained incapable of decisive actions.[61]

Unfortunately, Haig's departure did not guarantee instant harmony among the Reagan administration's foreign policy makers. In the months that followed, a well-publicized feud simmered between Caspar Weinberger and George Shultz.[62] The emergence of ANSA McFarlane as an "honest broker" among the competing factions within the administration was particularly important for restoring some order to the Reagan administration's foreign policy–making procedures.

Shultz's low-key, reserved style may have served him well in the sharply fought bureaucratic battles of the Reagan administration. Newspaper headlines of stories about the secretary of state's tenure are highly suggestive: "Watching Grass Grow, Paint Dry, and Shultz Wait," "Shultz Scores a Backstage Victory," "No Headlines, No Fanfare: This is Shultz," "Reticence and Foreign Policy."[63] However, after the combativeness of Haig and Weinberger on major international issues, Shultz's style must have seemed immensely reassuring to the senior White House staff, as well as to President Reagan. In particular, Shultz was willing to act simply as a "senior aide"—not even a primus inter pares, let alone a vicar—in the foreign policy–making process. He cultivated a good reputation for behind-the-scenes diplomacy, not only avoiding headlines but having the White House Press Office rather than the State Department issue all foreign policy announcements. After the mercurial Haig and the uncompromising Weinberger, Shultz must have seemed increasingly attractive to Reagan and Chief of Staff Donald Regan.

In the end, Shultz emerged as the administration's principal foreign policy official, not only because of his administrative tenacity and personal self-effacement but because of an important political alliance with the White House. As Robert McFarlane, as assistant for national security affairs, grew more self-assured and gained President Reagan's confidence (and, not inconsequentially, Mrs. Reagan's as well), he was able to use his influence to resolve many Shultz–Weinberger impasses. Moreover, as a former staff member on the Senate Armed Services Committee, Kissinger's former NSC deputy, and Haig's counselor at the State Department, McFarlane actually had experience in foreign affairs approximating that of Shultz or Weinberger, especially on arms control and the Middle East. At first, the national security adviser was content to mediate the conflict between Shultz and Weinberger; as this proved unsuccessful, he began tilting increasingly toward the more flexible Shultz.[64] This Shultz–McFarlane axis allowed the secretary of state to emerge as the administration's premier foreign policy maker while ensuring the prerequisite for that preeminence—White House support.

In surrendering any pretensions to a vicarage over American foreign policy, George Shultz defined a role for the secretary of state as part of a foreign policy team in which he and the national security adviser were approximately coequal. Shultz may have salvaged the best deal possible under the circumstances, and he clearly won a hard-fought victory over Weinberger in arms control negotiations. In an administration disposed toward collective decision making under a president who delegated broad authority over policy making to the departments, some sort of collegial arrangement for the management of foreign affairs, with the White House staff acting as umpire, was the most workable arrangement. Nonetheless, it must be acknowledged that Shultz accepted a more subservient status for the secretary of state and a more diminished role for the State Department in the making of foreign policy.

As we have seen, the administration of foreign policy under Carter and during Reagan's first term highlighted the difficulty of determining who is to have primacy in foreign policy making—the secretary of state or the national security adviser.

Zbigniew Brzezinski has argued that a "secretarial" model of foreign policy making, in which the secretary of state is responsible for directing and coordinating the making of policy, is clearly inferior to a "presidential" model, in which these tasks are performed by the assistant to the president for national security affairs. For Brzezinski, three reasons necessitate a "Presidential" model: (1) In an age of dramatic global crises, the nerve center for national security is increasingly the White House; (2) though foreign policy requires the integration of diplomacy, defense, intelligence, and international economics, the State Department is concerned largely with diplomatic issues; and (3) coordination is only effective when managed from the White House, which is better able to transcend narrow departmental concerns.[65] In sum, Brzezinski proposed giving up the pretense that the secretary of state can serve as the chief architect of foreign policy, because only a White House official close to the president can pull all the competing bureaucratic interests together.

Brzezinski's proposal smacks of justification for his own actions in the battles during the Carter administration for control of foreign policy making. Similarly, various structural reforms intended to better define the proper relationship of the president, secretary of state, and national security adviser generally reflect a priori conceptions of the proper scope of presidential responsibility for foreign policy making.[66]

Most important, no proposal for restructuring the policy making process can be effective unless it suits the incumbent president's preferences with regard to decision making. A strong secretary of state can be in full command when he is both diplomatically knowledgeable and enjoys the full confidence of the president (as with Dulles and Eisenhower); in such a situation the national security assistant is less likely to attempt to maximize his power potential.[67] In other situations, the national security assistant will seek to expand his power at the expense of the secretary of state, with the concurrence of the president (as with Bundy versus Rusk, under Kennedy). Alternatively, if the chief executive does not, or cannot, choose an appropriate model there will likely be a constant battle to control the president.[68] There is simply no substitute for a president sufficiently knowledgeable and self-assured to set policy and to determine how he or she wants to structure the policy-making process. This was a criticism of President Reagan that was to be made with particular vehemence in the aftermath of the Iran–Contra affair discussed in the next chapter.

NOTES

1. Dom Bonafede, "How the White House Helps Carter Make up His Mind," *National Journal,* April 15, 1978, p. 584.

2. Alexander George, *Presidential Decisionmaking in Foreign Policy: The Effective Use of Information and Advice* (Boulder, Colo.: Westview Press, 1980), p. 159.

3. Ibid., p. 160.

4. Jimmy Carter, *Keeping Faith* (New York: Bantam Books, 1982), p. 50.

5. I. M. Destler, "National Security II: The Rise of the Assistant," in *Illusion of Presidential Government,* ed. Hugh Heclo and Lester M. Salamon (Boulder, Colo.: Westview Press, 1981), p. 272.

6. Ibid.

7. Zbigniew Brzezinski, *Power and Principle* (New York: Farrar, Straus & Giroux, 1983), p. 12.

8. Destler, *Illusion of Presidential Government,* p. 273.

9. Carter, *Keeping Faith,* p. 54.

10. Brzezinski, *Power and Principle,* pp. 27 and 42–43; and Carter, *Keeping Faith,* p. 54.

11. Carter, *Keeping Faith,* p. 54.

12. George, *Presidential Decisionmaking in Foreign Policy,* p. 200.

13. Destler, *Illusion of Presidential Government,* p. 273.

14. The best single source on Brzezinski's performance as assistant for national security affairs during the first six months of the Carter administration is the profile "A Reporter at Large: Brzezinski," by Elizabeth Drew, *New Yorker,* May 1978, pp. 90–130.

15. Carter, *Keeping Faith,* p. 53.

16. Ibid., p. 54; and Destler, *Illusion of Presidential Government,* p. 274.

17. See Brzezinski, *Power and Principle,* pp. 36–43, and 219–225, and Vance, *Hard Choices,* pp. 24–44, 87–92, and 328–340.

18. Cyrus Vance, *Hard Choices: Critical Years in American Foreign Policy (New York: Simon & Schuster, 1983).*

19. See, for example, Stanley Hoffman, "The Hell of Good Intentions," *Foreign Policy* 29 (Winter 1977–1978): 3–26; and Thomas L. Hughes, "Carter and the Management of Contradictions," *Foreign Policy* 31 (Summer 1978): 34–55.

20. Exchange between Senator Zorinsky and Secretary Vance at a hearing of the Committee on Foreign Relations, March 27, 1980, in the *National Security Adviser: Role and Accountability* (Washington: Government Printing Office, 1980), p. 173.

21. *New York Times,* July 10, 1980.

22. Leslie H. Gelb, "The Struggle over Foreign Policy," *New York Times Magazine,* July 20, 1980, pp. 26–27.

23. Destler, *Illusion of Presidential Government,* p. 247.

24. Brzezinski, *Power and Principle,* p. 63. For a description of the NSC staff in the Carter administration, see ibid., pp. 74–78.

25. Henry Kissinger, *Years of Upheaval* (Boston: Little, Brown, 1980), p. 47.

26. Gelb, "The Struggle Over Foreign Policy," pp. 39–40.

27. See Kissinger, *Years of Upheaval,* pp. 107–110.

28. William Safire, *New York Times,* November 24, 1980.

29. Bob Woodward and Carl Bernstein, *The Final Days* (New York: Avon Books, 1976), p. 61.

30. Anthony Lewis, *New York Times,* December 4, 1980.

31. *New York Times,* February 8, 1981.

32. Ibid.

33. *New York Times,* December 18, 1980.

34. "A New Direction in U.S. Foreign Policy," a speech delivered by Secretary Haig before the American Society of Newspaper Editors (ASNE) on

April 24, 1981, as quoted in *Department of State Bulletin* 81, no. 2051 (June 1981): 5–7.

35. *Newsweek,* April 6, 1981, p. 32.

36. *New York Times,* July 2, 1981.

37. Haig must have been acting on the assumption that the Twentieth Amendment, which did provide for the secretary of state to succeed to the presidency after the vice-president, was still in effect. However, this constitutional provision had been superseded by the Twenty-fifth Amendment in 1967.

38. Roger Morris, *Haig: The General's Progress* (New York: Seaview Books, 1982), p. 399.

39. *New York Times,* March 29, 1981.

40. For the text of the White House statement, see *New York Times,* March 25, 1981.

41. *New York Times,* March 26, 1982.

42. *New York Times,* March 28, 1981.

43. *New York Times,* March 26, 1981.

44. Hedrick Smith in *New York Times,* March 29, 1981.

45. Destler, *Illusion of Presidential Government,* p. 282. See also *New York Times,* January 27, 1981. Haig apparently did not push this twenty-page memorandum on Reagan while the president was still in formal dress after viewing the parade. Instead, he submitted it to Edwin Meese to bring to Reagan's attention. Meese, for his part, deferred presidential consideration of Haig's memorandum until he had secured the reactions of other interested institutions.

46. *New York Times,* February 27, 1981.

47. *New York Times,* March 26, 1981.

48. Destler, *Illusion of Presidential Government,* p. 281.

49. *New York Times,* January 27, 1981.

50. *New York Times,* March 4, 1981.

51. *New York Times,* November 19, 1980.

52. One visible symbol of the difference in Allen's status as assistant for national security affairs compared to that of his predecessor was that his office was in the basement of the west wing whereas Meese occupied the corner suite that was once Brzezinski's, down the hall from the Oval Office.

53. *New York Times,* March 24, 1981; *Washington Post,* November 6, 1981.

54. Richard Halloran, "Reagan as Commander-in-Chief," *New York Times Magazine,* January 15, 1984, p. 57. For background on Allen's departure and replacement, see *New York Times,* January 5–8, 1982, January 10, 1982, and January 19, 1982.

55. *New York Times,* June 22, 1982. Leslie Gelb also reported, "Unlike Mr. Haig who seeks the limelight, 'Judge' Clark is always careful to insure that it is his boss, the President, who gets the credit for making foreign policy."

56. *New York Times,* June 27, 1981.

57. *U.S. News and World Report,* November 8, 1982.

58. Ibid.; *New York Times,* July 18, 1982.

59. *U.S. News and World Report,* September 19, 1983, p. 30.

60. Steven Weisman, "The Influence of William Clark," *New York Times Magazine,* August 14, 1983, pp. 17–20.

61. The quotations in the preceding paragraph are from Lesile Gelb, *New York Times,* August 1, 1983.

62. Philip Taubman, "The Shultz–Weinberger Feud," *New York Times,* April 14, 1985, p. 81.

63. *New York Times,* May 23, 1985; December 9, 1984; May 17, 1985; and October 8, 1985.

64. *U.S. News and World Report,* June 24, 1985, July 1, 1985, and July 8, 1985; Leslie H. Gelb, "Taking Charge," *New York Times Magazine,* May 26, 1985, pp. 20–21*ff.*

65. Brzezinski, *Power and Principle,* pp. 533–535. To legitimate the assistant's central role in coordination, Brzezinski thinks that the office should be subject to Senate confirmation. See ibid., p. 536.

66. For a discussion of the proper role of the national security assistant and the NSC staff, see the 1980 hearings of the Senate Committee on Foreign Relations, *The National Security Adviser: Role and Accountability.* See also I. M. Destler, "National Security Adviser to U.S. Presidents: Some Lessons from Thirty Years," *World Politics* 29 (January 1977): 143–176. See also R. Gordon Hoxie, *Command Decision and the Presidency* (New York: Reader's Digest Press, 1977).

67. Margaret J. Wyszomirski, "The De-Institutionalization of Presidential Staff Agencies," *Public Administration Review* 42 (Sept/Oct 1982): 453.

68. Stanley Hoffman, "In Search of a Foreign Policy," *New York Review of Books,* September 29, 1983, p. 51.

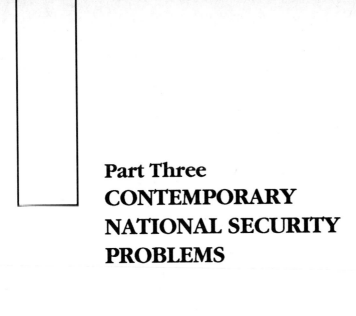

Part Three
CONTEMPORARY NATIONAL SECURITY PROBLEMS

CHAPTER 9

The Lessons of the Iran–Contra Affair for National Security Policy Making

Events in the last two years of the Reagan administration associated with the Iran–Contra affair dramatized certain problems in the making of national security policy. In particular, the roles of the assistant for national security affairs (ANSA) and the National Security Council staff in the policy-making process have come under close scrutiny. For all the importance of the ANSA and his staff in the conduct of American foreign affairs, the nature of this position and the patterns of presidential management of the policy-making process have received comparatively little attention. For example, how might the president, the secretaries of state and defense, the director of central intelligence, and the assistant for national security affairs structure their institutional relations? What is the appropriate mechanism for managing the policy-making process?

The Iran–Contra hearings suggested a number of lessons to be learned about the conduct of national security affairs. These lessons involved the responsibilities of the president as chief diplomat and commander in chief vis-à-vis the rights of Congress to collaborate in foreign relations, and the claiming of a privileged status with regard to national security concerns in contrast to the expectation that international covenants will be openly arrived at and politically reviewed. The lessons that concern us are admittedly more limited in scope. Specifically, we focus on the peculiar nature of the NSC as a decision-making body, examine the unique position of the president in the management of national security, and analyze in detail the roles that assistants for national security affairs have come to play in the policy-making process.

▌ The National Security Advisory System: A Typology

The administrative history of the Office of the Assistant for National Security since 1947 suggests the elements of a typology, admittedly one of several that might be constructed, that is useful in better understanding the general problem of policy making with regard to national security. We have used certain designations—administrator, coordinator, counselor, agent—to describe different roles that past national security assistants have played and that constitute a repertory available to future assistants. Of course, the particular role to be played by an ANSA is always a presidential prerogative. The Iran–Contra affair also suggests an aberrant role—the ANSA as insurgent—that serves as a warning as to what can happen when a national security policy–making system gets out of control.

It cannot be emphasized too strongly that the particular role that an ANSA will play is strictly determined by presidential preference. How the assistant for national security affairs is to be cast depends ultimately on what role the president has cast for him- or herself in the management of American foreign affairs. Similarly, an assistant's success will depend on his or her adapting to whatever role best suits the president's managerial preferences. The importance of the president's approach to managing the policy-making process and of clearly defining the role of the national security adviser will become abundantly clear in the course of our discussion.

In figure 9-1 we present a typology of the roles that national security assistants have played since the late 1940s, classifying them according to their patterns of responsibility. Before elaborating on the patterns represented, two limitations on the usefulness of such a typology should be noted. First, all such summary representations involve some oversimplification. Thus, our identification of a specific assistant with a single role might be more accurately understood as indicative of that assistant's dominant role.

Second, the variables associated with the typology—responsibility for policy making and responsibility for implementation of policy—are very broad measures selected from among the many that might be applied in defining the ANSA's role. Nonetheless, a formal construct such as our typology can call attention to certain identifiable patterns by which ANSAs have performed their duties, patterns that should remain management options. Furthermore, identifying these roles helps to clarify the consequences of each for the policy-making process.

Implementation Responsibility

		Low	High
Low *Policy-Making* *Responsibility*		**Administrator**	**Coordinator**
	High	**Counselor**	**Agent**

Figure 9-1.   A typology of national security assistants' roles.

In figure 9-2, we have categorized the sixteen national security advisers who have served between 1947 and 1988 according to our typology of roles.

We believe that our classifications generally accord with the historical record. The ideal types come quickly to mind: Souers as administrator, Cutler as coordinator, Bundy as counselor, Kissinger as agent. Understandably, however, there may be differences over the classification of particular ANSAs. Accordingly, we have used the placement of the ANSAs within the matrix to suggest ambiguities. For example, Brzezinski was a counselor who aspired to be an agent, but he never acquired Kissinger's mastery over the policy-making process. Allen and Clark were weak representatives of their respective roles. Poindexter is classified as an agent, but he might be better placed outside the typology. We will discuss this deviant case of the ANSA as insurgent in greater detail after the following elaboration of our typology of roles.

■ The Roles Played by National Security Assistants

The national security adviser as administrator has a low level of responsibility with regard to both implementation and policy making. Such an ANSA is essentially a servant of the NSC as a presidential institution, rather than a personal and political aide. The duties of this type of ANSA include briefing the president on the international situation, representing departmental proposals and viewpoints, scheduling matters for presidential decisions, and monitoring NSC directives. The role of administrator emphasizes the day-to-day business of the foreign policy-making process[1] and represents a pattern of management that radically curtails the stature of the ANSA and his staff. In this model, neither the preeminence of the State Department nor the position of the secretary of state as the "orchestra leader" and "first among equals" in national security policy making[2] is threatened.

The quintessential example of an ANSA who played the role of an administrator was Admiral Sidney W. Souers, President Truman's executive secretary of the NSC. Souers, a model of political rectitude and administrative

Allen			Clark
ADMINISTRATOR		**COORDINATOR**	
Souers		Cutler	
Lay		Anderson	
Powell			
Carlucci	Scowcroft	McFarlane	
COUNSELOR		**AGENT**	
Bundy		Kissinger	
Rostow			
	Brzezinski		Poindexter

Figure 9-2. National security assistants and their roles in the policy-making process, 1947–1988.

restraint, was extremely sensitive, even deferential, with regard to the position of the State Department. He must have perceived President Truman's high personal regard for his secretaries of state and defense and realized that Truman preferred the "classical model" of State Department dominance of foreign affairs.[3]

Souers's custodial role over the NSC advisory process was almost as highly circumscribed as his political role, which precluded attending White House staff meetings, despite efforts by some Truman aides to augment his political responsibilities. "The security assistant had little authority, staff capability or (often) desire to monitor the bureaucracy's implementation of the president's decisions; and his ability to coordinate defense and foreign policy was also constrained."[4] Essentially, Souers saw his role as that of a nonpolitical presidential official responsible for facilitating the NSC's advisory function.[5]

Another ANSA who falls into the category of administrator is General Brent Scowcroft under President Gerald Ford. General Scowcroft's operating style under President Bush will be discussed in the concluding section. It should be noted here, regardless, that Scowcroft's operating style under Ford was completely opposite to that of the preceding ANSA, Henry Kissinger. Scowcroft, who had served as Kissinger's deputy, saw his position as requiring a more self-effacing style, giving priority to organization and the faithful presentation of the views of NSC members. He did not act independently or negotiate for the president but functioned instead as a senior administrative aide and staff assistant. The qualities attributed to Scowcroft—"cool, hardworking, straightforward, a good administrator"—were precisely the qualities that appealed to Ford.[6] Scowcroft never appeared on a national interview show, and his name was rarely mentioned in the press.[7] Despite a more limited role as ANSA when compared to that of Kissinger, Scowcroft has often been singled out as the ideal type for the ANSA position.[8]

President Ronald Reagan's first ANSA, Richard Allen, was also essentially an administrator. As noted in chapter 8, Allen consistently endorsed a low-profile conception of his job and asserted that he had no interest in making policy. As he put it, "the policy formulation function of the national security adviser should be off-loaded to the Secretary of State."[9] On the other hand, Allen's diminished status as ANSA deprived the White House of an adviser who could compensate for the president's admitted deficiencies in foreign affairs.

The role of the ANSA as coordinator involves recognizing two enduring characteristics of national security policy making: (1) that even with a strong secretary of state, most decisions affecting the nation's security involve more than just diplomacy and cannot therefore remain the exclusive preserve of the State Department and (2) that interdepartmental policies and programs need active management, which will inevitably lead to some conflict among the principals involved. Overall coordination of this management process is necessarily a presidential task, with the ANSA a necessary presidential taskmaster.

As a coordinator, the ANSA facilitates the making of policy but does not initiate it. He is, instead, responsible for defining policy options for the NSC to consider. He also manages the flow of ideas, information, policies, and programs involved in national security. Although the ANSA may exercise considerable influence, it is as a presidential staff assistant, not as an independent actor. The ANSA's role entails reviewing policy and managing programs, while the principals (particularly the president and the secretary of state) make the final decisions.

Robert Cutler, President Eisenhower's special assistant for national security affairs, typified the ANSA as a coordinator of national security policy. As our earlier discussion emphasized, Eisenhower's national security system could be characterized as a "policy hill." On the up side, the NSC Planning Board considered policy recommendations to be submitted to the council, where they were debated prior to presidential approval. Approved policy went "down the other side of the policy hill to departments and agencies responsible for its execution,"[10] with the Operations Coordinating Board, or OCB, monitoring implementation. The NSC was the apex of this formalized and highly structured system, and Cutler was responsible for its direction.

Even though Cutler chaired the two interdepartmental committees that buttressed the NSC (the Planning Board and the OCB) and initiated discussions at council meetings, his primary responsibilities were to ensure that all points of view were considered and to summarize these findings at NSC meetings, "maintaining the quality and character of advising as a process, not simply . . . expressing those views he and his staff favored."[11] Cutler sought to ensure an orderly policy-making process by relating current and past NSC decisions, seeing that the council's discussion remained on track, and spelling out the implications of all options.[12] Cutler, along with his successors, Dillon Anderson and Gordon Gray, saw himself as a servant of the NSC rather than as an independent actor in the policy-making process, though at the same time, he institutionalized presidential staff involvement in the evolution and evaluation of national security policy.

Two of President Reagan's ANSAs also exemplified the role of coordinator: William P. Clark and Robert McFarlane. McFarlane, in particular, acted as an "honest broker" in the national security policy–making process. His ability to work as a team player allowed Secretary of State George Shultz to become the administration's premier foreign policy maker while maintaining the White House support that was prerequisite to such preeminence. For a two-year period (1983–1985), in fact, the Shultz–McFarlane axis lent coherence to the Reagan administration's foreign policy, in which disarray seemed more the order of the day.

The ANSA as counselor functions in a largely personal relationship to the president: evaluating, rather than simply presenting, policy alternatives; intervening in the departments to get information or other points of view; articulating the presidential perspective on proposed policy—generally seeking "to pinpoint and balance others' biases rather than to press his own."[13] The ANSA as counselor does not preside over a highly structured advisory system and is consequently allowed to spend more time on ad hoc policy making and serving immediate presidential needs.

The more-operational orientation of the NSC staff under a counselor is designed to introduce the widest possible range of alternative actions from which the president may choose. Though the ANSA might respect the secretary of state and his "formal prerogatives,"[14] he and his staff can venture deeply into State Department business—for example, clearing and drafting cables and monitoring the communications system. Moreover, as the NSC staff assumes greater operational responsibilities, the likelihood of conflict between "the president's prime agent of coordination" and the State Department over questions of which policies will meet presidential expectations increases.[15]

President Kennedy's ANSA, McGeorge Bundy, created and typified the role of presidential counselor. Bundy saw his job as clarifying alternatives set before the president, recording decisions, and monitoring follow-through. However, his work was not as without competition with the State Department as he may have thought. As Kennedy's frustrations with the State Department's bureaucratic routine mounted, the role of Bundy—"a crisp, terse intellectual operator"—grew.[16] Most important, Bundy (as well as his successor Walt W. Rostow) was close to "an aggressive, pragmatic President whose style meshed well with his own."[17]

Bundy's service as ANSA points up an aspect of White House staffing that has not been lost on subsequent advisers or secretaries of state: Physical proximity to the president creates special relationships. When Bundy maneuvered his office from the Executive Office Building to the west wing of the White House and established the situation room, he engineered a major administrative coup. He was now "at the end of the buzzer," at the president's immediate call, ensconced among the political staff, capable of access to the Oval Office without necessarily having an appointment or a specific agenda. No other national security policy maker has enjoyed such a potential advantage.

President Carter wanted Secretary of State Cyrus Vance to be his principal foreign policy adviser and ANSA Zbigniew Brzezinski to serve as a personal counselor. To Secretary Vance's disadvantage, Brzezinski proved to be aggressive in gaining both the president's confidence and access to his person. Brzezinski realized that, as the president's assistant, the ANSA was the guardian of the "presidential perspective" in decision making. As time passed, Brzezinski acted more and more as Carter's foreign policy spokesman and became increasingly involved in diplomatic operations. By mid-1978, Brzezinski had transformed his role as presidential counselor into one of vigorous public advocate for important foreign policy decisions.[18] Although Brzezinski never realized the policy-making preeminence of Kissinger—he never succeeded in becoming an *agent*—this was not for want of aspiration or effort.

The ANSA as agent combines the duties of a coordinator (directing the planning process) with those of a counselor (serving as a personal presidential adviser). As an agent, the ANSA dominates the process of formulating national security policy—making many decisions himself and advocating others—and acts as the primary presidential spokesman for foreign affairs. This virtually eliminates any distinction between the duties of the national security adviser and those of the secretary of state. Thus, the ANSA becomes "the key line operator in every important respect."[19] The overall purpose of this type of system is to strengthen the intellectual and bureaucratic resources of the White House to ensure direct presidential control over national security policy making.[20] Administratively, the State Department is displaced to the periphery, and the NSC staff, in effect, becomes a "rival State Department."

Henry Kissinger, ANSA under Richard Nixon, was, like McGeorge Bundy, an intellectual who was disposed to advance his own ideas. However, what distinguished Kissinger from other ANSAs before or since was the degree to which he transformed the scope of his office. Before the end of Nixon's first term, Kissinger was unquestionably the prime presidential adviser on foreign affairs: "If Bundy had intruded on the role of the Secretary of State, Kissinger obliterated it."[21] The actual Secretary of State, William P. Rogers, was eclipsed by Kissinger, who would eventually combine both positions in an unprecedented consolidation of policy-making powers.

As a presidential agent, Kissinger not only briefed Nixon daily on the nation's security but increasingly spoke on behalf of the president, and finally served as the prime negotiator for matters relating to Vietnam, China, and SALT I. These were the principal items on the Nixon foreign policy agenda, and Kissinger was the focal point for both their conception and their realization. The situation room provided the "backchannels" by which foreign policy could be conducted from the White House. Kissinger ultimately acquired decisive control over both the formulation and conduct of foreign affairs. By doing so he acquired de facto powers greater than the de jure authority of the secretaries of state and defense.

After his tenure at the State Department, Kissinger declared his conviction (while admitting that he had not held it when in the White House) that the secretary of state should be every administration's chief foreign policy spokesman. The ANSA, in contrast, he said, should play only a coordinating role in ensuring that all points of view on a proposed policy are heard. "If the security adviser becomes active in the development and articulation of policy, he must inevitably diminish the Secretary of State and reduce his effectiveness."[22] This, of course, was exactly Secretary Rogers's experience. Though successive presidents and national security assistants have announced themselves opposed to a Kissinger-type approach to national security policy making, the allures and successes of the agent role remain undeniable. Indeed, Admiral John Poindexter pushed the agent role one step further by acting on the basis of his personal assessment of the president's *intentions* rather than on expressed presidential policies.

■ The Iran–Contra Affair: The ANSA as Insurgent

In the last two years of the Reagan administration, great attention was focused on the structure and operation of the National Security Council, as highlighted by the Iran–Contra affair. We have designated the widely publicized activities of Admiral Poindexter and his aide, Lt. Colonel Oliver North, a case of insurgency in the formulation and implementation of national security policy. What principally distinguishes this model from the others we have identified is its status as an aberration that no student of the policy-making process could seriously recommend. The Iran–Contra episode is the clearest example to date of the NSC system out of control. In effect, the ANSA and members of the NSC staff mutinied: They attempted to seize control of the policy-making process to realize their own conception of American national security. Whether this was with the president's tacit consent or without his knowledge remains controversial.

President Reagan believed, with some accuracy, that a preoccupation with the details of foreign policy making had seriously weakened Jimmy Carter's standing and effectiveness as president. Reagan preferred, therefore, to focus on the "big picture," leaving his advisers to fill in the details of policy. Consequently, Reagan was more than ordinarily dependent on his advisers; however, with few exceptions, they were little better informed than he was. When no consensus existed among his advisers (as was the rule during most of his tenure in the White House), President Reagan appeared bewildered and uncertain of what to do about it. More than any president in recent memory, Reagan distanced himself from the policies undertaken in his name. His aides may well have concluded that this distancing was deliberate and then sought to assist him in achieving it.

Internal operating procedures within the NSC under Reagan were poorly defined and loosely supervised. For example, Admiral Poindexter said that Reagan would have approved the proposed sale of missiles to Iran for an exchange of American hostages "if he had been asked." Ronald Reagan said he would not have done so but maintained that he was never asked.[23] As with many NSC decisions President Reagan made, most concerning the Iranian arms deal were never recorded.[24] Reagan appeared not to have been really interested in the details of how the NSC staff was aiding the anti-Sandinista Contra cause in Nicaragua. According to Poindexter, the president knew about it but "in general terms."[25] Testifying to further examples of poorly supervised decision making, Colonel North contended that he sent President Reagan several memos concerning covert aid to the Contras. Admiral Poindexter said that these were never received, and President Reagan denied having seen or approved them.[26]

Under Reagan, there were six national security advisers. Two had prior experience in external policy making (Robert McFarlane and Frank Carlucci). Two others came from the military (Admiral Poindexter and Lt. General Colin Powell). Two had little or no background in the management of national security affairs (Richard Allen and William Clark). The average tenure of a Reagan ANSA was sixteen months. No other administration had such a high turnover in this important position. Lacking adequate preparation and expertise, the ANSAs and their staffs during the Reagan era were understandably uncertain about their proper roles.

This situation was exacerbated by President Reagan's inability or unwillingness to specify their duties. President Reagan was faulted by the Tower Commission for major deficiencies in what was termed his "management style."[27] Reagan was also likened to a modern-day James Buchanan: Faced with conflicts and competitiveness among his principal advisers, he was unable to make a decision. Failure to exercise this presidential responsibility puts the president at risk of losing control over the policy-making process. Ultimately, the Iran–Contra affair was attributable to a lack of presidential decisiveness.

Reagan, as noted, liked to make policy on the basis of staff consensus, approving agreements reached among his principal subordinates. Unfortunately, such consensus rarely existed—and perhaps never could have—on important issues such as arms control, Central America, and the Middle East. The long-standing feud between the Departments of State and Defense over intermediate nuclear weapons went largely unarbitrated by the White House. Both Secretaries Shultz and Weinberger also expressed serious reservations about White House initiatives concerning the arms-for-hostages deal with Iran. Adjudicating such disputes is a presidential responsibility. Most presidents since 1945 have had either a forceful secretary of state or a forceful ANSA to assist them in doing so, but most of the time Reagan had neither. The predictable outcome of such a state of affairs was drift and disarray in the policy-making process—conditions encouraging insurgency by members of the White House staff.

In the Reagan White House, the ANSA and other members of the NSC staff came to perform, often on their own initiative, interesting and novel functions. These included protecting the president from certain other advisers whose views they regarded as unwelcome, projecting a tough American image abroad and voicing a willingness to use force when necessary, preventing political damage to the president's reputation, and keeping peace among departmental rivals. As the details of the Iran–Contra affair indicate, some members of the NSC staff also seemed to interpret their responsibilities to include carrying out actions that other executive agencies were legally prohibited from conducting by virtue of the Boland Amendments. Poindexter and North, for example, conducted such activities in accordance with what they maintained was implicit presidential approval.[28] Regardless, directing covert actions involved the NSC staff in a variety of questionable activities: personally negotiating with foreign governments, diverting funds to selected Contra leaders from the sale of arms to Iran, attempting to influence congressional opinion for repeal of the Boland Amendments, and, using the NSC staff as a military strategy board to advise the Contras in their fight against the Sandinista government.

In the Iran–Contra affair Americans thus witnessed a dramatic perversion of the proper role of the NSC staff in the policy-making process as defined both by statute and tradition.[29] It was not just that the arms-for-hostages deal with Iran was "an inept policy, poorly implemented,"[30] or that the NSC system failed; even more damaging, the advisory process was ignored or not used at all.[31] Under Poindexter and North, the NSC became a "shadowy parallel government," operating with little or no supervision and without the limitations on executive actions that are normally assumed in a democratic system.[32] Accountability was further undermined by cabals within the executive branch that acted to keep major public officials (such as the CIA director and the secretaries of state and defense) from knowing the details of the Iran–Contra activities.[33] Admiral Poindexter testified that he deliberately withheld knowledge of the details from President Reagan so as to protect the president with "plausible deniability."[34] Deniability thus replaced constitutional accountability.

Irrespective of the particular national security advisory processes that a president may use, the record on the Iran–Contra affair suggests the need for a series of steps or established procedures to be followed in the decision-making process. These include:

1. clear and accurate identification of the problems confronting the United States in the area of national security,
2. comprehensive and objective intelligence gathering and evaluation,
3. consultation with experts
4. solicitation of the views of all major participants about proposed policy alternatives,
5. full evaluation of policy proposals at the highest level,
6. clear and objective identification of the consequences of all major policy options,
7. final decision by the president and wide communication of his decision at all levels of government,
8. observance of all legal restraints on the government's proposed action,
9. careful and systematic monitoring of policy implementation, and
10. periodic policy evaluation and program review.

As should be clear from the record on the Iran–Contra affair, few of these guidelines were observed or even acknowledged during the Reagan administration. Though the insurgency of Poindexter and North was an aberration in the history of national security advisory models, there is much to suggest that a precondition for this insurgency was the president's failure to take charge of the national security process. Whatever the ultimate legal judgments on his subordinates, President Reagan must bear the ultimate responsibility for the insurgency within his administration.

Despite the public scandal and breaches of the law involved in the Iran–Contra activities, the machinations of Admiral Poindexter and Colonel North may have had the unanticipated consequence of bringing about a reevaluation of the National Security Council, the NSC staff, and especially the role of the assistant for national security affairs. For example, there have been only two major congressional analyses of the NSC system: the comprehensive, if controversial, Jackson subcommittee report in 1960 and the Zorinsky hearings in 1978. Perhaps another subcommittee on national policy needs to be created to spell out in detail the substantive and structural reforms suggested by the particulars of the Iran–Contra hearings. For so important an agency of American foreign policy making, the NSC has been comparatively under-scrutinized and underlegislated, at least in relation to the Departments of State and Defense. In part, this fact can be explained as due to the traditional deference of Congress to "executive privilege" in the conduct of the presidential office. Of equal importance has been the tradition of deference—by Congress, the press, and the public—to the president's claims to primacy in the conduct of national security affairs.

▌ The Lessons of the Iran–Contra Affair

Deriving general lessons from specific events is among the more difficult of analytical undertakings. There is always a tendency to translate the conventional wisdom of one's time into an immutable principle. We do not offer any overarching law to guide presidential policy making in the always difficult sphere of national security. However, just as there were important lessons to be learned from Watergate about the constitutional and political role of the presidency in the American political system, the Iran–Contra affair too offers an opportunity for learning. What follows is an attempt to present some general observations—and to note some possible correctives—with regard to the nature of national security policy making. Though ours is a modest undertaking, we hope that the ten lessons drawn from "What Oliver North Hath Wrought" will assist future policy makers in the formulation and implementation of American national security.

1. After forty years, the National Security Council mechanism has not yet yielded a unified and coherent national security policy. Indeed, the level of intraexecutive disunity under President Reagan was higher than in any previous administration. Where disunity occurred under President Carter, it was largely a matter of personal competitiveness. Under Reagan, it was virtually institutionalized, with long-standing unresolved disagreements among key decision makers. In sum, the basic objective of an integrated national security policy, accepted by all major agencies, has remained elusive.

2. The Iran–Contra affair raises anew Juvenal's ancient question: "Who watches the watchmen?"[35] In Iran–Contra, the national security adviser and his staff, charged with the responsibility of unifying and monitoring the activities of the agencies concerned with national security, essentially ran amok. In effect, the national security adviser and the NSC staff under President Reagan led an insurgency aimed at taking national security policy making into their own hands, free from the constraints of public opinion, legislative oversight, and even presidential authority.

3. Among the many causes of the Iran–Contra affair was President Reagan's detached and uninvolved approach to decision making, as well as his evident lack of interest in, or understanding of, important national security

issues. President Reagan appeared to lack a specific game plan, so members of the NSC staff devised and implemented their own. Oliver North and his associates acted to fill this vacuum on the basis on two beliefs: (1) that the actions they initiated were fully compatible with the Reagan administration's ideological principles and (2) that though he may not have been consciously aware of their activities abroad President Reagan at least tacitly approved of them.

4. Though there are several models for the management of national security, each presupposes that the president will, in fact, discharge his constitutional responsibilities—one of which is to supervise his immediate staff and demand that his subordinates provide full and accurate information. Former Secretary of State Dean Rusk once observed that he would like to see Article II of the Constitution, which vests executive power in the person of the president, hung in the White House dining room for the staff to gaze upon. Since the Iran–Contra affair, one must also wonder if Article II should not also be displayed prominently in the Oval Office.

5. In general, the power of the White House staff has increased dramatically over the past twenty-five years. The size and importance of the White House Office requires presidents to be good managers of their own staff, as well as of the government. Designating a competent national security adviser and devising an effective national security advisory process are two of the president's most important management decisions. There are several models for the advisory process, as we have elaborated, and ultimately the "correct" choice is the one that works best for the particular president. Choosing an appropriate advisory process has obvious difficulties, but to shirk these responsibilities is an invitation to insurgency.

6. For all the unquestioned importance of presidential involvement in the making of national security policy, in the Reagan administration the officials and advisers involved had little background or knowledge in foreign affairs. The Iran–Contra affair is replete with evidence of uninformed aides giving bad advice to President Reagan, who, given a lack of personal background and manifest lack of interest in the substance of foreign affairs, was even more than ordinarily dependent on his advisers. This may be the most fundamental reason for the Iran–Contra scandal.

7. Ultimately, the national security adviser's power and effectiveness stem from one source: the president—specifically, the president's level of confidence in him and the similarity of their views. However, neither the ANSA nor any other aide can simply take this presidential confidence for granted; it must be clearly indicated and periodically reaffirmed. In particular, the ANSA cannot merely assume that the president wants a particular policy and then attempt to implement it according to his often highly subjective assumptions about what the president would want to do if he were really aware of the issue. Admiral Poindexter's role in the Iran–Contra affair points to the danger of such unilateral decision making by a presidential assistant. Inevitably, the president and the nation are badly served by such behavior.

8. A related lesson of the Iran–Contra affair is that the president's decisions must be clearly and unambiguously arrived at and duly recorded for communication to his subordinates. A recurrent question during the Iran–Contra hearings was "what precisely were President Reagan's wishes concerning the arms-for-hostages deal and aid for the Nicaraguan Contras?" Considerable confusion and uncertainty as to the answer to that question led subordinates to supply their own answers.

9. Another deficiency in national security policy making highlighted by Iran–Contra (although hardly confined to that event) was the absence of regular and objective policy review and program evaluation by disinterested advisers reporting directly to the president. Clearly, the American foreign policy process would benefit from more periodic and regularized assessments. Procedures that guaranteed strict accountability in policy making would have brought Oliver North and the other errant members of the NSC staff to heel sooner and with less damage to the nation's foreign relations.

10. As evidenced by the Iran–Contra affair, the Reagan administration failed to establish or enforce clear lines of accountability among the members of the White House staff responsible for national security policy making. The result was administrative chaos. Two kinds of administrative chaos should be identified—one relatively benign, the other disruptive. Benign chaos is calculated and intentional—as evident, for example, in the management style of Franklin Roosevelt, who used administrative "divide and rule" tactics to keep decision-making in his own hands. Disruptive chaos came to light during the Iran–Contra hearings. Reagan's pattern of administration, which was at best nondeliberate and unintentional—or, if President Reagan is not to be believed, deceptive and chaotic—resulted from a combination of factors, the most prominently cited of which was President Reagan's "detached" style of management. In FDR's case, administrative chaos greatly enhanced presidential power. In Reagan's case, it seriously weakened presidential control over decision making.

The disunity and disarray that was a constant feature of national security policy making during the Reagan administration had its origins in fundamental policy disagreements among the president's advisers on a range of issues. Internal policy disputes have, of course, also characterized other presidential administrations and, arguably, have led to the formulating of better policies. Nonetheless, it is the president's unique constitutional prerogative and responsibility to put an end to bureaucratic warfare among his subordinates and to articulate a unified policy both to the United States and to other nations. Ultimately, a president must make it his business to inform himself adequately about what his subordinates are undertaking in his name. Furthermore, the president must guarantee that his subordinates's actions are consonant with his political interests and the best interests of the American people. In the last analysis, President Reagan could not, or would not, accept the burden of this managerial responsibility.

■ Is There a Preferred ANSA Role?

Constitutional provisions, administrative precedents, and electoral promises collectively dictate that a newly elected president approach the organization of government from a personal perspective. Defining the president's perspective is a central responsibility of the White House staff; the management of national security is hardly an exception to this rule. Indeed, given the centrality of presidential decision making in the conduct of foreign affairs, how a president organizes for national security is one of his or her most crucial decisions. Clearly, mandating a particular mode of decision making for the president is also both impossible and inadvisable. Nevertheless, the evidence from this review of the historical record does suggest certain conclusions—and a few recommendations—with regard to the effective management of national security affairs.

The most obvious conclusion is that the ANSA has been institutionalized as part of the national security policy–making process on a level with the secretaries of state and defense and the CIA director. At the same time, we have observed rather dramatic oscillations in the ways in which presidents have used their national security assistants and the NSC staff. Almost as a rule, successive administrations have reactively reorganized, restructuring their national security advisory process to presumably correct the defects of their predecessors.[36] Kennedy, for example, deconstructed the Eisenhower machinery in light of the Jackson subcommittee's criticisms; Nixon reversed the collegiality of the Kennedy administration and reconstructed a hierarchial NSC staff.

To some extent these shifts in organizational structure reflect the conventional political wisdom of the day. As we have observed, the making of national security policy involves the exercise of presidential responsibilities in ways that are largely unfettered by constitutional or institutional constraints.[37] The ANSA's political and administrative role consequently varies, because the nature of this role "is primarily determined by the man [sic] it serves."[38]

Is there a preferred ANSA role? Though answering a question so dependent on personalities and politics is admittedly difficulty, both future presidents and the concerned public must still ask it. Figure 9-3, "Presidential Management Styles and ANSA Roles," represents an attempt to help answer this question.

Using the same values and variables as in figure 9-1, we can classify a president with little interest in the hands-on administration of foreign affairs and with few policies initiated by the White House as having a department-centered management style. This is the classical pattern of policy making and implementation, in which the State Department is the lead agency within the executive branch and the secretary of state is the president's chief foreign policy deputy and spokesperson to the international community. In this pattern, the president, though unquestionably in charge of external policy and of making the final decisions, designates the secretary of state his chief of staff for foreign affairs and supports the secretary in this role against bureaucratic

Implementation Responsibility

	Low	High
Low	**Department-Centered** Administrator	**Formalized** Coordinator
High	**Collegial** Counselor	**Palace Guard** Agent

Policy-Making Responsibility (row labels Low / High on left side)

Figure 9-3.   Presidential management styles and ANSA roles.

rivals and political criticisms. In turn, the secretary of state relies heavily on State Department personnel for analytical and operational support. In this model of presidential management, the ANSA appropriately plays the role of administrator.

A president who looks to the cabinet departments for policy proposals but maintains a high degree of personal control over the administration of foreign affairs is classified as having a formalized management style. With a president bent on considering the fullest range of policy proposals and implementation plans, the NSC becomes an interdepartmental forum for the presentation and elaboration of matters for presidential disposition. With formal briefings by standing committees of the NSC and a careful delineation of the different departmental perspectives, the president can survey the range of options available and evaluate the effectiveness of ongoing operations. In this model, the ANSA serves as a coordinator of the advisory machinery.

In contrast to the formalized management of national security policy making, in the collegial model of presidential management the president eschews direct administrative responsibility for an active part in shaping the content of the policy. Ad hoc working groups rather than a formal hierarchy of interdepartmental committees are typical. Presidents matching this model are presumed to distrust the State Department and the other national security bureaucracies (even if this is not expressed overtly). The president's goal is to shift the locus of decision making to the White House and to use the NSC staff as an independent analysis and review agency. Decision making is based on an open exchange among relative equals in the policy-making process. Without clearly demarcated areas of responsibility, NSC participants (at the council level and below) are encouraged to seek a preferred solution rather than protect bureaucratic turf. In this model, the ANSA, as the guardian of the president's interests, serves as a counselor.

In the "palace guard" pattern of presidential management, administrative and policy-making responsibilities are centralized within the confines of the White House. Virtually excluded from an active role, the State Department and its NSC colleagues are relegated to carrying out policies devised by the president and the national security adviser (within their "rival State Department"). In such a situation, the ANSA tends to be an articulate and ambitious aide with strongly held international views that complement those of the president. As the president's designated alter ego, the ANSA is free to operate as an agent with the authority to represent American security interests traditionally reserved for the secretary of state.

The question still remains: "Is there a preferred ANSA role?" This may be addressed in three ways. First, a president would be advised to define a role for the ANSA that is consistent with his or her preferences regarding the general management of the government. For example, if a president is committed to the principle of cabinet government—that is, the predominance of the State Department—the appointment of an ANSA with strong policy positions and personal ambitions would invite the kind of bureaucratic warfare that debilitated the Carter foreign policy. If President Carter really wished to have Secretary Vance direct the policy process, he should have appointed someone more like Brent Scowcroft instead of Zbigniew Brzezinski as his ANSA.

Second, the history of the NSC over the past forty years does suggest that neither the agent nor the administrator roles of the ANSA are to be recommended. The machinations of Admiral Poindexter, a self-appointed presidential agent, indicate how easily the exigencies of national security can provide a veil for insurgent operations—that is, operations without presidential authorization and uninformed by departmental expertise. On the other hand, the administrator role may easily prove too weak in providing the advice that the president needs to make transdepartmental decisions. For an ANSA who is an administrator to be effective, both the president and the secretary of state must be knowledgeable about foreign affairs and able hands-on administrators. This can prove a rare combination.

Third, whether a president chooses to manage national security policy with a coordinator or counselor is largely a matter of background and temperament. Yet, both of these models have costs as well as benefits. Not every president will be knowledgeable about the international situation, confident in voicing his or her opinion, or comfortable with the give-and-take of collegial decision making. Although a counselor can assist the president in managing the process, he or she will inevitably be tempted to do more than this. On the other hand, the structured character of formalized national security management may prove exasperating to presidents preferring a more flexible and freewheeling approach. Some presidents may perceive the benefits of a formalized approach—procedural regularity, predictability, and accountability—as stultifying wheel spinning.

The worst situation arises when a president vacillates in designating the ANSA's role or chooses a national security assistant with personality traits inconsistent with the demands of the designated role. For example, Carter seemingly could not choose between the roles of counselor and agent for his ANSA; Reagan, with six ANSAs, seemed unable to choose at all. It is hard to disagree with what Alexander George has concluded: "The experience of every president from Truman to Reagan makes one conclusion inescapable: a president must first define his own role in the national security policymaking system before he can design and manage the roles and relationships of the major participants."[39]

NOTES

1. Stanley L. Falk, "The National Security Council under Truman, Eisenhower, and Kennedy," *Political Science Quarterly* 79 (September 1964): 414.

2. U.S. Senate, Committee on Government Operations, Subcommittee on National Policy Machinery, *Organizing for National Security,* vol. 1 (Washington, D.C.: Government Printing Office, 1961), pp. 561 and 564.

3. Cecil V. Crabb, Jr., and Kevin V. Mulcahy, *Presidents and Foreign Policy Making: FDR to Reagan* (Baton Rouge: Louisiana State University Press, 1986), pp. 122–155.

4. Joseph G. Bock and Duncan L. Clarke, "The National Security Assistant and the White House Staff: National Security Policy Decisionmaking and Domestic Political Considerations, 1947–84," *Presidential Studies Quarterly* 16 (Spring 1986): 259.

5. Sidney W. Souers, "Policy Formulation for National Security," *American Political Science Review* 43 (Spring 1986): 537.

6. *New York Times,* November 4, 1975; Gerald Ford, *A Time to Heal* (New York: Harper & Row, 1979), p. 326.

7. I. M. Destler, "A Job That Doesn't Work," *Foreign Policy* 38 (Spring 1980): 89.

8. Ibid., p. 85.

9. *New York Times,* November 19, 1980.

10. Robert Cutler, "The Department of the National Security Council," *Foreign Affairs* 34 (April 1956): 448.

11. Fred I. Greenstein and John P. Burke, "Comparative Models of Presidential Decisionmaking: Eisenhower and Johnson." Paper presented at the annual meeting of the American Political Science Association, August 29–September 1, 1985, pp. 13–14.

12. Ibid., p. 15.

13. I. M. Destler, "National Security II: The Rise of the Assistant," in *The Illusion of Presidential Government,* ed. Hugh Heclo and Lester M. Salamon (Boulder, Colo.: Westview Press, 1981), p. 268.

14. I. M. Destler, Leslie Gelb, and Anthony Lake, *Our Own Worst Enemy: The Unmaking of American Foreign Policy* (New York: Simon & Schuster, 1984), p. 194.

15. I. M. Destler, *Presidents, Bureaucrats, and Foreign Policy* (Princeton, N.J.: Princeton University Press, 1972), pp. 102–103.

16. Destler, Gelb, and Lake, *Our Own Worst Enemy,* p. 184.

17. Ibid.

18. Alexander George, *Presidential Decision Making in Foreign Policy* (Boulder, Colo.: Westview Press, 1980), p. 200.

19. Destler, "National Security II," p. 271.

20. George, *Presidential Decision Making*, p. 177.

21. Destler, Gelb, and Lake, *Our Own Worst Enemy*, p. 208.

22. Henry Kissinger, *The White House Years* (Boston: Little, Brown, 1979), pp. 11–12.

23. *Report on the Congressional Committee Investigating the Iran–Contra Affair.* Joint Hearings before the Select Committee on Secret Military Assistance to Iran and the Nicaraguan Opposition, U.S. Senate, and the Select Committee to Investigate Covert Arms Transactions with Iran, U.S. House, 100th Cong., 1st sess. (Washington, D.C.: Government Printing Office, 1987), p. 13. Hereafter referred to as *Iran–Contra Report*.

24. *The Tower Commission Report: The Full Text of the President's Special Review Board* (New York: Times Books and Bantam Books, 1987), p. 70. Hereafter referred to as Tower Commission Report.

25. *Iran–Contra Report*, p. 77.

26. Ibid., p. 13; and *Tower Commission Report*, pp. 77–78.

27. *Tower Commission Report*, p. xv.

28. *Iran–Contra Report*, p. 21.

29. Ibid., p. 17.

30. *Tower Commission Report*, p. xv.

31. Ibid., p. 80.

32. Ibid., p. xv.

33. *Iran–Contra Report*, p. 14–16.

34. Ibid., p. 17.

35. *Tower Commission Report*, p. xvi.

36. Destler, Gelb, and Lake, *Our Own Worst Enemy*, p. 168; Anna Kasten Nelson, "National Security I: Inventing a Process," in *The Illusion of Presidential Government*, ed. Hugh Heclo and Lester M. Salamon, (Boulder, Colo.: Westview Press, 1981), p. 259; and Destler, "National Security II," pp. 263 and 272.

37. Bock and Clarke, "The National Security Assistant and the White House Staff," p. 258.

38. John E. Endicott, "The National Security Council," in *American Defense Policy*, ed. John E. Endicott and Roy W. Strafford, Jr. (Baltimore, Md.: Johns Hopkins University Press, 1981), p. 314.

39. George, *Presidential Decision Making*, p. 146.

CHAPTER 10

National Security Policy in the Post–Cold War Era: The Challenge of the 1990s

The Bush administration's approach to national security policy making, at least as judged by the early record, can be characterized as managerial, collegial, incremental, and pragmatic. Each of these elements will be considered in turn as part of a preliminary assessment of whether or not the Bush administration's approach to American national security is adequate to deal with the challenges that the United States will face in world affairs during the post–Cold War era of the 1990s.

▌ Bush's Management Style

In the aftermath of the Iran–Contra affair, much concern was voiced about the degree of direct presidential involvement in decision making. Whereas Jimmy Carter was faulted for being overly involved in the minutiae of policy, Ronald Reagan was judged by the Tower Commission to be too detached. The perception of a presidency on "remote control"—with a chief executive who was unwilling or unable to direct the policy process—has persisted in the minds of many observers despite Reagan's considerable foreign policy accomplishments in the last two years of his administration. Regardless of the accuracy of this characterization, George Bush appears to have entered the White House determined not to be faulted for a lack of personal direction in national security policy making. In contrast to his low profile as vice president, President Bush appears to want to be known as a take-charge commander of the ship of state.

Shortly after the start of the Bush administration, the following opinion about what was necessary for the proper conduct of international affairs was offered: "Washington badly needs a foreign-policy process under clear direction, with a clear chain of command and clear spheres of influence. It hasn't had one for a very long time."[1] Clear presidential direction of American foreign affairs has been a manifest goal of the Bush administration, with every effort being made to position the president at stage center managing the policy process. Indeed, "in his campaign for office, George Bush sought to project an image of himself as a pragmatically-oriented decision maker."[2] Whereas Reagan articulated a fervent anticommunist worldview and was open to charges of haphazard policy planning, Bush has substituted a declared commitment to sound policy planning in place of his predecessor's "ideological pontifications."[3] The Bush administration presents itself as an experienced team inspired more by a desire to forge effective policies than by a desire to crusade for ideological causes.[4] On the other hand, Bush's self-styled restraint in the face of dramatic movements toward democratization in the Soviet Union and Eastern bloc countries has left his administration open to charges of vacillation and vacuity.

Bush's preferred form of decision making was vividly demonstrated in the preparations for his visit to the North Atlantic Treaty Organization's fortieth anniversary meeting in Brussels in May 1989. According to the *New York Times* account, the president was displeased with the State Department's review of his foreign and defense policy options, especially in light of Mikhail Gorbachev's widely publicized proposals for reductions in strategic weapons. At a meeting with a handful of his aides—most prominently Secretary of State James Baker, National Security Adviser Brent Scowcroft, Secretary of Defense Dick Cheney, and White House Chief of Staff John Sununu—over a long weekend at Kennebunkport, Maine, President Bush hammered out a far-reaching address to the NATO summit that stabilized NATO relations and transformed the administration's standing with the Europeans.[5]

It should be recognized here that Bush's performance, especially the hastily arranged nature of the process, was not universally acclaimed in all of the national security bureaucracies. What is significant is that this weekend conference at Kennebunkport—a pragmatic response to a specific challenge, with calculated attention to media response and public opinion, and the visible participation of Baker and Scowcroft in their complementary roles—reflects the qualities that the Bush administration most values.

In sum, President Bush appears to have adopted a collegial approach to national security policy making and a counselor role for his national security adviser.[6] Such a collegial model has the following characteristics:

1. The president distrusts the national security bureaucracies, especially the State Department. As will be discussed in detail presently, the prestige of the Foreign Service under Secretary of State Baker has fallen to the low associated with the secretaryships of Henry Kissinger and John Foster Dulles.

2. The national security adviser and the NSC staff together serve as an independent analysis and review agency. Compared to the NSC staff under Reagan, that under Bush has been given high marks for its experience and professionalism.

3. Policy making is decision-oriented, with a minimum of fighting over bureaucratic turf. The Bush administration has not seen the degree of inter-

departmental rivalry that characterized the relations between the Departments of State and Defense over arms control in the Reagan administration or the competition between the secretary of state and the national security adviser that damaged the Carter administration's credibility with regard to policy making.

4. The national security adviser represents the interests of the president in the policy-making process—not advocating personal policy preferences, but exercising independent judgment if convinced that a department's proposal is inimical to the president's interests. General Scowcroft has been particularly distinguished in acting as a full partner with the secretaries of state and defense without usurping their departmental prerogatives or presuming to be the sole instrument of the president's will.

Overall, President Bush has made every effort to avoid the mistakes of previous administrations by defining a clear management style and appointing a national security team capable of working collegially. Indeed, the pattern of presidential–secretarial–White House staff relations represented by Bush–Baker–Scowcroft may prove to be one of the better examples of successful policy-making relations in the history of the presidency.[7] Though successful collegiality is, of course, no guarantee of successful policy, it is certainly to be preferred to a vague management style or to a management team staffed with inappropriate personnel.

▌ Bush's National Security Team

Lt. General Brent Scowcroft has the unique distinction of being the only assistant to the president for national security affairs to have served in two different administrations. (Robert Cutler served twice under President Eisenhower, and McGeorge Bundy was retained by President Johnson when he succeeded to the office, just as President Ford retained Henry Kissinger before appointing him secretary of state.) Having served under Gerald Ford from 1975 to 1977, Scowcroft is back twelve years later under George Bush. Given the uniqueness of the position and the national security adviser's special relationship with the president, Scowcroft's reemergence is both unprecedented and extraordinary. His appointment raises two lines of inquiry: What kind of role will Scowcroft play under George Bush, and how will it compare to his previous tenure in office?

Scowcroft played what can be described as an administrator role when he served as national security adviser under Ford. He acted in a decidedly low-key, low-profile advisory capacity and was responsible primarily for overseeing both the flow of interdepartmental proposals and all subsequent decisions. Scowcroft's performance as an administrator of the national security policy–making process has, along with that of President Reagan's last ANSA, General Colin Powell, received generally high marks. As a writer for the *New York Times* editorialized, "Two of the best people in this post have been happy to be 'inside' men: General Powell and retired Lieut. Gen. Brent Scowcroft. They let the Secretaries give the speeches and face the cameras while concentrating on getting decisions made at the right time—with all parties getting a full and fair hearing."[8] As noted in the previous chapter, whether the administrator role is to be recommended as adequate to the demands of the position of ANSA or not is questionable. Nonetheless, the role that Scowcroft played in the Ford administration was ideally suited to the policy-making situation. With a powerful secretary of state in Kissinger (under whom Scowcroft had been deputy national security adviser), the ANSA was appropriately more subordinate. While Secretary of State Kissinger dominated the advising of President Ford, Scowcroft operated most effectively in the supporting role of facilitating the process rather than shaping policy.

"Scowcroft Redux" has proved a very different commodity in response to a different policy-making configuration. In between his first and second terms as national security adviser, Scowcroft developed a reputation as a foreign policy intellectual in his own right. In chairing a special presidential commission on strategic-weapons policy in 1983, he achieved a workable solution on the issue of MX missile mobility that, while far from unanimously received, was politically acceptable to a broad range of ideological viewpoints. (Scowcroft himself has been an advocate of the single-warhead mobile ICBM, or Midgetman missile, that was much favored by opponents of the Reagan administration. While a member of Kissinger Associates, Scowcroft also took an antiadministration position in opposing the Intermediate Nuclear Forces (INF) Treaty. By contrast, he favored a "broad interpretation" of the Antiballistic Missile (ABM) Treaty to allow some deployment of the Strategic Defense Initiative.) Scowcroft's membership on the Tower Commission, which investigated the Iran–Contra affair, further confirmed his credentials as independent and fair-minded. Overall, Scowcroft achieved a front-rank status within the national security community for his expertise on complex questions of strategic weaponry and a balanced approach to the competing claims of the NCS staff and the Departments of State and Defense for policy preeminence.

Upon his appointment as President Bush's national security adviser, Scowcroft was widely acclaimed as the kind of "honest broker"[9] who was essential if the national security policy making process was to avoid the internecine warfare and interdepartmental stalemate that typified so much of the Carter and Reagan administrations. Under Bush, however, Scowcroft has defined a far more ambitious role for himself than he assumed in his earlier service as national security adviser. In the Ford administration, Scowcroft was inevitably in Kissinger's shadow. In the Bush administration, Scowcroft is a full partner in the policy-making process.

Although Secretary of State James A. Baker III may be the premier foreign policy actor under Bush, he is no Henry Kissinger dominating the process. Furthermore, President Bush, unlike Gerald Ford, has a strong background in foreign affairs. As noted earlier, Bush has opted for a management style that places the presidency in the midst of national security decision making. Inevitably, this places the White House staff—that is, the national security adviser—in a key position to influence policy, even allowing for Secretary Baker's close personal and political relationship with the president.

An important indicator of Scowcroft's influence is the highly professional nature of the NSC staff. Whereas the Reagan NSC staff was frequently criticized for being either too ideological or politically inexperienced, Scowcroft quickly assembled a group of individuals with acknowledged credentials in national security affairs. The deputy assistant for national security affairs, Robert M. Gates, had been deputy director of central intelligence under Reagan's director, William Casey. (Gates's nomination to the CIA directorship was withdrawn because of controversy concerning what he knew about the Iran–Contra affair.) In naming Gates, President Bush described him as a man who "knows the system, the critical importance of the inter-agency process for Presidential decision-making and the details of the management of that process."[10] Gates has also known Scowcroft since the Ford administration, when he served as a junior NSC staffer. Among the other senior appointments to the NSC staff were Robert D. Blackwill, former chief negotiator at the Mutual and Balanced Force Reductions Talks in Vienna from 1985 to 1987, as director of European and Soviet affairs; David C. Miller, Jr., former ambassador to Zimbabwe from 1984 to 1986, as director of African affairs; Karl D. Jackson, former deputy assistant secretary of defense for international security affairs, as director of Asian affairs; Richard Haas, former director of the Office of Regional Security Affairs in the State Department's Bureau of Politico-Military Affairs, as director of Near East and South Asian affairs; and William W. Working, former director of program and budget for the intelligence community staff, as director of intelligence affairs.[11]

In addition to appointing experienced diplomats and intelligence officers to the NSC staff, Scowcroft has carried out a far-reaching reorganization of the advisory structure for national security policy making. In place of the numerous interagency committees typical of the Reagan administration, Scowcroft has designed a three-tiered system. At the highest decision-making level is the existing National Security Council, or "principals committee," with the ANSA chairing in the president's absence. (The National Security Council members are still the president, the vice-president, and the secretaries of state and defense, with the director of central intelligence and the chairman of the Joint Chiefs of Staff serving as statutory advisers.) At the operational level that defines policy alternatives is the "deputies committee." This group, chaired by Gates, is made up of the under secretary of state for political affairs (or the deputy secretary), the under secretary of defense for policy (or the deputy secretary), the vice-chairman of the Joint Chiefs of Staff, and the deputy director of central intelligence. At the third level are about eight "policy coordination committees," composed of officials at the assistant-secretary level, that are responsible for examining and developing policy proposals. Each of these interagency committees has an NSC staff member serving as its executive secretary.

Overall, the goal of Scowcroft's approach to NSC management is to give "coherence and compatibility to the process."[12] This has entailed enhancing the role of the NSC staff and, not incidentally, that of the national security adviser, as presidential operatives. (Both had lost standing during the Reagan administration, in contrast to both Democratic and Republican presidencies in the 1960s and 1970s.) Though President Bush, like Reagan and most other presidents, has expressed a commitment to cabinet government, he has not made Reagan's mistake of downgrading the national security adviser's role (as was especially true with Richard Allen) and leaving the national security policy-making process without clear White House direction. Bush has also avoided appointing a national security adviser who would preempt the foreign policy prerogatives of the secretary of state, as did Zbigniew Brzezinski with Cyrus Vance in the Carter administration. Scowcroft, unlike Brzezinski, has shown no evidence of aspiring to the agent role of his former mentor, Henry Kissinger.

Scowcroft has acted to facilitate, not to dominate, the national security process. On the other hand, Scowcroft does not simply coordinate the machinery of policy making as he did in the Ford administration. Under Bush, Scowcroft has emerged as more of an internal counselor on national security matters. As the then president-elect said of his relationship with Scowcroft, "I will be the one who takes a keen interest in these matters. I have a lot of ideas. They will need to be tempered by his experience and judgment."[13] As with the best counselors—such as McGeorge Bundy to Kennedy, or W. W. Rostow to Johnson—Scowcroft is his president's man. He seeks to safeguard Bush's policy priorities and oversee the bureaucratic machinery without undermining the departmental collaboration necessary for effective policy making.

In the making of national security policy, the most often observed difficulty has arisen in the relations between the national security adviser and the secretary of state. The Bush administration may be distinguished by its success in avoiding this problem through its sensitivity to working relationships whose impact on policy outcomes may often be underestimated. First, Scowcroft has been frequently characterized as both "self-effacing" and not having "a Washington-size ego."[14] Risky as such psychological assessments may be, Scowcroft's low-key personality does seem to have obviated the potential for conflict between himself and the secretary of state.

Second, Scowcroft and Secretary of State Baker are good friends. Though the effect of friendship is difficult to measure, there is no doubt as to its importance. Moreover, as the party that has controlled the presidency for most of the past two decades, the Republicans have developed a corps of executive elites that are not strangers. Scowcroft, Baker, and their aides are known commodities who have been tested in extensive collaborations during their prior governmental experience.

Third, and perhaps most important, Scowcroft and Baker each appears to have delimited his own sphere of competence. Specifically, Baker has positioned himself as "Mister Outsider," handling external matters such as Gorbachev, Congress, and the press; Scowcroft, not surprisingly, serves as "Mister Insider," overseeing the policy-making process. Whether this division is by deliberate design or default must be a moot point.

In some ways, James Baker would seem an atypical choice for Secretary of State, since he lacks direct experience in foreign affairs. On the other hand, he enjoys an independent political stature unusual among recent secretaries of state. As a former White House chief of staff, secretary of the treasury, and presidential campaign manager, Baker is without equal in the Bush cabinet. Moreover, as a friend of President Bush's for more than thirty years and his most trusted political adviser, Baker enjoys an advantage of confidence and accessibility that equals that of Acheson with Truman, Dulles with Eisenhower, and Kissinger with Nixon. Indeed, Baker has been touted as a future presidential candidate to succeed Bush. Whatever the policy-making expertise of other administration officials, Baker must be granted pride of place in any decision-making forum. As the Republican political consultant Edward Rollins put it, "for all practical purposes, Jim Baker will be deputy President . . . No matter what the issue, Bush will go to him for advice and counsel."[15]

If Scowcroft is to be held responsible for the policy-making process, Baker must be held accountable for the direction of foreign affairs. This may prove to be a difficult undertaking, especially in relation to the transcendent issue of East–West relations. For all their manifest abilities, neither Baker nor Bush is considered a conceptualizer or visionary thinker. Like Bush, Baker is known as a pragmatist and a problem solver. Ordinarily, this should prove advantageous; however, in this extraordinary era of global *glasnost,* caution may appear to be timidity and incrementalism obstructionism. The prospects of the Bush–Baker approach to global politics and superpower relations will be the subject of some final observations.

In running the State Department, Baker has reverted to a management model reminiscent of Kissinger and Dulles: a powerful office of the secretary and, as was especially true under Dulles, a manifest distrust of the Foreign Service. In both respects, Baker stands in marked contrast to his predecessor, George Shultz, who made wide use of Foreign Service officers in policy-making positions. What is somewhat surprising about Baker's approach is that his is a "friendly takeover" of the State Department—that is, the succession of one Republican administration by another rather than an interparty transfer of power. When the Eisenhower administration came to power, for example, it followed two decades of Democratic presidents and foreign policies that had been the subject of sharp partisan debate. In particular, Truman's secretary of state from 1949 to 1953, Dean Acheson, along with other high State Department officials, were frequently criticized in Republican campaign oratory. Inevitably, Dulles was suspicious of career diplomatic officials, who were thought to be tainted by the policies of Truman and Acheson. President Nixon, who had a deep-seated distrust of the Foreign Service, sought to displace the State Department's influence with an all-powerful national security adviser. Later, when Kissinger became secretary of state, he exercised personal control over policy making through a private office that was largely staffed with departmental officials whose loyalties he had cultivated during their service on his NSC staff.

Despite the absence of hostility between the Bush administration and his predecessor's personnel and policies, Secretary Baker felt that Shultz depended too much on the State Department for senior personnel and policy agendas. "Baker made clear from the start that he intended to be President Bush's man at the State Department and not the State Department's man at the White House."[16] Accordingly, Baker has staffed the highest policy-making positions with an inner circle of young past associates. The under secretary of state for political affairs, Robert M. Kimmitt, got to know Baker while serving on the Reagan NSC staff. The State Department counselor, Robert B. Zoellick, worked for Richard Darman when he was Baker's deputy secretary of the treasury. Dennis B. Ross, the director of the Policy Planning Board, was a foreign policy adviser to the second Bush campaign that Baker directed. Assistant Secretary of State for Public Affairs Margaret D. Tutweiler has been associated with Baker since the late 1970s on Bush's 1980 presidential campaign and at the Treasury Department.

Because of its relative youth (the above-named officials are in their early forties or younger), the Baker inner circle is also relatively inexperienced in making foreign policy decisions. The outstanding exception is Baker's number-two man, Deputy Secretary of State Lawrence S. Eagleburger. As a longtime Foreign Service officer who served on the Nixon NSC staff, as under secretary for management under Kissinger, as ambassador to Yugoslavia under President Carter, and most recently as president of Kissinger Associates, Eagleburger has the depth of experience in foreign affairs needed to ensure orderly management of State Department business. This allows Baker to concentrate on the president's agenda, congressional relations, and public opinion. Arguably, "strong secretaries have been strong precisely because they ignored the department."[17] Still, the question of whether the tension between the political appointees surrounding the secretary and the career Foreign Service officers is conducive to effective policy making must be asked. As proved to be the case in earlier administrations, ignoring the professional expertise of State Department careerists may hinder the development of a coherent and cohesive foreign policy.

The most frequent criticism of Baker as secretary of state has been that his tenure has been long on politics and short on policy. When Senate Majority Leader George J. Mitchell (D–Maine), criticized the Bush administration's seeming "nostalgia for the Cold War" because of its overly cautious reaction to the new opportunities for improved East–West relations, Baker replied, "When a president is rocking along with a seventy percent approval rating on his handling of foreign policy, if I were the leader of the opposition, I might have something similar to say." Though Baker was careful to cast his aspersions as personal rather than presidential, the administration's credibility with regard to policy was inevitably called into question. For his part, Senator Mitchell retorted, "I remind the Secretary that this is not a political campaign."[18] By citing public approval as the only factor necessary to defend the president, Baker seemed to equate the Bush administration's foreign policy goals with short-term partisan success rather than with the transformation of superpower relations that might be possible (and necessary) in a post–Cold War era.

When Baker's remarks are considered along with the administration's description of itself as cautious and pragmatic, a sense emerges that Bush's foreign policy lacks an overall strategic vision. In the world arena, where appearances must be rated as at least as important as in the electoral arena, the Bush administration has been judged to be uncertain about how to handle the challenges inherent in a changing international order. This is especially the case concerning East–West relations, proposed strategic-arms reductions, and, more generally, the changing nature of American global leadership. An age that will almost certainly witness a continued reduction in superpower tensions, as well as a relative decline in superpower hegemony, may prove difficult to manage without an agonizing reappraisal of American national security priorities.

▮ Inching beyond the Cold War: A Preliminary Assessment

For better or worse, this nation has achieved a bipartisan consensus on the approximate level of resources that will be available to defense in the first part of the 1990s. The challenge for the Bush administration and Congress is to apply those resources in a way that relates them to a coherent strategy and a changing international environment."[19]

Neither the economy nor the public will sustain the buy-everything defense budgets of the Reagan era. Furthermore, the United States is "no longer the omnipotent power that emerged after World War II, or even the one that shared a bipolar world with the Soviet Union."[20] This statement is not meant to suggest that the United States has become another example of the decline and fall of a great power[21]—if applicable to either superpower, this thesis would more accurately describe the Soviet Union. Indeed, the Soviet economy is likely to decline ever more sharply over the next twenty years, with inevitable consequences to its ability to maintain an overabundance of strategic weaponry.

At the same time, American economic preeminence is giving way to a world in which the United States, Japan, and the European Community compete on a relatively equal basis. Whether or not this economic multipolarity will take on international political and military dimensions is the subject of great debate. Regardless, arrangements need to be made to accommodate the larger role of these new economic superpowers in the international system. Such an accommodation will also require the United States to develop a more consultative and collaborative approach to the management of its European and Asian alliances. William G. Hyland, the editor of *Foreign Affairs,* has argued as follows:

The main problems are structural. . . . They relate to the emergence of a new balance of power in the post–cold war era, a period in which America's role will necessarily be different—diminished by the rise of the other powers and limited by its own constrained resources. The Administration will eventually have to redefine U.S. relations with the permanent challenge of Japanese economic prowess. And it will have to settle the residual issues of the cold war.[22]

Does Bush have an identifiable national security policy that addresses the prospects of a multipolar international system in a post–Cold War world? The preliminary assessment must be "not yet." As noted, Bush—who "values conciliation over confrontation, prefers partial victories to glorious defeats and deals with the world as it is, not as American policymakers would like it to be"[23]—tends toward a self-conscious approach to national security. As President Bush put it, "Democrats on Capitol Hill have been calling me 'timid.' I have other, better words, like 'cautious,' 'diplomatic,' 'prudent.' We have a good team, well seasoned. We're unified."[24] Yet, the criticism still remains that these attributes relate almost exclusively to the process of policy making, not to its content. Critics continue to define the Bush administration as derivative, rather than creative. Is a pragmatic, incrementalist worldview adequate to guide the United States through on the international scene of the 1990s and beyond? Critics of the Bush administration are likely to contend that pragmatism and incrementalism are not substitutes for strategic vision and policy making with direction.

If the Bush administration's sense of national security policy remains reactive rather than innovative, serious reservations will persist about its ability to define successfully an adequate strategy for East–West and interalliance relations. Indeed, as the Cold War era comes to an end, "the world is becoming more complex and probably more dangerous."[25] Consequently, foreign affairs will persist as front-burner issues demanding fresh policy initiatives, rather than as residual legacies of the Reagan administration requiring only occasional fine-tuning. Yet, voicing a widely shared opinion, Joseph Nye of the Kennedy School of Government at Harvard judges the Bush team "an administration of extremely able managers who don't have a sense of strategy."[26]

The central issue is how the United States is to move beyond a national security posture dominated by the need to deter possible Soviet expansionism to a new posture of cooperation that reflects diminished military threats and ideological hostility between the superpowers. The implications for American diplomatic relations of this shift to a less confrontational and more pluralistic world order are twofold. First, any justification for strategic weapons systems must go beyond citing a need to modernize the existing arsenal in anticipation of Soviet aggression. The arms buildup of the 1980s and the mitigation of tensions associated with *glasnost* requires a new and publicly elaborated rationale for deterrence, one no longer based on anticommunism or strategic vulnerability.

Second, transforming a relationship of overt superpower rivalry into one of at least cautious cooperation requires that both the United States and the Soviet Union attend more closely to cultivating alliances. Just as the USSR must revise its security concerns to accommodate a more independent Eastern bloc, the United States must increasingly learn to collaborate with its economic rivals—Japan and the European Community—in the international system. If the world of the 1990s cannot precisely be called "multipolar" (because of the nuclear superiority still enjoyed by the superpowers), the global system will no longer be characterized by the radical bipolarity of the Cold War era.[27]

By way of conclusion, it is possible to offer three observations about the Bush administration's national security policy.[28]

First, concerning strategic planning, the Bush administration has failed to conduct a comprehensive policy review and appears to have avoided formulating either an overall conception of the international order (as did Carter) or a set of ideological goals that would define American interests abroad (as did Reagan). President Bush seems content to manage events as they arise rather than to shape alternatives and to fine-tune the changes needed in national security policy in response to the openness in East–West relations ushered in during the last few years.

Second, the absence of a post–Cold War national security policy has unquestionably hampered the Bush administration in obtaining congressional support for its strategic programs. After a massive buildup in nuclear weaponry in the 1980s and with a conciliatory Soviet Union under Gorbachev, further modernization of the American nuclear arsenal appears to many to be strategically unnecessary and financially wasteful. This will require "forced-choice" defense budgets for the foreseeable future. In particular, the choices that need to be made concerning strategic-weapons spending can be summarized as follows: Increase the survivability of the ICBMs by deploying the rail-mobile MX or the Midgetman but not both; fund Stealth technology, but limit B-2 bomber production; deploy advanced cruise missiles on existing long-range bombers; further strengthen the SLBM force with the improved Trident II; and support only research on SDI, not development.

Third, the structure of the Bush administration's national security policy–making process has reflected the organizational prescriptions suggested by the Iran–Contra affair and by the frequent decision-making disarray of the past two administrations. Thus far, Secretary of State James Baker and National Security Adviser Brent Scowcroft have shown no indication of political and personal rivalry like that between Cyrus Vance and Zbigniew Brzezinski. Moreover, President Bush, unlike President Reagan, has a highly engaged management style. A prevailing perception that the presidency is not on automatic pilot may do more than anything else to foster public support for President Bush's conduct of national security affairs. What is less certain is whether or not a pragmatic and incrementalist approach to national security policy will suffice to galvanize congressional and public support for continued spending on modernizing strategic weapons and to redefine America's external relations in what appears to be a post–Cold War world.

NOTES

1. Hodding Carter III, *Wall Street Journal,* February 16, 1989.
2. Charles W. Kegley, Jr., "The Bush Administration and the Future of American Foreign Policy: Pragmatism or Procrastination?" *Presidential Studies Quarterly,* 19 (Fall, 1989): 718.
3. Ibid.
4. Ibid.; and *U.S. News and World Report,* November 13, 1989, p. 22.

5. *New York Times,* June 4, 1989.

6. For a detailed analysis of the relationship between presidential management styles and national security adviser roles, see chapter 9 and especially figure 9-3.

7. For a representation of the different variations that the triangular relationship of president, secretary of state, and national security adviser can take, see Cecil V. Crabb, Jr., and Kevin V. Mulcahy, *Presidents and Foreign Policy Making: FDR to Reagan* (Baton Rouge: Louisiana State University, 1987), pp. 317–340.

8. *New York Times,* July 10, 1988.

9. *New York Times,* November 24, 1988.

10. *New York Times,* December 5, 1988.

11. *New York Times,* December 29, 1988.

12. *New York Times,* January 25, 1989; January 28, 1989; and February 2, 1989.

13. *New York Times,* November 24, 1988; and November 6, 1989.

14. *New York Times,* February 6, 1989.

15. *New York Times,* November 13, 1988; and November 3, 1989.

16. *New York Times,* July 27, 1989.

17. Bert A. Rockman, "America's Department of State: Irregular and Regular Syndromes of Policy Making," *American Political Science Review,* 75 (December 1981): 918.

18. *New York Times,* September 21, 1989.

19. William W. Kaufmann and Lawrence J. Korb, *The 1990 Defense Budget* (Washington, D.C.: The Brookings Institution, 1989), p. 8.

20. *U.S. News and World Report,* May 1, 1989, p. 42.

21. The reference is to Paul Kennedy's controversial book, *The Rise and Fall of the Great Powers: Economic Change and Military Conflict From 1500 to 2000* (New York: Random House, 1987).

22. *New York Times,* April 26, 1989.

23. *U.S. News and World Report,* April 17, 1989, p. 34.

24. *New York Times,* October 25, 1989.

25. *U.S. News and World Report,* October 2, 1989, p. 21.

26. Quoted in ibid., p. 22. See also Elizabeth Drew in the *New Yorker,* November 27, 1989, pp. 121–133.

27. For a more extended discussion of this issue, see Kevin V. Mulcahy, "Cooperation *and* Deterrence: American Foreign Policy Challenges in the Twenty-First Century" in *The Argument Book,* ed. John Shea (Pacific Grove, CA: Brooks/Cole, forthcoming).

28. For a review of the recent literature on this subject, see Kevin V. Mulcahy, "The Bush Administration and American National Security: Process, Programs, Policy," *Public Administration Review,* 50 (January/February 1990): 115–119.

INDEX